# Classics in
# Economic
# Thought

*A Reader*

**Robert B. Ekelund, Jr.**
**Robert F. Hebert**
Auburn University

The McGraw-Hill Companies, Inc.
College Custom Series

New York  St. Louis  San Francisco  Auckland  Bogotá
Caracas Lisbon  London  Madrid  Mexico  Milan  Montreal
New Delhi  Paris  San Juan  Singapore  Sydney  Tokyo  Toronto

*McGraw·Hill*

*A Division of The McGraw·Hill Companies*

Classics in Economic Thought
*A Reader*

McGraw-Hill's College Custom Series consists of products that are produced from camera-ready copy. Peer review, class testing, and accuracy are primarily the responsibility of the author(s).

4 5 6 7 8 9 HAM HAM 0 9 8 7 6 5 4 3 2 1

ISBN 0-07-034353-5

Editor: J. D. Ice
Cover Designer: Maggie Lytle
Printer/Binder: HAMCO/NETPUB Corporation

# CONTENTS

# CLASSICS IN ECONOMIC THOUGHT

A Collection of Readings to Accompany
*A History of Economic Theory and Method*
and Other Selected Texts

Cross References to Other Texts

| Ekelund Hebert | Selection | Blaug | Brue | Landreth Colander | Niehans | Rima | Roll | Screpanti Zamagni | Spiegel | Staley |
|---|---|---|---|---|---|---|---|---|---|---|
| 1 | Introduction | | | | | | | | | |
| 2 | Aristotle on Property, Trade and Money | | | 2 | | 1 | 1 | | 2 | 2 |
| 3 | Mandeville on Economics and Morality | 1 | 2 | 3 | 3 | 2 | 2 | 1 | 10 | 3 |
| 4 | Cantillon on Entrepreneurship | 1 | 4 | 3 | 4 | 3 | 3 | 1 | 8 | 3 |
| 5 | Smith on Growth, Trade and University Professors | 2 | 5 | 4 | 7 | 5 | 4 | 2 | 11 | 5 |
| 6 | Malthus on Population, Diminishing Returns, and Consumption | 3 | 6 | 5 | 8 | 6 | 4 | 3 | 12 | 6 |
| 7 | Ricardo on Value and Comparative Advantage | 4 | 7 | 5 | 9 | 7 | 4 | 3 | 14 | 8 |
| 8 | Mill on the Workability of Socialism | 6 | 8 | 6 | 11 | 8 | 7 | 3 | 16 | 10 |
| 9 | Chadwick on Competition | | | | | | | | | |
| 10 | Marx and Engels on the Nature of Communism | 7 | 10 | 7 | 12 | 10 | 6 | 4 | 20 | 11 |
| 11 | Cournot on Mathematical Method and Demand Theory | 8 | 12 | 8 | 15 | 11 | 7 | 3 | 22 | 12 |
| 12 | Menger on Money and Transaction Costs | 8 | 13 | 8 | 19 | 12 | 8 | 5 | 23 | 13 |
| 13 | Jevons on Sunspots and Business Cycles | 8 | 13 | 17 | 17 | 12 | 8 | 5 | 22 | 14 |
| 14 | Marshall on Elasticity | 9 | 15 | 11 | 20 | 14 | 8 | 6 | 25 | 16 |
| 15 | Hicks on the Walrasian System | 13 | 18 | 10 | 18 | 12 | 8 | 5 | 24 | 15 |
| 16 | Veblen on Conspicuous Consumption | 17 | 19 | 12 | | 18 | 9 | 8 | 27 | 17 |
| 17 | Chamberlin on Product Differentiation | 9 | 17 | 15 | 24 | 16 | 10 | 8 | 25 | 18 |
| 18 | Keynes on the Socialization of Investment | 16 | 21 | 16 | 27 | 20 | 10 | 7 | 26 | 19 |
| 19 | Friedman on the Quantity Theory of Money | 15 | 24 | 16 | 36 | 22 | 12 | 9 | | 20 |
| 20 | Hayek on Knowledge in Economics | | | 14 | | 24 | | 8 | | |
| 21 | Tullock on the Welfare Costs of Tariffs, Monopolies and Theft | 20 | 20 | 14 | | | | 11 | | |
| 22 | Stigler on the Economics of Information | 24 | 24 | | | 24 | | | | |
| 23 | Shackle on What Makes an Economist | | | | | | | | | |

# List of Alternate Texts for Concordance

Blaug, Mark. *Economic Theory in Retrospect*, 4th ed. Cambridge: Cambridge University Press, 1985. Pp. 737.

Brue, Stanley L. *The Evolution of Economic Thought*, 5th ed. New York: Dryden Press, 1994. Pp. 563.

Landreth, Harry, and Colander, D. C. *History of Economic Thought*, 3rd ed. Boston: Houghton Mifflin, 1994. Pp. 538.

Niehans, Jurg. *A History of Economic Theory: Classic Contributions, 1720-1980*. Baltimore: John Hopkins University Press, 1990. Pp. 578.

Rima, Ingrid H. *Development of Economic Analysis*, 5th ed. Homewood, IL: Irwin, 1991. Pp. 603.

Roll, Eric. *A History of Economic Thought*, 5th ed. London: Faber and Faber, 1992. Pp. 592.

Screpanti, Ernesto, and Stefano Zamagni. *An Outline of the History of Economic Thought*. Oxford: Clarendon Press, 1993. Pp. 441.

Spiegel, Henry W. *The Growth of Economic Thought*, 3rd ed. Durham, NC: Duke University Press, 1991. Pp. 868.

Staley, Charles E. *A History of Economic Thought: From Aristotle to Arrow*. Cambridge, MA: Basil Blackwell, 1989. Pp. 273.

# Chapter 1

## Introduction

This book of selected readings is designed for use with the text, *A History of Economic Theory and Method*, 4th edition, by Robert B. Ekelund, Jr. and Robert F. Hébert. Each of the following chapters contains a selection chosen for its relevance to chapters in the aforementioned text. However, the editors designed this readings book so that it may profitably be used with other texts in the history of economic thought as well as their own. Examine carefully the table of contents at the beginning of this volume and you shall find the chapters of readings herein that correspond most closely to chapters in other leading texts. Because the coverage of subjects by other texts does not necessarily coincide with that of Ekelund and Hébert, some of the selections herein do not match up easily with other texts in all respects. But on the whole, there is reasonable concordance among the leading texts.

The readings in this volume were chosen with several objectives in mind. First and foremost, there is no substitute for reading the ancient texts in the original. This assures not only accuracy but preservation of the author's unique substance and style. Another objective is to expand and elaborate, through the author's own words, on ideas presented in summary form in the text. Still another objective is to make available to you, the student, a carefully selected assemblage of readings in a convenient and easily accessible form.

The number of chapters in this book of readings matches the number of chapters in *A History of Economic Theory and Method*, 4th edition. At the end of each chapter in the text, you are directed to the appropriate selection in this volume. Preceding each reading is a brief introduction to the author and to the particular selection. The introduction attempts among other things to guide you toward important principles and/or ideas in the selected reading. If you are using this book of readings with another text, follow the table of contents at the front of this volume to guide you to reasonably close matches with your text.

The individual selections in this volume vary in length, style, and difficulty. One of the obvious lessons to be drawn from the progression of ideas over time is that economics inevitably has become more sophisticated and more complex as it has matured. While we make no apologies for this fact, we nevertheless have tried to choose readings that are understandable, as well as representative of what economics, both past and present, is all about.

# Chapter 2

## Aristotle on Property, Trade and Money

Aristotle (384-322 B.C.), student of Plato, and teacher of Alexander the Great, was one of the giants of Western thought. A thinker of extraordinary range and depth, he wrote important works on logic, ethics, philosophy, politics, rhetoric, history, psychology, metaphysics and the natural sciences. Although his style is somewhat obscure, all of his works are characterized by a deep respect for facts and attempted precision. None of his works are devoted purely to economic questions, but throughout his writings he remained alive to the relation between economics and the larger aspects of life, and he discussed many economic questions from this point of view. In the passages below Aristotle discusses property, trade and money, and their proper place in a 'good' society. These views had a major impact on medieval scholars and held wide sway in the eventual development of economic thought, even up to the time of Adam Smith and beyond.

Source: *Early Economic Thought: Selections from Economic Literature Prior to Adam Smith*, edited by A. E. Monroe. Cambridge, MA: Harvard University Press, 1924. Pages 13-25.

## *The Politics*

### Book I

Let us now enquire into property generally, and into the art of money-making, in accordance with our usual method [of resolving a whole into its parts]. The first question is whether the art of money-making is the same with the art of managing a household or a part of it, or instrumental to it; and if the last, whether in the way that the art of making shuttles is instrumental to the art of weaving, or in the way that the casting of bronze is instrumental to the art of the statuary, for they are not instrumental in the same way, but the one provides tools and the other material; and by material I mean the substratum out of which any work is made; thus wool is the material of the weaver, bronze of the statuary. Now it is easy to see that the art of household management is not identical with the art of money-making, for the one uses the material which the other provides. And the art which uses household stores can be no other than the art of household management. There is, however, a doubt whether the art of money-making is a part of household

3

management or a distinct art. [They appear to be connected]; for the money-maker has to consider whence money and property can be procured; but there are many sorts of property and wealth: there is husbandry and the care and provision of food in general; are these parts of the money-making art or distinct arts? Again, there are many sorts of food, and therefore there are many kinds of lives, both of animals and men; they must all have food, and the differences in their food have made differences in their ways of life. For of beasts, some are gregarious, others are solitary; they live in the way which is best adapted to sustain them, accordingly as they are carnivorous or herbivorous or omnivorous: and their habits are determined for them by nature in such a manner that they may obtain with greater facility the food of their choice. But, as different individuals have different tastes, the same things are not naturally pleasant to all of them; and therefore the lives of carnivorous or herbivorous animals further differ among themselves. In the lives of men too there is a great difference. The laziest are shepherds, who lead an idle life, and get their subsistence without trouble from tame animals; their flocks having to wander from place to place in search of pasture, they are compelled to follow them, cultivating a sort of living farm. Others support themselves by hunting, which is of different kinds. Some, for example, are pirates, others, who dwell near lakes or marshes or rivers or a sea in which there are fish, are fishermen, and others live by the pursuit of birds or wild beasts. The greater number obtain a living from the fruits of the soil. Such are the modes of subsistence which prevail among those whose industry is employed immediately upon the products of nature, and whose food is not acquired by exchange and retail trade there is the shepherd, the husbandman, the pirate, the fisherman, the hunter. Some gain a comfortable maintenance out of two employments, eking out the deficiencies of one of them by another: thus the life of a shepherd may be combined with that of a brigand, the life of a farmer with that of a hunter. Other modes of life are similarly combined in any way which the needs of men may require. Property, in the sense of a bare livelihood, seems to be given by nature herself to all, both when they are first born, and when they are grown up. For some animals bring forth, together with their offspring, so much food as will last until they are able to supply themselves; of this the vermiparous or oviparous animals are an instance; and the viviparous animals have up to a certain time a supply of food for their young in themselves, which is called milk. In like manner we may infer that, after the birth of animals, plants exist for their sake, and that the other animals exist for the sake of man, the tame for use and food, the wild, if not all, at least the greater part of them, for food, and for the provision of clothing and various instruments. Now if nature makes nothing incomplete, and nothing in vain, the inference must be that she has made all animals and plants for the sake of man. And so, in one point of view, the art of war is a natural art of acquisition, for it includes hunting, an art which we ought to practise against wild beasts, and against men who, though intended by nature to be governed, will not submit; for war of such a kind is naturally just.

Of the art of acquisition then there is one kind which is natural and is a part of the management of a household. Either we must suppose the necessaries of life to exist previously, or the art of household management must provide a store of them for the common use of the family or state. They are the elements of true wealth; for the amount of property which is needed for a good life is not unlimited, although Solon in one of his poems says that,

No bound to riches has been fixed for man.

But there is a boundary fixed, just as there is in the arts; for the instruments of any art are never unlimited, either in number or size, and wealth may be defined as a number of instruments to be used in a household or in a state. And so we see that there is a natural art of acquisition which is practised by managers of households and by statesmen, and what is the reason of this.

There is another variety of the art of acquisition which is commonly and rightly called the art of making money, and has in fact suggested the notion that wealth and property have no limit. Being nearly connected with the preceding, it is often identified with it. But though they are not very different, neither are they the same. The kind already described is given by nature, the other is gained by experience and art.

Let us begin our discussion of the question with the following considerations:

Of everything which we possess there are two uses: both belong to the thing as such, but not in the same manner, for one is the proper, and the other the improper or secondary use of it. For example, a shoe is used for wear, and is used for exchange; both are uses of the shoe. He who gives a shoe in exchange for money or food to him who wants one, does indeed use the shoe as a shoe, but this is not its proper or primary purpose, for a shoe is not made to be an object of barter. The same may be said of all possessions, for the art of exchange extends to all of them, and it arises at first in a natural manner from the circumstance that some have too little, others too much. Hence we may infer that retail trade is not a natural part of the art of money-making; had it been so, men would have ceased to exchange when they had enough. And in the first community, which is the family, this art is obviously of no use, but only begins to be useful when the society increases. For the members of the family originally had all things in common; in a more divided state of society they still shared in many things, but they were different things which they had to give in exchange for what they wanted, a kind of barter which is still practised among barbarous nations who exchange with one another the necessaries of life and nothing more; giving and receiving wine, for example, in exchange for corn and the like. This sort of barter is not part of the money-making art and is not contrary to nature, but is needed for the satisfaction of men's natural wants. The other or more complex form of exchange grew out of the simpler. When the inhabitants of one country became more dependent on those of another, and they imported what they needed, and exported the

5

surplus, money necessarily came into use. For the various necessaries of life are not easily carried about, and hence men agreed to employ in their dealings with each other something which was intrinsically useful and easily applicable to the purposes of life, for example, iron, silver, and the like. Of this the value was at first measured by size and weight, but in process of time they put a stamp upon it, to save the trouble of weighing and to mark the value.

When the use of coin had once been discovered, out of the barter of necessary articles arose the other art of money-making, namely, retail trade; which was at first probably a simple matter, but became more complicated as soon as men learned by experience whence and by what exchanges the greatest profit might be made. Originating in the use of coin, the art of money-making is generally thought to be chiefly concerned with it, and to be the art which produces wealth and money; having to consider how they may be accumulated. Indeed, wealth is assumed by many to be only a quantity of coin, because the art of money-making and retail trade are concerned with coin. Others maintain that coined money is a mere sham, a thing not natural, but conventional only, which would have no value or use for any of the purposes of daily life, if another commodity were substituted by the users. And, indeed, he who is rich in coin may often be in want of necessary food. But how can that be wealth of which a man may have a great abundance and yet perish with hunger, like Midas in the fable, whose insatiable prayer turned everything that was set before him into gold?

Men seek after a better notion of wealth and of the art of making money than the mere acquisition of coin, and they are right. For natural wealth and the natural art of money-making are a different thing; in their true form they are part of the management of a household; whereas retail trade is the art of producing wealth, not in every way, but by exchange. And it seems to be concerned with coin; for coin is the starting-point and the goal of exchange. And there is no bound to the wealth which springs from this art of money-making. As in the art of medicine there is no limit to the pursuit of health, and as in the other arts there is no limit to the pursuit of their several ends, for they aim at accomplishing their ends to the uttermost; (but of the means there is a limit, for the end is always the limit), so, too, in this art of money-making there is no limit of the end, which is wealth of the spurious kind, and the acquisition of money. But the art of household management has a limit; the unlimited acquisition of money is not its business. And, therefore, in one point of view, all wealth must have a limit; nevertheless, as a matter of fact, we find the opposite to be the case; for all money-makers increase their hoard of coin without limit. The source of the confusion is the near connexion between the two kinds of money-making; in either, the instrument [i.e., wealth] is the same, although the use is different, and so they pass into one another; for each is a use of the same property, but with a difference: accumulation is the end in the one case, but there is a further end in the other. Hence some persons are led to believe that making money is the object of household management, and the whole idea of their lives is that they ought either to increase their money without limit, or at any rate not to lose it. The origin of this disposition in men is that they are intent upon living only, and not upon living well; and, as their desires are unlimited, they also desire that the means of gratifying them should be without limit. Even those who aim at a good life seek the means of obtaining bodily pleasures; and, since the enjoyment of these appears to depend on property, they are absorbed in making money: and so there arises the second species of money-making. For, as their enjoyment is in excess, they seek an art which produces the excess of enjoyment; and, if they are not able to supply their pleasures by the art of money-making, they try other arts, using in turn every faculty in a manner contrary to nature. The quality of courage, for example, is not intended to make money, but to inspire confidence; neither is this the aim of the general's or of the physician's art; but the one aims at victory and the other at health. Nevertheless, some men turn every quality or art into a means of making money; this they conceive to be the end, and to the promotion of the end all things must contribute.

Thus, then, we have considered the art of money-making, which is unnecessary, and why men want it; and also the necessary art of money-making, which we have seen to be different from the other, and to be a natural part of the art of managing a household, concerned with the provision of food, not, however, like the former kind, unlimited, but having a limit.

And we have found the answer to our original question, Whether the art of money-making is the business of the manager of a household and of the statesman or not their business?— viz., that it is an art which is presupposed by them. For political science does not make men, but takes them from nature and uses them; and nature provides them with food from the element of earth, air, or sea. At this stage begins the duty of the manager of a household, who has to order the things which nature supplies; he may be compared to the weaver who has not to make but to use wool, and to know what sort of wool is good and serviceable or bad and unserviceable. Were this otherwise, it would be difficult to see why the art of money-making is a part of the management of a household and the art of medicine not; for surely the members of a household must have health just as they must have life or any other necessary. And as from one point of view the master of the house and the ruler of the state have to consider about health, from another point of view not they but the physician; so in one way the art of household management, in another way the subordinate art, has to consider about money. But strictly speaking, as I have already said, the means of life must be provided beforehand by nature; for the business of nature is to furnish food to that which is born, and the food of the offspring always remains over in the parent. Wherefore the art of making money out of fruits and animals is always natural.

Of the two sorts of money-making one, as I have just said, is a part of household management, the other is retail trade: the former necessary and honourable, the latter a kind of exchange which is justly censured; for it is unnatural, and a mode by which men gain from one another. The most hated sort, and with the greatest reason, is usury, which makes a gain out of money itself, and not from the natural use of it. For money was intended to be used in exchange, but not to increase at interest. And this term usury, which means the birth of money from money, is applied to the breeding of money because the offspring resembles the parent. Wherefore of all modes of making money this is the most unnatural.

Enough has been said about the theory of money-making; we will now proceed to the practical part. The discussion of such matters is not unworthy of philosophy, but to be engaged in them practically is illiberal and irksome. The useful parts of money-making are, first, the knowledge of live stock,—which are most profitable, and where, and how,—as, for example, what sort of horses or sheep or oxen or any other animals are most likely to give a return. A man ought to know which of these pay better than others, and which pay best in particular places, for some do better in one place and some in another. Secondly, husbandry, which may be either tillage or planting, and the keeping of bees, and of fish, or fowl, or of any animals which may be useful to man. These are the divisions of the true or proper art of money-making and come first. Of the other, which consists in exchange, the first and most important division is commerce (of which there are three kinds—commerce by sea, commerce by land, selling in shops—these again differing as they are safer or more profitable), the second is usury, the third, service for hire—of this, one kind is employed in the mechanical arts, the other in unskilled and bodily labour. There is still a third sort of money-making intermediate between this and the first or natural mode which is partly natural, but is also concerned with exchange of the fruits and other products of the earth. Some of these latter, although they bear no fruit, are nevertheless profitable; for example, wood and minerals. The art of mining, by which minerals are obtained, has many branches, for there are various kinds of things dug out of the earth. Of the several divisions of money-making I now speak generally; a minute consideration of them might be useful in practice, but it would be tiresome to dwell upon them at greater length now.

Those occupations are most truly arts in which there is the least element of chance; they are the meanest in which the body is most deteriorated, the most servile in which there is the greatest use of the body, and the illiberal in which there is the least need of excellence.

Works have been written upon these subjects by various persons; for example, by Chares the Parian, and Apollodorus the Lemnian, who have treated of Tillage and Planting, while others have treated of other branches; any one who cares for such matters may refer to their writings. It would be well also to collect the scattered stories of the ways in which individuals have succeeded in amassing a fortune; for all this is useful to persons who value the art of making money. There is the anecdote of Thales the Milesian and his financial device, which involves a principle of universal application, but is attributed to him on account of his reputation for wisdom. He was reproached for his poverty, which was supposed to show that philosophy was of no use. According to the story, he knew by his skill in the stars while it was yet winter that there would be a great harvest of olives in the coming year; so, having little capital, he gave earnest money for the use of all the olive presses in Chios and Miletus, which he hired at a low price because no one bid against him. When the harvest time came, and many wanted them all at once and of a sudden, he let them out at any rate which he pleased, and made a quantity of money. Thus he showed the world that philosophers can easily be rich if they like, but that their ambition is of another sort. He is supposed to have given a striking proof of his wisdom, but, as I was saying, his device for getting money is of universal application, and is nothing but the creation of a monopoly. It is an art often practised by cities when they are in want of money; they make a monopoly of provisions.

There was a man of Sicily, who, having money deposited with him, bought up all the iron from the iron mines; afterwards, when the merchants from their various markets came to buy, he was the only seller, and without much increasing the price he gained 200 per cent. Which when Dionysius heard, he told him that he might take away his money, but that he must not remain at Syracuse, for he thought that the man had discovered a way of making money which was injurious to his own interests. He had the same idea as Thales; they both contrived to create a monopoly for themselves. And statesmen ought to know these things; for a state is often as much in want of money and of such devices for obtaining it as a household, or even more so; hence some public men devote themselves entirely to finance.

## Book II

Next let us consider what should be our arrangements about property: should the citizens of the perfect state have their possessions in common or not ? This question may be discussed separately from the enactments about women and children. Even supposing that the women and children belong to individuals, according to the custom which is at present universal, may there not be an advantage in having and using possessions in common ? Three cases are possible: (1) the soil may be appropriated, but the produce may be thrown for consumption into the common stock; and this is the practice of some nations. Or (2), the soil may be common, and may be cultivated in common, but the produce divided among individuals for their private use; this is a form of common property which is said to exist among certain barbarians. Or (3), the soil and the produce may be alike common.

When the husbandmen are not the citizens, the case will be different and easier to deal with; but when the citizens till the ground themselves the question of ownership will give a world of trouble. If they do not share equally in enjoyments and toils, those who labour much and get little will necessarily complain of those who labour little and receive or consume much. There is always a difficulty in men living together and having things in common, but especially in their having common property. The partnerships of fellow-travellers are an example to the point; for they generally fall out by the way and quarrel

9

about any trifle which turns up. So with servants: we are most liable to take offence at those with whom we most frequently come into contact in daily life.

These are only some of the disadvantages which attend the community of property; the present arrangement, if improved as it might be by good customs and laws, would be far better, and would have the advantages of both systems. Property should be in a certain sense common, but, as a general rule, private; for, when every one has a distinct interest, men will not complain of one another, and they will make more progress, because every one will be attending to his own business. And yet among the good, and in respect of use, 'Friends,' as the proverb says, 'will have all things common.' Even now there are traces of such a principle, showing that it is not impracticable, but, in well-ordered states, exists already to a certain extent and may be carried further. For, although every man has his own property, some things he will place at the disposal of his friends, while of others he shares the use with them. The Lacedaemonians, for example, use one another's slaves, and horses and dogs, as if they were their own; and when they happen to be in the country, they appropriate in the fields whatever provisions they want. It is clearly better that property should be private, but the use of it common; and the special business of the legislator is to create in men this benevolent disposition. Again, how immeasurably greater is the pleasure, when a man feels a thing to be his own; for the love of self is a feeling implanted by nature and not given in vain, although selfishness is rightly censured; this, however, is not the mere love of self, but the love of self in excess, like the miser's love of money; for all, or almost all, men love money, and other such objects in a measure. And further, there is the greatest pleasure in doing a kindness or service to friends or guests or companions, which can only be rendered when a man has private property. The advantage is lost by the excessive unification of the state. Two virtues are annihilated in such a state: first, temperance towards women (for it is an honourable action to abstain from another's wife for temperance sake); secondly, liberality in the matter of property. No one, when men have all things in common, will any longer set an example of liberality or do any liberal action; for liberality consists in the use which is made of property.

Such legislation may have a specious appearance of benevolence; men readily listen to it, and are easily induced to believe that in some wonderful manner everybody will become everybody's friend, especially when some one is heard denouncing the evils now existing in states, suits about contracts, convictions for perjury, flatteries of rich men and the like, which are said to arise out of the possession of private property. These evils, however, are due to a very different cause—the wickedness of human nature. Indeed, we see that there is much more quarrelling among those who have all things in common, though there are not many of them when compared with the vast numbers who have private property.

# Chapter 3

## Mandeville on Economics and Morality

A few intellectual works owe their importance more to the controversy and furor they stirred than to the number of converts they were able to win over. Such is the case of Bernard Mandeville (1670-1733) and his *Fable of the Bees*, first published in 1714, and expanded in 1723. In this work, Mandeville turned contemporary morality upside down, causing outrage in some quarters and admiration in others. One commentator referred to him as MAN-DEVIL, in an obvious play on his name. But neither friend nor foe could ignore Mandeville's writings, for in them he brutally exposed the follies of his countrymen and lashed their vices. *The Fable of the Bees* started as an allegorical poem, but grew into a book-length satirical treatment. Its chief paradox is underscored by its sub-title: 'Private Vices, Public Benefits.' The essence of this paradox is that full employment (the basis of national prosperity), and vigorous trade (which is necessary to the continuance of prosperity), are the immediate consequences of immorality. Criminal activities, for example, support the employment of many people: lawyers, policemen, jurists, jailers, bailiffs, court reporters, locksmiths, handwriting experts, and so forth. Whereas the vices of luxury, prodigality, avarice, pride, envy, and vanity displayed by the more respectable members of society promote trade by creating wants, which enterprising merchants continually seek to supply.

In defending the necessity of vice Mandeville had in mind a certain kind of economy, namely, "a populous, rich, wide, extended Kingdom...a trading country." He also recognized another kind of economy, unspoiled by commercial vices, which he described as "a small, indigent state or principality...a frugal and honest society". Mandeville refused to exalt one over the other, insisting that he was not championing vice for its own sake but merely recognizing its importance to the emerging capitalist economy. It is as though he provided a recipe for prosperity without endorsing the product.

The following excerpts from *The Fable of the Bees* show two sides of Mandeville's thought. On the one hand (*Remark L*), he endorses the mercantilist idea that government must carefully regulate commerce by means of tariffs. On the other hand (*Remark Q*), he scorns the mercantilist tendency to link morality with economics (e.g., the denunciation of luxury as both immoral and a threat to trade imbalance). We also confront in these pages the "utility of poverty" argument described in the text.

Source:   *The Fable of the Bees, or Private Vices, Public Benefits.* F. B. Kaye edition, Vol. 1. Indianapolis: Liberty Classics, 1988. Pages 107-123; 181-198.

## Remark (L.)

*------While Luxury Employ'd a Million of the Poor, &c.*


If every thing is to be Luxury (as in strictness it ought) that is not immediately necessary to make Man subsist as he is a living Creature, there is nothing else to be found in the World, no not even among the naked Savages; of which it is not probable that there are any but what by this time have made some Improvements upon their former manner of Living; and either in the Preparation of their Eatables, the ordering of their Huts, or otherwise, added something to what once sufficed them. This Definition every body will say is too rigorous; I am of the same Opinion; but if we are to abate one Inch of this Severity, I am afraid we shan't know where to stop. When People tell us they only desire to keep themselves sweet and clean, there is no understanding what they would be at; if they made use of these Words in their genuine proper literal Sense, they might soon be satisfy'd without much cost or trouble, if they did not want Water: But these two little Adjectives are so comprehensive, especially in the Dialect of some Ladies, that no body can guess how far they may be stretcht. The Comforts of Life are likewise so various and extensive, that no body can tell what People mean by them, except he knows what sort of Life they lead. The same obscurity I observe in the words Decency and Conveniency, and I never understand them unless I am acquainted with the Quality of the Persons that make use of them. People may go to Church together, and be all of one Mind as much as they please, I am apt to believe that when they pray for their daily Bread, the Bishop includes several things in that Petition which the Sexton does not think on.

By what I have said hitherto I would only shew, that if once we depart from calling every thing Luxury that is not absolutely necessary to keep a Man alive, that then there is no Luxury at all; for if the wants of Men are innumerable, then what ought to supply them has no bounds; what is call'd superfluous to some degree of People, will be thought requisite to those of higher Quality; and neither the World nor the Skill of Man can produce any thing so curious or extravagant, but some most Gracious Sovereign or other, if it either eases or diverts him, will reckon it among the Necessaries of Life; not meaning every Body's Life, but that of his Sacred Person.

It is a receiv'd Notion, that Luxury is as destructive to the Wealth of the whole Body Politic, as it is to that of every individual Person who is guilty of it, and that a National Frugality enriches a Country in the same manner as that which is less general increases the Estates of private Families. I confess, that tho' I have found Men of much better Understanding than my self of this Opinion, I cannot help dissenting from them in this Point. They argue thus: We send, say they, for Example to *Turkey* of Woollen Manufactury, and other things of our own Growth, a Million's worth every Year; for this we bring back Silk, Mohair, Drugs, &c. to the value of Twelve Hundred Thousand

12

Pounds, that are all spent in our own Country. By this, say they, we get nothing; but if most of us should be content with our own Growth, and so Consume but half the quantity of those Foreign Commodities, then those in *Turkey,* who would still want the same quantity of our Manufactures, would be forc'd to pay ready Money for the rest, and so by the Balance of that Trade only, the Nation should get Six Hundred Thousand Pounds per Annum.

To examine the force of this Argument, we'll suppose (what they would have) that but half the Silk, &c. shall be consumed in *England* of what there is now; we'll suppose likewise, that those in *Turkey,* tho' we refuse to buy above half as much of their Commodities as we used to do, either can or will not be without the same quantity of our Manufactures they had before, and that they'll pay the Balance in Money; that is to say, that they shall give us as much Gold or Silver, as the value of what they buy from us exceeds the value of what we buy from them. Tho' what we suppose might perhaps be done for one Year, it is impossible it should last: Buying is Bartering, and no Nation can buy Goods of others that has none of her own to purchase them with. *Spain* and *Portugal,* that are yearly supply'd with new Gold and Silver from their Mines, may for ever buy for ready Money as long as their yearly increase of Gold or Silver continues, but then Money is their Growth and the Commodity of the Country. We know that we could not continue long to purchase the Goods of other Nations, if they would not take our Manufactures in Payment for them; and why should we judge otherwise of other Nations? If those in *Turkey* then had no more Money fall from the Skies than we, let us see what would be the consequence of what we supposed The Six Hundred Thousand Pounds in Silk, Mohair, &c. that are left upon their Hands the first Year, must make those Commodities fall considerably: Of this the *Dutch* and *French will* reap the Benefit as much as our selves; and if we continue to refuse taking their Commodities in Payment for our Manufactures, they can Trade no longer with us, but must content themselves with buying what they want of such Nations as are willing to take what we refuse, tho' their Goods are much worse than ours, and thus our Commerce with *Turkey* must in few Years be infallibly lost.

But they'll say, perhaps, that to prevent the ill consequence I have shew'd, we shall take the *Turkish* Merchandizes as formerly, and only be so frugal as to consume but half the quantity of them our selves, and send the rest Abroad to be sold to others. Let us see what this will do, and whether it will enrich the Nation by the balance of that Trade with Six Hundred Thousand Pounds. In the first Place, I'll grant them that our People at Home making use of so much more of our own Manufactures, those who were employ'd in Silk, Mohair, &c. will get a living by the various Preparations of Woollen Goods. But in the second, I cannot allow that the Goods can be sold as formerly; for suppose the Half that is wore at Home to be sold at the same Rate as before, certainly the other Half that is sent Abroad will want very much of it: For we must send those Goods to Markets already supply'd; and besides that there must be Freight, Insurance, Provision, and all other Charges deducted, and the Merchants in general must lose much more by this Half that is reshipp'd, than they got by the Half that is consumed here. For tho' the Woollen Manufactures are our own Product, yet they stand the Merchant that ships them off to Foreign Countries, in as much as they do the Shopkeeper here that retails them: so that if the Returns for what he sends Abroad repay him not what his Goods cost him here, with all other Charges, till he has the Money and a good Interest for it in Cash, the Merchant must run out, and the Upshot would be, that the Merchants in general finding they lost by the *Turkish* Commodities they sent Abroad, would ship no more of our Manufactures than what would pay for as much Silk, Mohair, &c. as would be consumed here. Other Nations would soon find Ways to supply them with as much as we should send short, and some where or other to dispose of the Goods we should refuse: So that all we should get by this Frugality would be, that those in *Turkey* would take but half the Quantity of our Manufactures of what they do now, while we encourage and wear their Merchandizes, without which they are not able to purchase ours.

......................................................

What is laid to the Charge of Luxury besides, is, that it increases Avarice and Rapine: And where they are reigning Vices, Offices of the greatest Trust are bought and sold; the Ministers that should serve the Publick, both great and small, corrupted, and the Countries every Moment in danger of being betray'd to the highest Bidders: And lastly, that it effeminates and enervates the People, by which the Nations become an easy Prey to the first Invaders. These are indeed terrible Things; but what is put to the Account of Luxury belongs to Male-Administration, and is the Fault of bad Politicks. Every Government ought to be thoroughly acquainted with, and stedfastly to pursue the Interest of the Country. Good Politicians by dextrous Management, laying heavy Impositions on some Goods, or totally prohibiting them, and lowering the Duties on others, may always turn and divert the Course of Trade which way they please; and as they'll ever prefer, if it be equally considerable, the Commerce with such Countries as can pay with Money as well as Goods, to those that can make no Returns for what they buy, but in the Commodities of their own Growth and Manufactures, so they will always carefully prevent the Traffick with such Nations as refuse the Goods of others, and will take nothing but Money for their own. But above all, they'll keep a watchful Eye over the Balance of Trade in general, and never suffer that all the Foreign Commodities together, that are imported in one Year, shall exceed in Value what of their own Growth or Manufacture is in the same exported to others. Note, that I speak now of the Interest of those Nations that have no Gold or Silver of their own Growth, otherwise this Maxim need not to be so much insisted on.

If what I urg'd last be but diligently look'd after, and the Imports are never allow'd to be superior to the Exports, no Nation can ever be impoverish'd by Foreign Luxury; and they may improve it as much as they please, if they can but in proportion raise the Fund of their own that is to purchase it.

14

Trade is the Principal, but not the only Requisite to aggrandize a Nation: there are other Things to be taken care of besides. The *Meum* and *Tuum* must be secur'd, Crimes punish'd, and all other Laws concerning the Administration of Justice, wisely contriv'd, and strictly executed. Foreign Affairs must be likewise prudently manag'd, and the Ministry of every Nation ought to have a good Intelligence Abroad, and be well acquainted with the Publick Transactions of all those Countries, that either by their Neighbourhood, Strength or Interest, may be hurtful or beneficial to them, to take the necessary Measures accordingly, of crossing some and assisting others, as Policy and the Balance of Power direct. The Multitude must be aw'd, no Man's Conscience forc'd, and the Clergy allow'd no greater Share in State Affairs than our Saviour has bequeathed them in his Testament. These are the Arts that lead to worldly Greatness: what Sovereign Power soever makes a good Use of them, that has any considerable Nation to govern, whether it be a Monarchy, a Commonwealth, or a Mixture of both, can never fail of making it flourish in spight of all the other Powers upon Earth, and no Luxury or other Vice is ever able to shake their Constitution. But here I expect a full-mouth'd Cry against me; What! has God never punish'd and destroy'd great Nations for their Sins? Yes, but not without Means, by infatuating their Governors, and suffering them to depart from either all or some of those general Maxims I have mentioned; and of all the famous States and Empires the World has had to boast of hitherto, none ever came to Ruin whose Destruction was not principally owing to the bad Politicks, Neglects, or Mismanagements of the Rulers.

There is no doubt but more Health and Vigour is to be expected among a People, and their Offspring, from Temperance and Sobriety, than there is from Gluttony and Drunkenness; yet I confess, that as to Luxury's effeminating and enervating a Nation, I have not such frightful Notions now as I have had formerly. When we hear or read of Things which we are altogether Strangers to, they commonly bring to our Imagination such Ideas of what we have seen, as (according to our Apprehension) must come the nearest to them: And I remember, that when I have read of the Luxury of *Persia, Egypt,* and other Countries where it has been a reigning Vice, and that were effeminated and enervated by it, it has sometimes put me in mind of the cramming and swilling of ordinary Tradesmen at a City Feast, and the Beastliness their overgorging themselves is often attended with; at other Times it has made me think on the Distraction of dissolute Sailors, as I had seen them in Company of half a dozen lewd Women roaring along with Fiddles before them; and was I to have been carried into any of their great Cities, I would have expected to have found one Third of the People sick a-bed with Surfeits; another laid up with the Gout, or crippled by a more ignominious Distemper; and the rest, that could go without leading, walk along the Streets in Petticoats.

It is happy for us to have Fear for a Keeper, as long as our Reason is not strong enough to govern our Appetites: And I believe that the great Dread I had more particularly against the Word, *to enervate,* and some consequent Thoughts on the

15

Etymology of it, did me Abundance of Good when I was a Schoolboy: But since I have seen something of the World, the Consequences of Luxury to a Nation seem not so dreadful to me as they did. As long as Men have the same Appetites, the same Vices will remain. In all large Societies, some will love Whoring and others Drinking. The Lustful that can get no handsome clean Women, will content themselves with dirty Drabs; and those that cannot purchase true *Hermitage* or *Pontack,* will be glad of more ordinary *French* Claret. Those that can't reach Wine, take up with worse Liquors, and a Foot Soldier or a Beggar may make himself as drunk with Stale-Beer or Malt-Spirits, as a Lord with *Burgundy,* Champaign or Tockay. The cheapest and most slovenly way of indulging our Passions, does as much Mischief to a Man's Constitution, as the most elegant and expensive.

...................................................

There is nothing refines Mankind more than Love and Honour. Those two Passions are equivalent to many Virtues, and therefore the greatest Schools of Breeding and good Manners are Courts and Armies; the first to accomplish the Women, the other to polish the Men. What the generality of Officers among civiliz'd Nations affect is a perfect Knowledge of the World and the Rules of Honour; an Air of Frankness, and Humanity peculiar to Military Men of Experience, and such a mixture of Modesty and Undauntedness, as may bespeak them both Courteous and Valiant. Where good Sense is fashionable, and a genteel Behaviour is in esteem, Gluttony and Drunkenness can be no reigning Vices. What Officers of Distinction chiefly aim at is not a Beastly, but a Splendid way of Living, and the Wishes of the most Luxurious in their several degrees of Quality, are to appear handsomely, and excel each other in Finery of Equipage, Politeness of Entertainments, and the Reputation of a judicious Fancy in every thing about them.

But if there should be more dissolute Reprobates among Officers than there are among Men of other Professions, which is not true, yet the most debauch'd of them may be very serviceable, if they have but a great Share of Honour. It is this that covers and makes up for a multitude of Defects in them, and it is this that none (how abandon'd soever they are to Pleasure) dare pretend to be without. But as there is no Argument so convincing as Matter of Fact, let us look back on what so lately happen'd in our two last Wars with *France.* How many puny young Striplings have we had in our Armies, tenderly Educated, nice in their Dress, and curious in their Diet, that underwent all manner of Duties with Gallantry and Chearfulness ?

...................................................

Those that understand their Business, and have a sufficient Sense of Honour, as soon as they are used to Danger will always be capable Officers: And their Luxury, as long as they spend no Body's Money but their own, will never be prejudicial to a Nation.

By all which I think I have proved what I design'd in this Remark on Luxury. First, That in one Sense everything may be call'd so, and in another there is no such Thing. Secondly, That with a wise Administration all People may swim in as much Foreign Luxury as their Product can purchase, without being impoverish'd by it. And Lastly, That where Military Affairs are taken care of as they ought, and the Soldiers well paid and kept in good Dislcipline, a wealthy Nation may live in all the Ease and Plenty imaginable; and in many Parts of it, shew as much Pomp and Delicacy, as Human Wit can invent, and at the same Time be formidable to their Neighbours, and come up to the Character of the Bees in the Fable, of which I said, That

> *Flatter'd in Peace, and fear'd in Wars,*
> *They were th' Esteem of Foreigners,*
> *And lavish of their Wealth and Lives,*
> *The Balance of all other Hives.*

## Remark (Q.)

------*For frugally They now liv'd on their Salary.*

When People have small comings in, and are honest withal, it is then that the Generality of them begin to be frugal, and not before. Frugality in *Ethicks* is call'd that Virtue from the Principle of which Men abstain from Superfluities, and despising the operose Contrivances of Art to procure either Ease or Pleasure, content themselves with the natural Simplicity of things, and are carefully temperate in the Enjoyment of them without any Tincture of Covetousness. Frugality thus limited, is perhaps scarcer than many may imagine; but what is generally understood by it is a Quality more often to be met with, and consists in a *Medium* between Profuseness and Avarice, rather leaning to the latter. As this prudent Oeconomy, which some People call *Saving,* is in private Families the most certain Method to increase an Estate, so some imagine that whether a Country be barren or fruitful, the same Method, if generally pursued (which they think practicable) will have the same Effect upon a whole Nation, and that, for Example, the *English* might be much richer than they are, if they would be as frugal as some of their Neighbours. This, I think, is an Error, which to prove I shall first refer the Reader to what has been said upon this head in Remark (L.) and then go on thus.

17

Experience teaches us first, that as People differ in their Views and Perceptions of Things, so they vary in their Inclinations; one Man is given to Covetousness, another to Prodigality, and a third is only *Saving*. Secondly, that Men are never, or at least very seldom, reclaimed from their darling Passions, either by Reason or Precept, and that if any thing ever draws 'em from what they are naturally propense to, it must be a Change in their Circumstances or their Fortunes. If we reflect upon these Observations, we shall find that to render the generality of a Nation lavish, the Product of the Country must be considerable in proportion to the Inhabitants, and what they are profuse of cheap; that on the contrary, to make a Nation generally frugal, the Necessaries of Life must be scarce, and consequently dear; and that therefore let the best Politician do what he can, the Profuseness or Frugality of a People in general, must always depend upon, and will in spite of his Teeth, be ever proportion'd to the Fruitfulness and Product of the Country, the Number of Inhabitants, and the Taxes they are to bear. If any body would refute what I have said, let him only prove from History, that there ever was in any Country a National Frugality without a National Necessity.

Let us examine then what things are requisite to aggrandize and enrich a Nation. The first desirable Blessings for any Society of Men are a fertile Soil and a happy Climate, a mild Government, and more Land than People. These Things will render Man easy, loving, honest and sincere. In this Condition they may be as Virtuous as they can, without the least Injury to the Publick, and consequently as happy as they please themselves. But they shall have no Arts or Sciences, or be quiet longer than their Neighbours will let them; they must be poor, ignorant, and almost wholly destitute of what we call the Comforts of Life, and all the Cardinal Virtues together won't so much as procure a tolerable Coat or a Porridge-Pot among them: For in this State of slothful Ease and stupid Innocence, as you need not fear great Vices, so you must not expect any considerable Virtues. Man never exerts himself but when he is rous'd by his Desires: While they lie dormant, and there is nothing to raise them, his Excellence and Abilities will be for ever undiscover'd, and the lumpish Machine, without the Influence of his Passions, may be justly compar'd to a huge Wind-mill without a breath of Air.

Would you render a Society of Men strong and powerful, you must touch their Passions. Divide the Land, tho' there be never so much to spare, and their Possessions will make them Covetous: Rouse them, tho' but in Jest, from their Idleness with Praises, and Pride will set them to work in earnest: Teach them Trades and Handicrafts, and you'll bring Envy and Emulation among them: To increase their Numbers, set up a Variety of Manufactures, and leave no Ground uncultivated; Let Property be inviolably secured, and Privileges equal to all Men; Suffer no body to act but what is lawful, and every body to think what he pleases; for a Country where every body may be maintained that will be employ'd, and the other Maxims are observ'd, must always be throng'd and can never want People, as long as there is any in the World. Would you have them bold and Warlike, turn to Military Discipline, make good use of their Fear, and flatter their Vanity with Art and

Assiduity: But would you moreover render them an opulent, knowing and polite Nation, teach 'em Commerce with Foreign Countries, and if possible get into the Sea, which to compass spare no Labour nor Industry, and let no Difficulty deter you from it: Then promote Navigation, cherish the Merchant, and encourage Trade in every Branch of it; this will bring Riches, and where they are, Arts and Sciences will soon follow, and by the Help of what I have named and good Management, it is that Politicians can make a People potent, renown'd and flourishing.

But would you have a frugal and honest Society, the best Policy is to preserve Men in their Native Simplicity, strive not to increase their Numbers; let them never be acquainted with Strangers or Superfluities, but remove and keep from them every thing that might raise their Desires, or improve their Understanding.

Great Wealth and Foreign Treasure will ever scorn to come among Men, unless you'll admit their inseparable Companions, Avarice and Luxury: Where Trade is considerable Fraud will intrude. To be at once well-bred and sincere, is no less than a Contradiction; and therefore while Man advances in Knowledge, and his Manners are polish'd, we must expect to see at the same time his Desires enlarg'd, his Appetites refin'd, and his Vices increas'd.

..............................................................

To convince the Champions for National Frugality by another Argument, that what they urge is impracticable, we'll suppose that I am mistaken in every thing which in *Remark (L)*. I have said in behalf of Luxury, and the necessity of it to maintain Trade: after that let us examine what a general Frugality, if it was by Art and Management to be forc'd upon People whether they have Occasion for it or not, would produce in such a Nation as ours. We'll grant then that all the People in *Great Britain* shall consume but four Fifths of what they do now, and so lay by one Fifth part of their Income; I shall not speak of what Influence this would have upon almost every Trade, as well as the Farmer, the Grazier and the Landlord, but favourably suppose (what is yet impossible) that the same Work shall be done, and consequently the same Handicrafts be employ'd as there are now. The Consequence would be, that unless Money should all at once fall prodigiously in Value, and every thing else, contrary to Reason, grow very dear, at the five Years end all the working People, and the poorest of Labourers, (for I won't meddle with any of the rest) would be worth in ready Cash as much as they now spend in a whole Year; which, by the by, would be more Money than ever the Nation had at once.

Let us now, overjoy'd with this increase of Wealth, take a View of the Condition the working People would be in, and reasoning from Experience, and what we daily observe of them, judge what their Behaviour would be in such a Case. Every Body knows that there is a vast number of Journey-men Weavers, Tailors, Clothworkers, and twenty other Handicrafts; who, if by four Days Labour in a Week they can maintain themselves, will hardly be persuaded to work the fifth; and that there are Thousands of labouring Men of all sorts, who will, tho' they can hardly subsist, put themselves to fifty Inconveniences disoblige their Masters, pinch their Bellies, and run in Debt, to make Holidays. When Men shew such an extraordinary proclivity to Idleness and Pleasure, what reason have we to think that they would ever work, unless they were oblig'd to it by immediate Necessity? When we see an Artificer that cannot be drove to his Work before *Tuesday,* because the *Monday* Morning he has two Shillings left of his last Week's Pay; why should we imagine he would go to it at all, if he had fiffteen or twenty Pounds in his Pocket?

What would, at this rate, become of our Manufactures? If the Merchant would send Cloth Abroad, he must make it himself, for the Clothier cannot get one Man out of twelve that used to work for him. If what I speak of was only to befal the Journeymen Shoemakers, and no body else, in less than a Twelve-month half of us would go barefoot. The chief and most pressing use there is for Money in a Nation, is to pay the Labour of the Poor, and when there is a real Scarcity of it, those who have a great many Workmen to pay, will always feel it first; yet notwithstanding this great Necessity of Coin, it would be easier, where Property was well secured, to live without Money than without Poor; for who would do the Work? For this Reason the quantity of circulating Coin in a Country ought always to be proportion'd to the number of Hands that are employ'd; and the Wages of Labourers to the Price of Provisions. From whence it is demonstrable, that whatever procures Plenty makes Labourers cheap, where the Poor are well managed; who as they ought to be kept from starving, so they should receive nothing worth saving. If here and there one of the lowest Class by uncommon Industry, and pinching his Belly, lifts himself above the Condition he was brought up in, no body ought to hinder him; Nay it is undeniably the wisest course for every Person in the Society, and for every private Family to be frugal; but it is the Interest of all rich Nations, that the greatest part of the Poor should almost never be idle, and yet continually spend what they get.

All Men, as Sir *William Temple* observes very well, are more prone to Ease and Pleasure than they are to Labour, when they are not prompted to it by Pride or Avarice, and those that get their Living by their daily Labour, are seldom powerfully influenc'd by either: So that they have nothing to stir them up to be serviceable but their Wants, which it is Prudence to relieve, but Folly to cure. The only thing then that can render the labouring Man industrious, is a moderate quantity of Money; for as too little will, according as his Temper is, either dispirit or make him Desperate, so too much will make him Insolent and Lazy.

A Man would be laugh'd at by most People, who should maintain that too much Money could undo a Nation. Yet this has been the Fate of *Spain;* to this the learned Don *Diego Savedra* ascribes the Ruin of his Country. The Fruits of the Earth in former Ages had made *Spain* so rich, that King *Lewis* XI of *France* being come to the Court of *Toledo,* was astonish'd at its Splendour, and said, that he had never seen any thing to be compar'd to it, either in *Europe* or *Asia;* he that in his Travels to the *Holy Land* had run through every

20

Province of them. In the Kingdom of *Castille* alone, (if we may believe some Writers) there were for the *Holy War* from all Parts of the World got together one hundred thousand Foot, ten thousand Horse, and sixty thousand Carriages for Baggage, which *Alonso* III maintain'd at his own Charge, and paid every Day as well Soldiers as Officers and Princes, every one according to his Rank and Dignity: Nay, down to the Reign of *Ferdinand* and *Isabella,* (who equipp'd *Columbus*) and some time after, *Spain* was a fertile Country, where Trade and Manufactures flourished, and had a knowing industrious People to boast of. But as soon as that mighty Treasure, that was obtain'd with more Hazard and Cruelty than the World 'till then had kown, and which to come at, by the *Spaniard's* own Confession, had cost the Lives of twenty Millions of *Indians*; as soon, I say, as that Ocean of Treasure came rolling in upon them, it took away their Senses, and their Industry forsook them. The Farmer left his Plough, the Mechanick his Tools, the Merchant his Compting-house, and every body scorning to work took his Pleasure and turn'd Gentleman. They thought they had reason to value themselves above all their Neighbours, and now nothing but the Conquest of the World would serve them.

The Consequence of this has been, that other Nations have supply'd what their own Sloth and Pride deny'd them; and when every body saw, that notwithstanding all the Prohibitions the Government could make against the Exportation of Bullion, the *Spaniard* would part with his Money, and bring it you aboard himself at the hazard of his Neck, all the World endeavoured to work for Spain. Gold and Silver being by this Means yearly divided and shared among all the trading Countries, have made all Things dear, and most Nations of *Europe* industrious, except their Owners, who ever since their mighty Acquisitions, sit with their Arms across, and wait every Year with impatience and anxiety, the arrival of their Revenues from Abroad, to pay others for what they have spent already: and thus by *too much Money,* the making of Colonies and other Mismanagements, of which it was the occasion, *Spain is* from a fruitful and well-peopled Country, with all its mighty Titles and Possessions, made a barren and empty Thorough-fare, thro' which Gold and Silver pass from *America* to the rest of the World; and the Nation, from a rich, acute, diligent and laborious, become a slow, idle, proud and beggarly People; so much for *Spain.* The next Country where Money may be called the Product is *Portugal,* and the Figure which that Kingdom with all its Gold makes in *Europe,* I think is not much to be envied.

The great Art then to make a Nation happy and what we call flourishing, consists in giving every Body an Opportunity of being employ'd; which to compass, let a Government's first care be to promote as great a variety of Manufactures, Arts, and Handicrafts, as Human Wit can invent; and the second to encourage Agriculture and Fishery in all their Branches, that the whole Earth may be forc'd to exert it self as well as Man; for as the one is an infallible Maxim to draw vast Multitudes of People into a Nation, so the other is the only Method to maintain them.

It is from this Policy, and not the trifling Regulations of Lavishness and Frugality, (which will ever take their own Course, according to the Circumstances of the People) that the Greatness and Felicity of Nations must be expected; for let the Value of Gold and Silver either rise or fall, the Enjoyment of all Societies will ever depend upon the Fruits of the Earth, and the Labour of the People; both which joined together are a more certain, a more inexhaustible, and a more real Treasure, than the Gold of *Brazil,* or the Silver of *Potosi.*

# Chapter 4

## Cantillon on Entrepreneurship

Richard Cantillon (1680?-1734?) wrote sparingly but with great insight into the workings of the market economy. His *Essay on the Nature of Trade*, written around 1730 but not published until 1755, was an attempt to explain the world of his day. From our perspective it seems a distant and quaint world, of kings and princes, of large landed estates owned by nobles, and of small businessmen peddling their wares. The French Revolution (1789) was still over fifty years away and the property rights and privileges of the nobility were respected and accepted almost as a consequence of nature itself. Nevertheless, Cantillon's world already had many of the characteristics of our own, so that we can still learn from his analysis. Cantillon focused on the nature of commercial activity, which already by the eighteenth century held the key to understanding what superficially looked like a chaotic jumble of activities.

Cantillon's method of analysis was remarkably modern. He engaged in theoretical comparative-systems analysis. In the first instance he sets forth a model in which economic decision-making is centralized. This first model consists of only one great estate. The proprietor undertakes cultivation by himself, and his wishes alone count. In the second model, proprietors still "lead" the market in terms of setting demand, but the centralized decision-making of the proprietor is replaced by a decentralized form of decision-making in which supply is adjusted to demand by trial and error. In this decentralized model, the proprietor delegates responsibility to "overseers of labor" and his "overseers of mechanics" such that they become *entrepreneurs*. Otherwise, everything goes on as before. However, the consequences for the economy are dramatic. By employing the great estate as an analytical device, Cantillon is able to reveal the essential features of economic activity in a way that would be easily understood by his contemporaries. In the following extracts, see if you can identify the two models Cantillon employed, and trace their consequences on economic activity.

Source: *Essai sur la Nature du Commerce en Général by Richard Cantillon*, edited by Henry Higgs. New York: Augustus M. Kelley, 1964. Pages 43-65).

# CHAPTER XII

## *All Classes and Individuals in a State Subsist or are Enriched at the Expense of the Proprietors of Land*

Only the Prince and the landowners live independently; all other classes and inhabitants are hired or are entrepreneurs. The proof and the specifics of this statement will become obvious in the following chapter.

Obviously, if the Prince and the landowners close their estates and do not allow them to be cultivated, there would be neither food nor clothing for any of the inhabitants of a State; consequently all individuals in society are supported not only by the produce of the land which is cultivated for the benefit of the owners, but also at the expense of these same owners, from whose property the inhabitants derive whatever they get.

The farmers generally receive two thirds of the produce of the land, one third to cover their costs and the support of their assistants, the other third as profit for their own efforts. From this two-thirds share, the farmer usually provides, directly or indirectly, subsistence for all those who live in the country, and also for several artisans or entrepreneurs in the city who produce merchandise there that is consumed in the country.

The proprietor usually keeps one third of the produce of his land and on this third he maintains all the artisans and others whom he employs in the city, often including as well the shippers who carry the country's produce to the city.

It is generally assumed that one half of the inhabitants of a kingdom live and subsist in cities, and the other half in the country. On this assumption the farmer, who receives two thirds, or four sixths, of the produce of the land, pays out one sixth, either directly or indirectly, to the citizens from whom he buys merchandise. This sixth, along with the one third or two sixths which the landowner spends in the city, makes up three sixths or one half of the produce of the land. This rough calculation is only meant to convey a general idea of the division of income; in fact, if half of the inhabitants live in cities they will consume more than half of the produce of the land, because they will likely be artisans or dependents of the proprietors, and are thereby better maintained than the assistants and the dependents of the farmers, who live in the country.

However this division turns out, if we trace back to its roots the means by which an inhabitant is supported we always find that these means originate in the land held by the proprietor, either in the two thirds that goes to the farmer or the one third reserved for the landlord.

If all a proprietor's land were leased to a single farmer the farmer would get a better living out of it than the proprietor himself; but the nobles and large landowners in the cities often lease to several hundreds of farmers, while they are themselves very few in number compared to all the inhabitants of the State.

Admittedly it is often the case that some entrepreneurs and artisans in the city engage in foreign trade, and therefore live at the expense of foreign landowners, but at present I shall confine myself to a State without external trade, so as not to complicate my argument unnecessarily.

The land belongs to the proprietors but would be useless to them if it were not cultivated. The more labor expended on it, other things equal, the more it produces; and the more its products are worked up, other things being equal, the more value they have as merchandise. Hence the proprietors depend upon the inhabitants, just as the inhabitants depend upon the proprietors; but in this economy it is the proprietors who exercise control and supervision of landed capital, which is what gives the most advantageous turn and movement to the whole. Also everything in a State depends on the fancy, methods, and fashions of the landowners, as I will try to make clear later in this essay.

Need and necessity enable farmers, all manner of manufacturers, merchants, officers, soldiers, sailors, domestic servants and all the other classes engaged in economic activity in the State, to exist. All these working people serve not only the Prince and the landowners, but also each other, so that there are many of them who do not work directly for the landowners; thus, it is not obvious that they subsist on the capital of these landowners and live at their expense. Insofar as professional people are concerned, such as dancers, actors, painters, musicians, etc., they are only maintained in society for pleasure or for ornament, and their number is always a very small proportion of the total inhabitants.

## CHAPTER XIII

*The Circulation and Exchange of Goods and Merchandise as well as their Production are Carried on in Europe by Entrepreneurs, and at a Risk*

The farmer is an entrepreneur who promises to pay to the landowner, for his farm or land, a fixed sum of money (generally supposed to be equal in value to a third of the produce) without any assurance of receiving a profit from his enterprise. He uses part of the land to feed livestock, produce grain, wine, hay, etc., according to his judgment, but without being able to foresee which of these will pay best. The price of these products will depend partly on the weather, partly on demand. If wheat is abundant relative to its consumption it will be dirt cheap. If there is a scarcity it will be dear. Who can foresee the number of births and deaths of the people in a State in the course of the year? Who can foresee the increase or reduction of expense which may come about in the families? And yet the price of the farmer's produce depends naturally upon these unforeseen circumstances. Consequently, he conducts the enterprise of his farm at uncertainty.

More than half of agricultural output is consumed in the city. The farmer carries his produce to market there or sells it in the market of the nearest town; or perhaps to a few individuals who set themselves up as carriers. These individuals commit themselves to pay the farmer a fixed price for his produce, according to the current market circumstances, and thereafter they sell in the city at an uncertain price, which must nevertheless defray the cost of carriage and leave them a profit. But the daily variation in the price of products in the city, though not considerable, makes their profit uncertain.

The entrepreneur or merchant who carries produce from the country to the city cannot usually remain behind to sell it in dribs and drabs as people wish to consume. And no city family will burden itself with the purchase of all its needs at once, each family being susceptible to increase or decrease in number and in consumption, or to variation in the choice of products it will consume. Wine is almost the only article of consumption which families ordinarily stock. In any case, the majority of citizens who live from day to day, as well as even the largest consumers, cannot lay in a stock of produce from the country.

For this reason many city dwellers set themselves up as merchants or entrepreneurs to buy the country produce from those who bring it into the city, or to order it to be brought explicitly on their own account. They pay a certain price according to local conditions, in order to resell it wholesale or retail at an uncertain price.

Examples of such entrepreneurs are the wholesalers in wool and grain, bakers, butchers, manufacturers and merchants of all kinds, who buy country produce and raw materials to work them up and resell them piecemeal as the inhabitants require them.

These entrepreneurs can never know how great will be the demand in their city, nor how long their customers will buy from them, because their rivals will try all sorts of means to steal customers away. All this causes so much uncertainty among these entrepreneurs that every day witnesses one bankruptcy or another.

The manufacturer who buys wool from the wool merchant or directly from the farmer cannot predict the profit he will make in selling clothes and other dry goods to the merchant tailor. If the latter doesn't have brisk sales, he will not build much inventory through purchases of clothes and dry goods from the manufacturer, especially if fashions change quickly.

The draper [i.e., dealer in dry goods] is an entrepreneur who buys clothes and dry goods from the manufacturer at a certain price in order to sell them again at an uncertain price, because he cannot foresee the extent of his demand. He can, of course, fix a price and withhold sales until he gets it, but if his customers leave him to buy cheaper elsewhere he will be consumed by expenses while waiting to sell at the price he demands, and that will ruin him as soon as or sooner than if he sold without a profit.

Shopkeepers and retailers of every kind are entrepreneurs who buy at a certain price and sell in their shops or in the markets at an uncertain price. What encourages and maintains them in a State is that the consumers who are their customers prefer paying a little more to get what they want in small quantities when they want them rather than stockpile larger quantities; moreover, most of the consumers do not have the wherewithal to lay in such a stock by buying in quantity.

All these entrepreneurs become consumers and customers of each other, the draper of the wine merchant, and vice versa. They proportion themselves in a State to the extent of demand. If there are too many hatters in a city or in a street for the number of people who buy hats there, those who are least patronized must go out of business; if there be too few, the resulting profits will encourage new hatters to open shops there; and so it is that the entrepreneurs of all kinds adjust themselves to the prevailing risks in a State.

All the other entrepreneurs live at uncertainty and proportion themselves to their customers; like those who direct mines, theaters, construction, etc., the merchants by sea and land, etc., cook-shop keepers, pastry cooks, innkeepers, etc., as well as the entrepreneurs of their own labor who need no capital to establish themselves, like journeyman artisans, coppersmiths, needlewomen, chimney sweeps, and water carriers. Inasmuch as their customers may forsake them from one day to another, the master craftsmen like shoemakers, tailors, carpenters, wigmakers, etc., who employ journeymen according to the amount of work they have, live at the same uncertainty. The entrepreneurs of their own labor in the arts and sciences, like painters, physicians, lawyers, etc., live in similar uncertainty. If one attorney or barrister makes 5,000 pounds sterling yearly in the service of his clients and another earns only 500 pounds they may be regarded as having so much uncertain wages from those who employ them.

It might be argued by some that in their capacity as entrepreneurs, such persons try to get the better of their customers and snatch all they can from them, but this is outside my subject.

By all these inductions and many others that could be made concerning the inhabitants of a State, it may be asserted that with the exception of the Prince and the landowners, all the inhabitants of a State are dependent; that they can be divided into two classes, entrepreneurs and hirelings; and that all the entrepreneurs are as it were on unfixed wages and all the others are on fixed wages, so long as they receive them, even though their functions and ranks be very unequal. The general who draws his salary, the courtier who receives his pension and the domestic servant who earns his wages all fall into this last class. All the rest are entrepreneurs, whether they set up with a capital to conduct their enterprise, or are entrepreneurs of their own labor without capital; and they may be regarded as living at uncertainty; even beggars and robbers are of this class. Finally, all the inhabitants of a State derive their living and their advantages from the property of the landowners and are dependent upon them.

It is true, however, that someone with high wages or a successful entrepreneur who has accumulated capital or wealth may be justly considered independent so far as this capital goes: if he has stores of grain, wool, copper, gold, silver, or some goods or merchandise that is in constant demand, having a real or intrinsic value. He may use it to acquire a mortgage, receive interest from land or from public loans secured by land, and he may live even better than the small landowner, and may even buy the property of some of them.

Nevertheless, produce and merchandise, even gold and silver, are much more susceptible to accident and loss than the ownership of land; and however one may have gained or saved these forms of wealth they are always derived from land currently owned, either by accumulating profits or by saving out of the income otherwise earmarked for living expenses.

The number of people who hold money in a large State is often considerable enough; and though the value of all the money which circulates in the State barely exceeds the ninth or tenth part of the value of the produce drawn from the soil yet, as the owners of money lend considerable amounts for which they receive interest either by mortgage or public bonds, the sums due to them usually exceed all the money in the State, and they often become so powerful a body that, in certain instances they rival the owners of land, if they are not the same people; and if the owners of large sums of money did not always seek to become landowners themselves.

It is nevertheless always true that all the sums gained or saved have been drawn from land which is currently owned; but inasmuch as many of these landowners ruin themselves daily and their place is taken by others who acquire their property, the independence bestowed by the ownership of land applies only to those who keep possession of it. Inasmuch as all land always has a current owner, I assume throughout that it is from their property that all the inhabitants of the State derive their living and all their wealth. This would be incontrovertible if these landowners confined themselves to living on their rents, and in that case it would be much more difficult for the other inhabitants to enrich themselves at their expense.

I will therefore lay it down as a principle that in society only landowners are naturally independent: that all other classes are dependent whether entrepreneurs or hired, and that all the exchange and circulation of the State is conducted by the intercession of these entrepreneurs.


## CHAPTER XIV

*The Fancies, the Fashions and the Modes of Living of the Prince,
and Especially of the Landowners, Determine the Use to Which Land
is Put in a State and Cause the Variations in the Market Price of All Things*


If the owner of a large estate (which I wish to consider here as if it were the only one in the world) cultivates it himself he will follow his own desires in the use to which he puts it. (1) He will necessarily use some part of it for grain to feed his workers, artisans and overseers; another part to feed the cattle, sheep and other animals necessary for their clothing and food, or other commodities according to the way in which he wishes to maintain them. (2)

He will convert part of the land into parks, gardens, fruit trees, or vines as he feels inclined, and into pasture for the maintenance of those horses he keeps for his pleasure, etc.

Let us now suppose that to avoid so much care and trouble he strikes a deal with his overseers of labor, gives them land to cultivate and leaves to them the responsibility of maintaining in the usual manner all the workers they supervise. In effect, the overseers now become farmers or entrepreneurs, giving the fieldworkers a third of the produce for their food, clothing, and other needs, just as they had when the owner formerly employed them.

Assume further that the owner makes a similar bargain with the overseers of the artisans for the food and other things that he formerly gave them, so that the overseers become master-craftsmen, and that he establishes a common standard, like silver, to settle the price at which the farmers will supply them with wool and they will him with cloth, and that the prices are such as to give the master-craftsmen the same advantages and enjoyments that they had when they were overseers, and that the journeymen artisans are also maintained as before: their work regulated by the day or by the piece; their output, whether hats, stockings, shoes, clothes, etc. being sold to the landlord, the farmer, the workers and to other artisans as well, at a price that leaves all of them as well off as before. Finally, the farmers continue to sell their produce and raw material at a suitable price.

What happens, therefore, is that the overseers become entrepreneurs, the absolute masters of those who work under them, and they will take more care and satisfaction in working on their own account. We assume then that after this change all the people on this large estate live just as they did before, and that therefore all the parts and farms of this great estate will be put to the same use as it formerly was.

Thus, if some of the farmers sowed more grain than usual they must feed fewer sheep, and have less wool and mutton to sell. Then there will be too much grain and too little wool for the inhabitants to consume. Wool will therefore be dear, which will force the inhabitants to wear their clothes longer than usual, and there will be an oversupply of grain, and a surplus for the next year. And as we assume that the landlord has stipulated that a third of the produce be paid to him in silver, the farmers who have too much grain and too little wool will not be able to pay him his rent. If he excuses them this year, they will be careful the next year to produce less grain and more wool, for farmers always take care to use their land for the production of things which they think will fetch the best price at market. If, however, next year they have too much wool and too little grain for the demand, they will not fail to change from year to year the use of the land until they have adjusted their production more or less to the consumption of the inhabitants. Thus, a farmer who has adjusted his output to the level of consumption will have part of his farm in grass, for hay, another in wheat, wool, and so on, and he will not change his plan unless he sees some considerable change in demand; but in this example we have assumed that all the people live in the same way as when the landowner cultivated the land for himself, and consequently the farmers will employ the land in the same manner as before.

The owner, who has at his disposal one third of the produce of the land, is the principal agent in the changes that might occur in demand. Workmen and artisans who live from day to day change their mode of living only from necessity. If a few farmers, master-craftsmen, or other entrepreneurs in wealthy circumstances vary their expense and consumption they always pattern their behavior on that of the lords and landowners. They imitate them in their dress, food, and mode of life. If the landowners choose to wear fine linen, silk, or lace, the consumption of these things will therefore be greater than it would have been for the proprietors alone.

If a lord or landowner who has leased out all his lands to farming decides to change his mode of living in a significant way; if for instance he decreases the number of his domestic servants and increases the number of his horses; not only will his servants be forced to leave the estate but so will a proportionate number of artisans and workers who worked to maintain them. The portion of land that was used to maintain these inhabitants will then be planted in grass for the new horses, and if all landowners in a State did the same it would soon lead to an increase in the number of horses and a reduction in the number of men.

When a landowner has dismissed a large number of domestic servants and increased the number of his horses, there will then be too much wheat for the needs of the inhabitants, making wheat cheap and hay expensive. Consequently, the farmers will increase their grass land and diminish their wheat to adjust it to the demand. In this way the tastes and preferences of landowners determine the use of the land and produce the variations of demand that cause the variations of market prices. If all the landowners of a State cultivated their estates they would use them to produce what they want; and as the variations of demand are chiefly caused by their mode of living the prices that are offered in the market determine all the changes which the farmers make in the employment and use of land.

I am considering here a State in its natural and stable condition, choosing to ignore the variations that may arise from the good or bad harvest of any one year, or the extraordinary consumption that accompanies occupation by foreign troops, or other accidents, so as not to complicate my subject.

# Chapter 5

# Smith on Growth, Trade and University Professors

Adam Smith (1723-1790), the "father of economics," was one of the greatest thinkers in an age blessed with great minds (Voltaire, Kant, and Jefferson were his contemporaries). In his classic work, An Inquiry into the Nature and Causes of the Wealth of Nations, Smith espoused the "system of natural liberty" which promised economic abundance via the free play of individual motives aimed at self-betterment. The book was an extraordinary success in its day. It went through five editions during Smith's lifetime and was translated into many different languages.

A central feature of Smith's theory of economic development was capital accumulation and the division of labor it encouraged. In Book III, Chapter 1 of the *Wealth of Nations*, Smith gives a clear exposition of how economic growth takes place with regard to the American colonies. The justification and advantages of free international trade are outlined in part in Book IV, Chapter 2.

Above all else, Smith understood the nature and effects of incentives on human behavior. Nowhere is this more amply illustrated than in his discussion of education in Book V, Chapter 1. Notice in particular why Smith believes that the incentives prevailing in colleges and universities favor professors (i.e., "masters") rather than students.

Source:    *An Inquiry into the Nature and Causes of the Wealth of Nations by Adam Smith*, edited by E. Cannan.  New York:  Modern Library, 1937.  Pages 356-360; 420-425; 716-721.

## BOOK III

### Chapter I

*Of the Natural Progress of Opulence*

The great commerce of every civilized society, is that carried on between the inhabitants of the town and those of the country. It consists in the exchange of rude for manufactured produce, either immediately, or by the intervention of money, or of some sort of paper which represents money The country supplies the town with the means of subsistence, and the materials of manufacture. The town repays this supply by sending back a part of the manufactured produce to the inhabitants of the country. The town, in which there neither is nor can be any reproduction of substances, may very properly be said to gain its whole wealth and subsistence from the country. We must not, however, upon this account, imagine that the gain of the town is the loss of the country. The gains of both are mutual and reciprocal, and the division of labour is in this, as in all other cases, advantageous to all the different persons employed in the various occupations into which it is subdivided. The inhabitants of the country purchase of the town a greater quantity of manufactured goods, with the produce of a much smaller quantity of their own labour, than they must have employed had they attempted to prepare them themselves. The town affords a market for the surplus produce of the country, or what is over and above the maintenance of the cultivators, and it is there that the inhabitants of the country exchange it for something else which is in demand among them. The greater the number and revenue of the inhabitants of the town, the more extensive is the market which it affords to those of the country; and the more extensive that market, it is always the more advantageous to a great number. The corn which grows within a mile of the town, sells there for the same price with that which comes from twenty miles distance. But the price of the latter must generally, not only pay the expense of raising and bringing it to market, but afford too the ordinary profits of agriculture to the farmer. The proprietors and cultivators of the country, therefore, which lies in the neighborhood of the town, over and above the ordinary profits of agriculture, gain, in the price of what they sell, the whole value of the carriage of the like produce that is brought from more distant parts, and they save, besides, the whole value of this carriage in the price of what they buy. Compare the cultivation of the lands in the neighborhood of any considerable town, with that of those which lie at some distance from it, and you will easily satisfy yourself how much the country is benefited by the commerce of the town. Among all the absurd speculations that have been propagated concerning the balance of trade, it has never been pretended that either the country loses by its commerce with the town, or the town by that with the country which maintains it.

As subsistence is, in the nature of things, prior to conveniency and luxury, so the industry which procures the former, must necessarily be prior to that which ministers to the latter. The cultivation and improvement of the country, therefore, which affords subsistence, must, necessarily, be prior to the increase of the town, which furnishes only the means of conveniency and luxury. It is the surplus produce of the country only, or what is over and above the maintenance of the cultivators, that constitutes the subsistence of the town, which can therefore increase only with the increase of this surplus produce. The town, indeed, may not always derive its whole subsistence from the country in its neighborhood, or even from the territory to which it belongs, but from very distant countries; and this, though it forms no exception from the general rule, has occasioned considerable variations in the progress of opulence in different ages and nations.

That order of things which necessity imposes in general, though not in every particular country, is, in every particular country, promoted by the natural inclinations of man. If human institutions had never thwarted those natural inclinations the towns could nowhere have increased beyond what the improvement and cultivation of the territory in which they were situated could support; till such time, at least, as the whole of that territory was completely cultivated and improved. Upon equal, or nearly equal profits, most men will chuse to employ their capitals rather in the improvement and cultivation of land, than either in manufactures or in foreign trade. The man who employs his capital in land, has it more under his view and command, and his fortune is much less liable to accidents, than that of the trader, who is obliged frequently to commit it, not only to the winds and the waves, but to the more uncertain elements of human folly and injustice, by giving great credits in distant countries to men, with whose character and situation he can seldom be thoroughly acquainted. The capital of the landlord, on the contrary, which is fixed in the improvement of his land, seems to be as well secured as the nature of human affairs can admit of. The beauty of the country besides, the pleasures of a country life, the tranquillity of mind which it promises, and wherever the injustice of human laws does not disturb it, the independency which it really affords, have charms that more or less attract every body; and as to cultivate the ground was the original destination of man, so in every stage of his existence he seems to retain a predilection for this primitive employment.

Without the assistance of some artificers, indeed, the cultivation of land cannot be carried on but with great inconveniency and continual interruption. Smiths, carpenters, wheel-wrights, and plough-wrights, masons, and bricklayers, tanners, shoemakers, and taylors, are people, whose service the farmer has frequent occasion for. Such artificers too stand, occasionally, in need of the assistance of one another; and as their residence is not, like that of the farmer, necessarily tied down to a precise spot, they naturally settle in the neighborhood of one another, and thus form a small town or village. The butcher, the brewer, and the baker, soon join them, together with many other artificers and retailers, necessary or useful for supplying their occasional wants, and who contribute still further to augment the town. The inhabitants of the town and those of the country are mutually the servants of one another. The town is a continual fair or market, to which the inhabitants of the country resort, in order to exchange their rude for manufactured produce. It is this commerce which supplies the inhabitants of the town both with the materials of their work, and the means of their subsistence. The quantity of the finished work which they sell to the inhabitants of the country, necessarily regulates the quantity of the materials and provisions which they buy. Neither their employment nor subsistence, therefore, can augment, but in proportion to the augmentation of the demand from the country for finished work; and this demand can augment only in proportion to the extension of improvement and cultivation. Had human institutions, therefore, never disturbed the natural course of things, the progressive wealth and increase of the towns would, in every political society, be consequential, and in proportion to the improvement and cultivation of the territory or country.

In our North American colonies, where uncultivated land is still to be had upon easy terms, no manufactures for distant sale have ever yet been established in any of their towns. When an artificer has acquired a little more stock than is necessary for carrying on his own business in supplying the neighboring country, he does not, in North America, attempt to establish with it a manufacture for more distant sale, but employs it in the purchase and improvement of uncultivated land. From artificer he becomes planter, and neither the large wages nor the easy subsistence which that country affords to artificers, Can bribe him rather to work for other people than for himself. He feels that an artificer is the servant of his customers, from whom he derives his subsistence; but that a planter who cultivates his own land, and derives his necessary subsistence from the labour of his own family, is really a master, and independent of all the world.

In countries, on the contrary, where there is either no uncultivated land, or none that can be had upon easy terms, every artificer who has acquired more stock than he can employ in the occasional jobs of the neighborhood, endeavors to prepare work for more distant sale. The smith erects some sort of iron, the weaver some sort of linen or woolen manufactory. Those different manufactures come, in process of time, to be gradually subdivided, and thereby improved and refined in a great variety of ways, which may easily be conceived, and which it is therefore unnecessary to explain any further.

In seeking for employment to a capital, manufactures are, upon equal or nearly equal profits, naturally preferred to foreign commerce, for the same reason that agriculture is naturally preferred to manufactures. As the capital of the landlord or farmer is more secure than that of the manufacturer, so the capital of the manufacturer, being at all times more within his view and command, is more secure than that of the foreign merchant. In every period, indeed, of every society, the surplus part both of the rude and manufactured produce, or that for which there is no demand at home, must be sent abroad in order to be exchanged for something for which there is some demand at home. But whether the capital, which carries this surplus produce abroad, be a foreign or a domestic one, is of very little importance. If the society has not acquired sufficient capital both to cultivate all its lands, and to manufacture in the completest manner the whole of its rude produce, there is even a considerable advantage that that rude produce should be exported by a foreign capital, in order that the whole stock of the society may be employed in more useful purposes. The wealth of ancient Egypt, that of China and Indostan, sufficiently demonstrate that a nation may attain a very high degree of opulence, though the greater part of its exportation trade be carried on by foreigners. The progress of our North American and West Indian colonies would have been much less rapid, had not capital but what belonged to themselves been employed in exporting their surplus produce.

According to the natural course of things, therefore, the greater part of the capital of every growing society is, first, directed to agriculture, afterwards to manufactures, and last of all to foreign commerce. This order of things is so very natural, that in every society that had any territory, it has always, I believe, been in some degree observed. Some of their lands must have been cultivated before any considerable towns could be established, and some sort of coarse industry of the manufacturing kind must have been carried on in those towns, before they could well think of employing themselves in foreign commerce.

But though this natural order of things must have taken place in some degree in every such society, it has, in all the modern states of Europe, been, in many respects, entirely inverted. The foreign commerce of some of their cities has introduced all their finer manufactures, or such as were fit for distant sale; and manufactures and foreign commerce together, have given birth to the principal improvements of agriculture. The manners and customs which the nature of their original government introduced, and which remained after that government was greatly altered, necessarily forced them into this unnatural and retrograde order.

# BOOK IV

## Chapter II

*Of Restraints Upon the Importation from Foreign Countries of Such Goods as can be Produced at Home*

By restraining, either by high duties, or by absolute prohibitions, the importation of such goods from foreign countries as can be produced at home, the monopoly of the home market is more or less secured to the domestic industry employed in producing them. Thus the prohibition of importing either live cattle or salt provisions from foreign countries secures to the graziers of Great Britain the monopoly of the home market for butcher's meat. The high duties upon the importation of corn, which in times of moderate plenty amount to a prohibition, give a like advantage to the growers of that commodity. The prohibition of the importation of foreign woollens is equally favourable to the woollen manufacturers. The silk manufacture, though altogether employed upon foreign materials, has lately obtained the same advantage. The linen manufacture has not yet obtained it, but is making great strides towards it. Many other sorts of manufacturers have, in the same manner, obtained in Great Britain, either altogether, or very nearly a monopoly against their countrymen. The variety of goods of which the importation into Great Britain is prohibited, either absolutely, or under certain circumstances, greatly exceeds what can easily be suspected by those who are not well acquainted with the laws of the customs.

That this monopoly of the home-market frequently gives great encouragement to that particular species of industry which enjoys it, and frequently turns towards that employment a greater share of both the labour and stock of the society than would otherwise have gone to it, cannot be doubted. But whether it tends either to increase the general industry of the society, or to give it the most advantageous direction, is not, perhaps, altogether so evident.

The general industry of the society never can exceed what the capital of the society can employ. As the number of workmen that can be kept in employment by any particular person must bear a certain proportion to his capital, so the number of those that can be continually employed by all the members of a great society, must bear a certain proportion to the whole capital of that society, and never can exceed that proportion. No regulation of commerce can increase the quantity of industry in any society beyond what its capital can maintain. It can only divert a part of it into a direction into which it might not otherwise have gone; and it is by no means certain that this artificial direction is likely to be more advantageous to the society than that into which it would have gone of its own accord.

Every individual is continually exerting himself to find out the most advantageous employment for whatever capital he can command. It is his own advantage, indeed, and not that of the society, which he has in view. But the study of his own advantage naturally, or rather necessarily leads him to prefer that employment which is most advantageous to the society.

First, every individual endeavours to employ his capital as near home as he can, and consequently as much as he can in the support of domestic industry; provided always that he can thereby obtain the ordinary, or not a great deal less than the ordinary profits of stock.

Thus, upon equal or nearly equal profits, every wholesale merchant naturally prefers the home-trade to the foreign trade of consumption, and the foreign trade of consumption to the carrying trade. In the home-trade his capital is never so long out of his sight as it frequently is in the foreign trade of consumption. He can know better the character and situation of the persons whom he trusts, and if he should happen to be deceived, he knows better the laws of the country from which he must seek redress. In the carrying trade, the capital of the merchant is, as it were, divided between two foreign countries, and no part of it is ever necessarily brought home, or placed under his own immediate view and command. The capital which an Amsterdam merchant employs in carrying corn from Konnigsberg to Lisbon, and fruit and wine from Lisbon to Konnigsberg, must generally be the one-half of it at Konnigsberg and the other half at Lisbon. No part of it need ever come to Amsterdam. The natural residence of such a merchant should either be at Konnigsberg or Lisbon, and it can only be some very particular circumstances which can make him prefer the residence of Amsterdam. The uneasiness, however, which he feels at being separated so far from his capital, generally determines him to bring part both of the Konnigsberg goods which he destines for the market of Lisbon, and of the Lisbon goods which he destines for that of Konnigsberg, to Amsterdam: and though this necessarily subjects him to a double charge of loading and unloading, as well as to the payment of some duties and customs, yet for the sake of having some part of his capital always under his own view and command, he willingly submits to this extraordinary charge; and it is in this manner that every country which has any considerable share of the carrying trade, becomes always the emporium, or general market, for the goods of all the different countries whose trade it carries on. The merchant, in order to save a second loading and unloading, endeavours always to sell in the home-market as much of the goods of all those different countries as he can, and thus, so far as he can, to convert his carrying trade into a foreign trade of consumption. A merchant, in the same manner, who is engaged in the foreign trade of consumption, when he collects goods for foreign markets, will always be glad, upon equal or nearly equal profits, to sell as great a part of them at home as he can. He saves himself the risk and trouble of exportation, when, so far as he can, he thus converts his foreign trade of consumption into a home-trade. Home is in this manner the center, if I may say so, round which the capitals of the inhabitants of every country are continually circulating, and towards which they are always tending, though by particular causes they may sometimes be driven off and repelled from it towards more distant employments. But a capital employed in the home-trade, it has already been shown, necessarily puts into motion a greater quantity of domestic industry, and gives revenue and employment to a greater number of the inhabitants of the country, than an equal capital employed in the foreign trade of consumption: and one employed in the foreign trade of consumption has the same advantage over an equal capital employed in the carrying trade. Upon equal, or only nearly equal profits, therefore, every individual naturally inclines to employ his capital in the manner in which it is likely to afford the greatest support to domestic industry, and to give revenue and employment to the greatest number of people of his own country.

Secondly, every individual who employs his capital in the support of domestic industry, necessarily endeavours so to direct that industry, that its produce may be of the greatest possible value. The produce of industry is what it adds to the subject or materials upon which it is employed. In proportion as the value of this produce is great or small, so will likewise be the profits of the employer. But it is only for the sake of profit that any man employs a capital in the support of industry; and he will always, therefore, endeavour to employ it in the support of that industry of which the produce is likely to be of the greatest value, or to exchange for the greatest quantity either of money or of other goods.

But the annual revenue of every society is always precisely equal to the exchangeable value of the whole annual produce of its industry, or rather is precisely the same thing with that exchangeable value. As every individual, therefore, endeavours as much as he can both to employ his capital in the support of domestic industry, and so to direct that industry that its produce may be of the greatest value; every individual necessarily labours to render the annual revenue of the society as great as he can. He generally, indeed, neither intends to promote the public interest, nor knows how much he is promoting it. By preferring the support of domestic to that of foreign industry, he intends only his own security; and by directing that industry in such a manner as its produce may be of the greatest value, he intends only his own gain, and he is in this, as in many other cases, led by an invisible hand to promote an end which was no part of his intention. Nor is it always the worse for the society that it was no part of it. By pursuing his own interest he frequently promotes that of the society more effectually than when he really intends to promote it. I have never known much good done by those who affected to trade for the public good. It is an affectation, indeed, not very common among merchants, and very few words need be employed in dissuading them from it.

What is the species of domestic industry which his capital can employ, and of which the produce is likely to be of the greatest value, every individual, it is evident, can, in his local situation, judge much better than any statesman or lawgiver can do for him. The statesman, who should attempt to direct private people in what manner they ought to employ their capitals, would not only load himself with a most unnecessary attention, but assume an authority which could safely be trusted, not only to no single person, but to no council or senate whatever, and which would nowhere be so dangerous as in the hands of a man who had folly and presumption enough to fancy himself fit to exercise it.

To give the monopoly of the home-market to the produce of domestic industry, in any particular art or manufacture, is in some measure to direct private people in what manner they ought to employ their capitals, and must, in almost all cases, be either a useless or a hurtful regulation. If the produce of domestic can be brought there as cheap as that of foreign industry, the regulation is evidently useless. If it cannot, it must generally be hurtful. It is the maxim of every prudent master of a family, never to attempt to make at home what it will cost him more to make than to buy. The taylor does not attempt to make his own shoes, but buys them of the shoemaker. The shoemaker does not attempt to make his own clothes, but employs a taylor. The farmer attempts to make neither the one nor the other, but employs those different artificers. All of them find it for their interest to employ their whole industry in a way in which they have some advantage over their neighbours, and to purchase with a part of its produce, or what is the same thing, with the price of a part of it, whatever else they have occasion for.

What is prudence in the conduct of every private family, can scarce be folly in that of a great kingdom. If a foreign country can supply us with a commodity cheaper than we ourselves can make it, better buy it of them with some part of the produce of our own industry, employed in a way in which we have some advantage. The general industry of the country, being always in proportion to the capital which employs it, will not thereby be diminished, no more than that of the above-mentioned artificers; but only left to find out the way in which it can be employed with the greatest advantage. It is certainly not employed to the greatest advantage, when it is thus directed towards an object which it can buy cheaper than it can make. The value of its annual produce is certainly more or less diminished, when it is thus turned away from producing commodities evidently of more value than the commodity which it is directed to produce. According to the supposition, that commodity could be purchased from foreign countries cheaper than it can be made at ome. It could, therefore, have been purchased with a part only of the commodities, or, what is the same thing, with a part only of the price of the commodities, which the industry employed by an equal capital would have produced at home, had it been left to follow its natural course. The industry of the country, therefore, is thus turned away from a more, to a less advantageous employment, and the exchangeable value of its annual produce, instead of being increased, according to the intention of the lawgiver, must necessarily be diminished by every such regulation.

By means of such regulations, indeed, a particular manufacture may sometimes be acquired sooner than it could have been otherwise, and after a certain time may be made at home as cheap or cheaper than in the foreign country. But though the industry of the society may be thus carried with advantage into a particular channel sooner than it could have been otherwise, it will by no means follow that the sum total either of its industry, or of its revenue, can ever be augmented by any such regulation. The industry of the society can augment only in proportion as its capital augments, and its capital can augment only in proportion to what can be gradually saved out of its revenue. But the immediate effect of every such regulation is to diminishes its revenue, and what diminishes its revenue is certainly not very likely to augment its capital faster than it would have augmented of its own accord, had both capital and industry been left to find out their natural employments.

Though for want of such regulations the society should never acquire the proposed manufacture, it would not, upon that account, necessarily be the poorer in any one period of its duration. In every period of its duration its whole capital and industry might still have been employed, though upon different objects, in the manner that was most advantageous at the time. In every period its revenue might have been the greatest which its capital could afford, and both capital and revenue might have been augmented with the greatest possible rapidity.

## BOOK V

### Chapter I

*Of the Expence of the Institutions for the Education of Youth*

The institutions for the education of the youth may, in the same manner, furnish a revenue sufficient for defraying their own expence. The fee or honorary which the scholar pays to the master naturally constitutes a revenue of this kind.

Even where the reward of the master does not arise altogether from this natural revenue, it still is not necessary that it should be derived from that general revenue of the society, of which the collection and application are, in most countries, assigned to the executive power. Through the greater part of Europe, accordingly, the endowment of schools and colleges makes either no charge upon that general revenue, or but a very small one. It every where arises chiefly from some local or provincial revenue, from the rent of some landed estate, or from the interest of some sum of money allotted and put under the management of trustees for this particular purpose, sometimes by the sovereign himself, and sometimes by some private donor.

Have those public endowments contributed in general to promote the end of their institution? Have they contributed to encourage the diligence, and to improve the abilities of the teachers? Have they directed the course of education towards objects more useful, both to the individual and to the public, than those to which it would naturally have gone of its own accord? It should not seem very difficult to give at least a probable answer to each of those questions.

In every profession, the exertion of the greater part of those who exercise it, is always in proportion to the necessity they are under of making that exertion. This necessity is greatest with those to whom the emoluments of their profession are the only source from which they expect their fortune, or even their ordinary revenue and subsistence. In order to acquire this fortune, or even to get this subsistence, they must, in the course of a year, execute a certain quantity of work of a known value; and, where the competition is free, the rivalship of competitors, who are all endeavouring to justle one another out of employment, obliges every man to endeavour to execute his work with a certain degree of exactness. The greatness of the objects which are to be acquired by success in some particular professions may, no doubt, sometimes animate the exertion of a few men of extraordinary spirit and ambition. Great objects, however, are evidently not necessary in order to occasion the greatest exertions. Rivalship and emulation render excellency, even in mean professions, an object of ambition, and frequently occasion the very greatest exertions. Great objects, on the contrary, alone and unsupported by the necessity of application, have seldom been sufficient to occasion any considerable exertion. In England, success in the profession of the law leads to some very great objects of ambition; and yet how few men, born to easy fortunes, have ever in this country been eminent in that profession?

The endowments of schools and colleges have necessarily diminished more or less the necessity of application in the teachers. Their subsistence, so far as it arises from their salaries, is evidently derived from a fund altogether independent of their success and reputation in their particular professions.

In some universities the salary makes but a part, and frequently but a small part of the emoluments of the teacher, of which the greater part arises from the honoraries or fees of his pupils. The necessity of application, though always more or less diminished, is not in this case entirely taken away. Reputation in his profession is still of some importance to him, and he still has some dependency upon the affection, gratitude, and favourable report of those who have attended upon his instructions; and these favourable sentiments he is likely to gain in no way so well as by deserving them, that is, by the abilities and diligence with which he discharges every part of his duty.

In other universities the teacher is prohibited from receiving any honorary or fee from his pupils, and his salary constitutes the whole of the revenue which he derives from his office. His interest is, in this case, set as directly in opposition to his duty as it is possible to set it. It is the interest of every man to live as much at his ease as he can: and if his emoluments are to be precisely the same, whether he does, or does not perform some very laborious duty, it is certainly his interest, at least as interest is vulgarly understood, either to neglect it altogether, or, if he is subject to some authority which will not suffer him to do this, to perform it in as careless and slovenly a manner as that authority will permit. If he is naturally active and a lover of labour, it is his interest to employ that activity in any way, from which he can derive some advantage, rather than in the performance of his duty, from which he can derive none.

If the authority to which he is subject resides in the body corporate, the college, or university, of which he himself is a member, and in which the greater part of the other members are, like himself persons who either are, or ought to be teachers; they are likely to make a common cause, to be all very indulgent to one another and every man to consent that his neighbor may neglect his duty, provided he himself is allowed to neglect his own. In the university of Oxford, the greater part of the public professors have, for these many years, given up altogether even the pretence of teaching.

If the authority to which he is subject resides, not so much in the body corporate of which he is a member, as in some other extraneous persons, in the bishop of the diocese for example; in the governor of the province; or, perhaps, in some minister of state; it is not indeed in this case very likely that he will be suffered to neglect his duty altogether. All that such superiors, however, can force him to do, is to attend upon his pupils a certain number of hours, that is, to give a certain number of lectures in the week or in the year. What those lectures shall be, must still depend upon the diligence of the teacher; and that diligence is likely to be proportioned to the motives which he has for exerting it. An extraneous jurisdiction of this kind, besides, is liable to be exercised both ignorantly and capriciously. In its nature it is arbitrary and discretionary and the persons who exercise it, neither attending upon the lectures of that teacher themselves, nor perhaps understanding the sciences which it is his business to teach, are seldom capable of exercising it with judgment. From the insolence of office too they are frequently indifferent how they exercise it, and are very apt to censure or deprive him of his office wantonly, and without any just cause. The person subject to such jurisdiction is necessarily degraded by it, and, instead of being one of the most respectable, is rendered one of the meanest and most contemptible persons in the society. It is by powerful protection only that he can effectually guard himself against the bad usage to which he is at all times exposed; and this protection he is most likely to gain, not by ability or diligence in his profession, but by obsequiousness to the will of his superiors, and by being ready, at all times, to sacrifice to that will the rights, the interest, and the honour of the body corporate of which he is a member. Whoever has attended for any considerable time to the administration of a French university, must have had occasion to remark the effects which naturally result from an arbitrary and extraneous jurisdiction of this kind.

Whatever forces a certain number of students to any college or university, independent of the merit or reputation of the teachers, lends more or less to diminish the necessity of that merit or reputation.

The privileges of graduates in arts, in law, physic and divinity, when they can be obtained only by residing a certain number of years in certain universities, necessarily force a certain number of students to such universities, independent of the merit or reputation of the teachers. The privileges of graduates are a sort of statutes of apprenticeship, which have contributed to the improvement of education, just as the other statutes of apprenticeship have to that of arts and manufactures.

The charitable foundations of scholarships, exhibitions, bursaries, &c. necessarily attach a certain number of students to certain colleges, independent altogether of the merit of those particular colleges. Were the students upon such charitable foundations left free to chuse what college they liked best, such liberty might perhaps contribute to excite some emulation among different colleges. A regulation, on the contrary, which prohibited even the independent members of every particular college from leaving it, and going to any other, without leave first asked and obtained of that which they meant to abandon, would tend very much to extinguish that emulation.

If in each college the tutor or teacher, who was to instruct each student in all arts and sciences, should not be voluntarily chosen by the student, but appointed by the head of the college; and if, in case of neglect, inability, or bad usage, the student should not be allowed to change him for another, without leave first asked and obtained; such a regulation would not only tend very much to extinguish all emulation among the different tutors of the same college, but to diminish very much in all of them the necessity of diligence and of attention to their respective pupils. Such teachers, though very well paid by their students might be as much disposed to neglect them as those who are not paid by them at all, or who have no other recompence but their salary.

If the teacher happens to be a man of sense, it must be an unpleasant thing to him to be conscious, while he is lecturing his students, that he is either speaking or reading nonsense, or what is very little better than nonsense. It must too be unpleasant to him to observe that the greater part of his students desert his lectures or perhaps attend upon them with plain enough marks of neglect, contempt, and derision. If he is obliged, therefore, to give a certain number of lectures, these motives alone, without any other interest, might dispose him to take some pains to give tolerably good ones. Several different expedients, however may be fallen upon, which will effectually blunt the edge of all those incitements to diligence. The teacher, instead of explaining to his pupils himself the science in which he proposes to instruct them, may read some book upon it; and if this book is written in a foreign and dead language, by interpreting it to them into their own; or, what would give him still less trouble, by making them interpret it to him, and by now

d then making an occasional remark upon it, he may flatter himself that he is giving a
:ture. The slightest degree of knowledge and application will enable him to do this,
ithout exposing himself to contempt or derision, or saying any thing that is really foolish,
•surd, or ridiculous. The discipline of the college, at the same time, may enable him to
rce all his pupils to the most regular attendance upon this sham-lecture, and to maintain
e most decent and respectful behaviour during the whole time of the performance.

The discipline of colleges and universities is in general contrived, not for the benefit of
e students, but for the interest, or more properly speaking, for the ease of the masters.
; object is, in all cases, to maintain the authority of the master, and whether he neglects
performs his duty, to oblige the students in all cases to behave to him as if he performed
with the greatest diligence and ability. It seems to presume perfect wisdom and virtue in
e one order, and the greatest weakness and folly in the other. Where the  masters,
•wever, really perform their duty, there are no examples, I believe, that the greater part
' the students ever neglect theirs. No discipline is ever requisite to force attendance upon
ctures which are really worth the attending, as is well known wherever any such lectures
e given. Force and restraint may, no doubt, be in some degree requisite in order to
lige children, or very young boys, to attend to those parts of education which it is
ought necessary for them to acquire during that early period of life; but after twelve or
irteen years of age, provided the master does his duty, force or restraint can scarce ever
: necessary to carry on any part of education. Such is the generosity of the greater part
' young men, that, so far from being disposed to neglect or despise the instructions of
eir master, provided he shows some serious intention of being of use to them, they are
:nerally inclined to pardon a great deal of incorrectness in the performance of his duty,
id sometimes even to conceal from the public a good deal of gross negligence.

Those parts of education, it is to be observed, for the teaching of which there are no
iblic institutions, are generally the best taught. When a young man goes to a fencing or a
incing school, he does a not indeed always learn to fence or to dance very well; but he
:ldom fails of learning to fence or to dance. The good effects of the riding school are not
•mmonly so evident. The expence of a riding school is so great, that in most places it is a
iblic institution. The three most essential parts of literary education, to read, write, and
:count, it still continue to be more common to acquire in private than in public schools;
id it very seldom happens that any body fails of acquiring them to the degree in which it
 necessary to acquire them.

# Chapter 6

# Malthus on Population, Diminishing Returns and Consumption

Thomas Robert Malthus (1766-1834) achieved instant fame in 1798 with his essay on population, even though it was originally published anonymously. But his fame in this one area of social thought should not be allowed to overshadow the fact that he was an important contributor to classical economic theory in general. Malthus helped to lay two of the most important cornerstones of classical macroeconomics. His population theory was readily adopted by Ricardo and made a part of classical wage theory. And the principle of diminishing returns is clearly exposed in Malthus's theory of land rent. The selections reproduced below reveal Malthus's ideas on these two issues.

On population, we see Malthus exposing the ultimate check to increasing numbers (limited food supply) as well as the "vice" entailed in the "positive" and "preventive" checks. On rent, we find Malthus cognizant of the limits to "the bountiful gift of Providence" and eager to propound a scientific truth; namely, as an economy grows, the behavior of land rent is defined by "a law that is as invariable as the action of the principle of gravity." Note that in Malthus's formulation, rent can emerge on land *before* new plots of lesser fertility are cultivated. (Is this the same reasoning as Ricardo?). The third and final excerpt contains Malthus's view of "underconsumption" and the role that the "unproductive" consumer plays in the economy. In these passages you should be alert to ideas that reappear much later in the macroeconomic theory of John Maynard Keynes, who professed great admiration for Malthus.

Source 1:      T. R. Malthus, *An Essay on the Principle of Population, or a View of its past and present Effects on Human Happiness; With an Inquiry into our Prospects respecting the future Removal or Mitigation of the Evils which it occasions.* Selected and introduced by Donald Winch. Cambridge: Cambridge University Press, 1992. Pages 21-26.

Source 2:      T. R. Malthus, *An Inquiry into the Nature and Progress of Rent and the Principles by Which it is Regulated.* New York: Greenwood Press, 1969. Pages 17-21.

Source 3:     T. R. Malthus, *Principles of Political Economy Considered with a View to their Practical Application*, 2d ed.   New York:   Augustus M. Kelley, 1951.  Pages 35-42.

# AN ESSAY ON THE PRINCIPLE OF POPULATION

## Chapter II

*Of the general Checks to Population, and the Model of their Operation*

The ultimate check to population appears then to be a want of food, arising necessarily from the different ratios according to which population and food increase. But this ultimate check is never the immediate check, except in cases of actual famine.

The immediate check may be stated to consist in all those customs, and all those diseases, which seem to be generated by a scarcity of the means of subsistence; and all those causes, independent of this scarcity, whether of a moral or physical nature, which tend prematurely to weaken and destroy the human frame.

These checks to population, which are constantly operating with more or less force in every society, and keep down the number to the level of the means of subsistence, may be classed under two general heads—the preventive and the positive checks.

The preventive check, as far as it is voluntary, is peculiar to man, and arises from that distinctive superiority in his reasoning faculties which enables him to calculate distant consequences. The checks to the indefinite increase of plants and irrational animals are all either positive, or, if preventive, involuntary. But man cannot look around him and see the distress...

The checks to population, which are constantly operating with more or less force in every society, and keep down the number to the level of the means of subsistence, may be classed under two general heads; the preventive, and the positive checks.

The preventive check is peculiar to man, and arises from that distinctive superiority in his reasoning faculties, which enables him to calculate distant consequences. Plants and animals have apparently no doubts about the future support of their offspring. The checks to their indefinite increase, therefore, are all positive. But man cannot look around him, and see the distress which frequently presses upon those who have large families; he cannot contemplate his present possessions or earnings, which he now nearly consumes himself, and calculate the amount of each shirt when with very little addition they must be divided, perhaps, among seven or eight, without feeling a doubt, whether if he follow the bent of his inclinations, he may be able to support the offspring which he will probably bring into the world. In a state of equality, if such can exist, this would be the simple question. In the present state of society other considerations occur. Will he not lower his rank in life, and be obliged to give up in great measure his former society? Does any mode of employment present itself by which he may reasonably hope to maintain a family? Will he not at any rate subject himself to greater difficulties, and more severe labour than in his single state? Will he not be unable to transmit to his children the same advantages of education and improvement that he had himself possessed? Does he even feel secure that, should he have a large family, his utmost exertions can save them from rags, and squalid poverty, and their consequent degradation in the community? And may he not be reduced to the grating necessity of forfeiting his independence, and of being obliged to the sparing hand of charity for support?

These considerations are calculated to prevent, and certainly do prevent, a great number of persons in all civilized nations from pursuing the dictate of nature in an early attachment to one woman.

If this restraint do not produce vice, as in many instances is the case, and very generally so among the middle and higher classes of women, it is undoubtedly the least evil that can arise from the principle of population. Considered as a restraint on an inclination otherwise innocent, and always natural, it must be allowed to produce a certain degree of temporary unhappiness; but evidently slight, compared with the evils which result from any of the other checks to population.

When this restraint produces vice, as it does most frequently among men and among a numerous class of females, the evils which follow are but too conspicuous.

A promiscuous intercourse to such a degree as to prevent the birth of children, seems to lower in the most marked manner the dignity of human nature. It cannot be without its effect on men, and nothing can be more obvious than its tendency to degrade the female character, and to destroy all its most amiable and distinguishing characteristics. Add to which, that among those unfortunate females with which all great towns abound, more real distress and aggravated misery are perhaps to be found than in any other department of human life.

When a general corruption of morals, with regard to the sex, pervades all the classes of society, its effects must necessarily be to poison the springs of domestic happiness, to weaken conjugal and parental affection, and to lessen the united exertions and ardour of parents in the care and education of their children; effects which cannot take place without a decided diminution of the general happiness and virtue of the society; particularly as the necessity of art in the accomplishment and conduct of intrigues, and in the concealment of their consequences, necessarily leads to many other vices.

The positive checks to population are extremely various, and include every cause, whether arising from vice or misery, which in any degree contributes to shorten the natural duration of human life. Under this head therefore may be enumerated, all unwholesome occupations, severe labour and exposure to the seasons, extreme poverty, bad nursing of children, great towns, excesses of all kinds, the whole train of common diseases and epidemics, wars, pestilence, plague, and famine.

On examining these obstacles to the increase of population which I have classed under the heads of preventive and positive checks, it will appear that they are all resolvable into moral restraint, vice, and misery.

Of the preventive checks, the restraint from marriage which is not followed by irregular gratifications may properly be termed moral restraint.

Promiscuous intercourse, unnatural passions, violations of the marriage bed, and improper arts to conceal the consequences of irregular connexions, clearly come under the head of vice.

Of the positive checks, those which appear to arise unavoidably from the laws of nature may be called exclusively misery; and those which we obviously bring upon ourselves, such as wars, excesses, and many others which it would be in our power to avoid, are of a mixed nature. They are brought upon us by vice, and their consequences are misery.

The sum of all these preventive and positive checks, taken together, forms the immediate check to population; and it is evident that, in every country where the whole of the procreative power cannot be called into action, the preventive and the positive checks must vary inversely as each other; that is, in countries either naturally unhealthy, or subject to a great mortality, from whatever cause it may arise, the preventive check will prevail very little. In those countries, on the contrary, which are naturally healthy, and where the preventive check is found to prevail with considerable force, the positive check will prevail very little, or the mortality be very small.

In every country some of these checks are, with more or less force, in constant operation; yet notwithstanding their general prevalence, there are few states in which there is not a constant effort in the population to increase beyond the means of subsistence. This constant effort as constantly tends to subject the lower classes of society to distress, and to prevent any great permanent amelioration of their condition.

These effects, in the present state of society, seem to be produced in the following manner. We will suppose the means of subsistence in any country just equal to the easy support of its inhabitants. The constant effort towards population, which is found to act even in the most vicious societies, increases the number of people before the means of subsistence are increased. The food, therefore, which before supported eleven millions, must now be divided among eleven millions and a half. The poor consequently must live much worse, and many of them be reduced to severe distress. The number of labourers also being above the proportion of work in the market, the price of labour must tend to fall, while the price of provisions would at the same time tend to rise. The labourer therefore must do more work to earn the same as he did before. During this season of distress, the discouragements to marriage and the difficulty of rearing a family are so great, that population is nearly at a stand. In the meantime, the cheapness of labour, the plenty of labourers, and the necessity of an increased industry among them, encourage cultivators to employ more labour upon their land, to turn up fresh soil, and to manure and improve more completely what is already in tillage, till ultimately the means of subsistence may become in the same proportion to the population as at the period from which we set out. The situation of the labourer being then again tolerably comfortable, the restraints to population are in some degree loosened; and, after a short period, the same retrograde and progressive movements, with respect to happiness, are repeated.

## AN INQUIRY INTO THE NATURE AND PROGRESS OF RENT

In the early periods of society, or more remarkably perhaps, when the knowledge and capital of an old society are employed upon fresh and fertile land, this surplus produce, this bountiful gift of Providence, shews itself chiefly in extraordinary high profits, and extraordinary high wages, and appears but little in the shape of rent. While fertile land is in abundance, and may be had by whoever asks for it, nobody of course will pay a rent to a landlord. But it is not consistent with the laws of nature, and the limits and quality of the earth, that this state of things should continue. Diversities of soil and situation must necessarily exist in all countries. All land cannot be the most fertile: all situations cannot be the nearest to navigable rivers and markets. But the accumulation of capital beyond the means of employing it on land of the greatest natural fertility, and the greatest advantage of situation, must necessarily lower profits; while the tendency of population to increase beyond the means of subsistence must, after a certain time, lower the *wages of* labour.

The expense of production will thus be diminished, but the value of the produce, that is, the quantity of labour, and of the other products of labour besides corn, which it can command, instead of diminishing will be increased. There will be an increasing number of people demanding subsistence, and ready to offer their services in any way in which they can be useful. The exchangeable value of food will, therefore, be in excess above the cost of production, including in this cost the full profits, of the stock employed upon the land, according to the actual rate of profit, at the time being. And this excess is rent.

Nor is it possible that these rents should permanently remain as parts of the profit of stock, or of the wages of labour. If such an accumulation were to take place, decidedly to lower the general profit of stock, and, consequently, the *expenses* of cultivation, so as to make it answer to cultivate poorer land; the cultivators of the richer land, if they paid no rent, would cease to be mere farmers, or persons living upon the profits of agricultural stock. They would unite the characters of farmers and landlords, a union by no means uncommon; but which does not alter, in any degree, the nature of rent, or its essential separation from profits. If the general profits of stock were 20 per cent. and particular portions of land would yield 30 per cent. on the capital employed, 10 per cent. of the 30 would obviously be rent, by whomsoever received.

It happens, indeed, sometimes, that from bad government, extravagant habits, and a faulty constitution of society, the accumulation of capital is stopped, while fertile land is in considerable plenty, in which case profits may continue permanently very high; but even in

49

this case wages must necessarily fall, which by reducing the expenses of cultivation must occasion rents. There is nothing so absolutely unavoidable in the progress of society as the fall of wages, that is such a fall as, combined with the habits of the labouring classes, will regulate the progress of population according to the means of subsistence. And when, from the want of an increase of capital, the increase of produce is checked, and the means of subsistence come to a stand, the wages of labour must necessarily fall so low, as only just to maintain the existing population, and to prevent any increase.

We observe in consequence, that in all those countries, such as Poland, where, from the want of accumulation, the profits of stock remain very high, and the progress of cultivation either proceeds very slowly, or is entirely stopped, the wages of labour are extremely low. And this cheapness of labour, by diminishing the expenses of cultivation, as far as labour is concerned, counteracts the effects of the high profits of stock, and generally leaves a larger rent to the landlord than in those countries, such as America, where, by a rapid accumulation of stock, which can still find advantageous employment, and a great demand for labour, which is accompanied by an adequate increase of produce and population, profits cannot be low, and labour for some considerable time remains very high.

It may be laid down, therefore, as an incontrovertible truth, that as a nation reaches any considerable degree of wealth, and any considerable fullness of population, which of course cannot take place without a great fall both in the profits of stock and the wages of labour, the separation of rents, as a kind of fixture upon lands of a certain quality, is a law as invariable as the action of the principle of gravity. And that rents are neither a mere nominal value, nor a value unnecessarily and injuriously transferred from one set of people to another; but a most real and essential part of the whole value of the national property, and placed by the laws of nature where they are, on the land, by whomsoever possessed, whether the landlord, the crown, or the actual cultivator.

Rent then has been traced to the same common nature with that general surplus from the land, which is the result of certain qualities of the soil and its products; and it has been found to commence its separation from profits, as soon as profits and wages fall, owing to the comparative scarcity of fertile land in the natural progress of a country towards wealth and population.

## PRINCIPLES OF POLITICAL ECONOMY

### Chapter I

Section II

*On Productive Labor*

Labour may then be distinguished into two kinds, productive labour, and personal services, meaning by productive labour that labour which is so directly productive of material wealth as to be capable of estimation in the quantity or value of the object produced, which object is capable of being transferred without the presence of the producer; and meaning by personal services that kind of labour or industry, which however highly useful and important some of it may be, and however much it may conduce *indirectly* to the production and security of material wealth, does not realize itself on any object which can be valued and transferred without the presence of the person performing such service, and cannot therefore be made to enter into an estimate of national wealth.

This, though differing in name, is essentially the doctrine of Adam Smith. It has been controverted by two opposite parties, one of which has imputed to him an incorrect and unphilosophical extension of the term productive to objects which it ought not to include, and the other has accused him of a similar want of precision, for attempting to establish a distinction between two different sorts of labour where no distinction is to be found.

In proceeding to give my reasons for adopting the opinion of Adam Smith with the modification above suggested, I shall first endeavour to show that some such classification of the different sorts of labour is really called for in an inquiry into the causes of the wealth of nations, and that a considerable degree of confusion would be introduced into the science Of political economy by an attempt to proceed without it. We shall be less disposed to be disturbed by plausible cavils, or even by a few just exceptions to the complete accuracy of a definition, if we are convinced that the want of precision which is imputed to it, is beyond comparison less in amount and importance than the want of precision which would result from the rejection of it.

In the first place, then, it will readily be granted, that as material capital is the specific source of that great department of the national revenue, peculiarly called profits, and is further absolutely necessary to that division of labour, and extended use of machinery, which so wonderfully increases the productive powers of human industry, its vast influence on the progress of national wealth must be considered as incontrovertibly established. But in tracing the cause of the different effects of the produce which is employed as capital, and the produce which is consumed as revenue, we shall find that it arises principally from the different kinds of labour directly maintained by each. It is obvious, for instance, that it is only the productive labour of Adam Smith, which can keep up, restore, or increase, the material capital of a country. It is also this kind of labour alone, that is, the labour which is realized in the production, or increased value of material objects, which requires a considerable amount of capital for its continued employment; but that, for which there is an effectual demand, will generally be supplied, and the practical consequence is such as might naturally be expected. In those countries which abound in the number, and especially in the skill of their productive labourers, capital and wealth abound. In those where personal services predominate, capital and wealth are comparatively deficient.

It is true, that what is called capital, is sometimes employed in the maintenance of labour, which is not called productive; as by the managers of theatrical exhibitions, and in the payment of the expenses of education. In regard to the first kind of expenditures however, it would be excluded from coming under the head of capital, if capital were defined, as I have defined it, namely, that portion of the stock or material possessions of a country which is kept or employed with a view to profit in the production or distribution of wealth. But at all events, the amount of it is too inconsiderable to be allowed to interfere with a classification in other respects correct, and in the highest degree useful.

In regard to the expense of education, it should be recollected that no small portion of it is employed in acquiring the skill necessary to the production and distribution of material objects, as in the case of most apprenticeships; and as the persons who have the means of teaching this skill, are themselves employed in this sort of production and distribution; and that the skill so acquired will finally be realized, according to its value on material objects, the capital so employed must clearly be considered as maintaining productive labour, in the most natural sense of the term. The same may be said of all that is expended in the maintenance of those kinds of labour which, though they appear to have the same general character as personal services, are yet so necessary to the production and distribution of material objects, as to be estimated in the value of those objects when they reach the consumer.

In regard to the remaining expenditure in education, it will be excluded from coming under the denomination of capital, by the definition of capital above adverted to: and it may fairly be questioned whether the expenses of general education, and even, for the most part, the education for the learned professions, ought not properly to be considered as being paid from revenue rather than from capital. Practically they seem to be so considered. But in whatever light we view the expenditure upon these services, which are not realized upon any material products, it must be allowed that the great source of what is peculiarly called profits, and the great mass of what is usually called wealth, is directly derived from the employment of material capital in the maintenance of what Adam Smith has called productive labour. In speaking therefore, and treating of capital, it seems highly useful to have some term for the kind of labour which it generally employs, in contradistinction to the kind of labour which in general is employed directly by revenue, in order to explain the nature of productive labour, and its peculiar efficiency in causing the increase of wealth.

Secondly, it is stated by Adam Smith, that the produce which is annually saved is as regularly consumed, as that which is annually spent, but that it is consumed by a different set of people. If this be the case, and if saving be allowed to be the immediate cause of the increase of capital, it must be desirable in all questions relating to the progress of wealth, to distinguish by some particular title a set of people who appear to act so important a part n accelerating this progress. Almost all the lower classes of people of every society are employed in some way or other, and if there were no grounds of distinction in their employments with reference to their effects on the national wealth, it is difficult to conceive what would be the use of saving from revenue to add to capital, as it would be merely employing one set of people in preference to another. How in such a case are we to explain the nature of saving, and the different effects of parsimony and extravagance upon the national capital? No political economist of the present day can by saving mean mere hoarding; and beyond this contracted and inefficient proceeding, no use of the term in reference to the national wealth can well be imagined, but that which must arise from a different application of what is saved, founded upon a real distinction between the different kinds of labour maintained by it.

If the labour of menial servants be as productive of wealth as the labour of manufacturers, why should not savings be employed in their maintenance, not only without being dissipated, but with a constant increase of their amount? But menial servants, lawyers, or physicians, who save from their salaries are fully aware that *their* savings would be immediately dissipated again if they were advanced to persons like themselves, instead of being employed in the maintenance of persons of a different description. To consider the expenditure of the unproductive labourers of Adam Smith as advances made to themselves, and of the same nature as the advances of the master manufacturer to his workmen, would be at once to confound the very useful and just distinction between those who live upon wages, and those who live upon profits, and would render it quite impossible to explain the frequent and important operations of saving from revenue to add to capital, so absolutely necessary to the continued increase of wealth.

Some writers who refuse to adopt the classification of Adam Smith, endeavour to explain the nature of saving by substituting the term productive, or reproductive consumption for productive labour; but it does not seem to be agreed who are to be called the productive or reproductive consumers.

If, as some affirm, every person is a reproductive consumer who obtains for himself a value equal to that which he consumes, it is obvious that all menial servants kept for pomp or pleasure will be productive consumers; but it is quite impossible that a saving, or an increase of wealth and capital can result to any individual from the employment of a great number of such reproductive consumers. If on the other hand, a more correct meaning be given to the expression productive consumption, if it be considered as a present sacrifice with a view to a future advantage, still every species of education should be included in the definition; and certainly it would be impossible to explain the nature of saving by stating that a country gentleman would equally increase his own and the national wealth and capital, whether he employed a considerable part of his revenue in improving his farms and increasing their saleable value, or in paying masters to teach his sons and daughters the most fashionable accomplishments. The latter sort of expenditure, to a certain extent, might be quite as proper and creditable as the former, or even more so; but that is not the question. The question is, what is saving? Now every body would readily pronounce that the first kind of expenditure judiciously applied, was a saving from revenue to add to capital; but few, I apprehend, could expect to be understood, if they pronounced to its extent, was an equal saving from revenue, and an equal addition to individual and national capital.

It appears then upon examination, that the use of the term productive consumption will not enable us to explain what is most usually and most correctly meant by individual and national saving, unless when it is so defined as to mean the very same thing that Adam Smith means by the employment of productive labour.

It has been said, that many of the unproductive labourers of Adam Smith save, and add to the national capital in the usual sense of the term. This is no doubt true; and it is equally true that any person who received a portion of wealth as a gift might save some of it, and add to the national capital. The power of saving, which is equally possessed by both, is not necessarily connected with the means by which their wealth was obtained. But on this point there is another circumstance not sufficiently noticed, which draws a marked line of distinction between productive labour and personal services. Workmen and mechanics who receive the common wages, and various higher salaries, which are realized upon material objects, have the means of saving just in the same manner as menial servants, and others engaged in personal services. In this respect the two classes are precisely on a level. But the productive labourers at the same time that they obtain wealth, and the means of accumulation for themselves, furnish a large surplus to that other most important class of society which lives upon the profits of capital. This distinction alone is quite sufficient to place in a different point of view the productive labourers of Adam Smith, and those engaged in personal services.

Thirdly, it has been stated by Adam Smith, and it is allowed to have been stated truly, that there is a balance very different from the balance of trade, which according as it is favourable or unfavourable, occasions the prosperity or decay of every nation. This is the balance of the annual production and consumption. If in given periods the produce of a country exceeds in a certain degree the consumption of those employed in its production, the means of increasing its capital will be provided; its population will increase, or the actual numbers will be better accommodated, and probably both. If the consumption in such periods fully equals the produce, no means of increasing the capital will be afforded, and the society will be nearly at a stand. If the consumption continually exceeds the produce, every succeeding period will see the society worse supplied, and its prosperity and population will be evidently on the decline.

But if a balance of this kind be so important; if upon it depends the progressive, stationary, or declining state of a society, surely it must be of importance to distinguish those who mainly contribute to render this balance favourable, from those who chiefly contribute to make the opposite scale preponderate. Without some such distinction we shall not be able to trace the causes why one nation is thriving, and another is declining; nor will the superior riches of countries where merchants and manufacturers abound, compared with those in which the retainers of a court and of a feudal aristocracy predominate, admit of an intelligible explanation. To such an explanation it is absolutely necessary, that by the balance of production and consumption, we should mean the production and consumption of material objects; for, if all the gratifications derived from personal services were to be included in the term produce, it would be quite impossible either to estimate such a balance, or even to say what was to be understood by it.

# Chapter 7

## Ricardo on Value and Comparative Advantage

David Ricardo (1772-1823), of Dutch-Jewish lineage, entered his father's stock brokerage firm in London at 14 and had amassed a personal fortune by the time he reached 21, at which point he took a Quaker wife and converted to Christianity against his family's wishes. Ricardo traced his interest in economic theory to a casual reading of Adam Smith while on vacation. Possessed of a keen analytical mind, but poor expository skills, he eventually bent to the wishes of his friend, James Mill (father of John Stuart Mill, who became the most famous British economist of the next generation), and wrote a treatise that by sheer force of logic had a dominant impact on the formation of classical economics. Ricardo was a founding member of London's Political Economy Club. He also was elected to Parliament, where he entered into the lively economic debates of the day.

A fundamental difference between Ricardo and Malthus was the former's belief in a labor theory of value--a view encouraged by a durable passage from Smith's *Wealth of Nations*. Decades later, Karl Marx made the labor theory of value (much of it derived from Ricardo) the centerpiece of his analysis of capitalism. The excerpts reproduced here detail Ricardo's labor theory of value and the ingenious way in which he got around problems caused by the introduction of different qualities of capital and different proportions of "fixed" to "circulating" capital in the formulation of his theory.

The most durable contribution of Ricardo to economic theory was the concept of comparative advantage which he explicated for the first time in 1817. Although Ricardo couched his discussion in terms of international trade, this key principle applies with equal force to individuals, regions, and nations. Pay particular attention to his numerical example of the exchange of Portuguese wine for British cloth. It is one of the most famous examples of trade in the history of economic thought.

Source:  *The Works and Correspondence of David Ricardo*, edited by Piero Sraffa. Volume 1, *On the Principles of Political Economy and Taxation*. Cambridge: Cambridge University Press, 1951. Pages 11-14; 20-24; 30-34; 128-148.

# CHAPTER I

## ON VALUE

### Section I

*The value of a commodity, or the quantity of any other commodity for which it will exchange, depends on the relative quantity of labour which is necessary for its production, and not on the greater or less compensation which is paid for that labour.*

It has been observed by Adam Smith, that "the word Value has two different meanings, and sometimes expresses the utility of some particular object, and sometimes the power of purchasing other goods which the possession of that object conveys. The one may be called *value in use;* the other *value in exchange.* The things," he continues, "which have the greatest value in use, have frequently little or no value in exchange; and, on the contrary, those which have the greatest value in exchange, have little or no value in use." Water and air are abundantly useful; they are indeed indispensable to existence, yet, under ordinary circumstances, nothing can be obtained in exchange for them. Gold, on the contrary, though of little use compared with air or water, will exchange for a great quantity of other goods.

Utility then is not the measure of exchangeable value, although it is absolutely essential to it. If a commodity were in no way useful,—in other words, if it could in no way contribute to our gratification,—it would be destitute of exchangeable value, however scarce it might be, or whatever quantity of labour might be necessary to procure it.

Possessing utility, commodities derive their exchangeable value from two sources: from their scarcity, and from the quantity of labour required to obtain them.

There are some commodities, the value of which is determined by their scarcity alone. No labour can increase the quantity of such goods, and therefore their value cannot be lowered by an increased supply. Some rare statues and pictures, scarce books and coins, wines of a peculiar quality, which can be made only from grapes grown on a particular soil, of which there is a very limited quantity, are all of this description. Their value is wholly independent of the quantity of labour originally necessary to produce them, and varies with the varying wealth and inclinations of those who are desirous to possess them.

These commodities, however, form a very small part of the mass of commodities daily exchanged in the market. By far the greatest part of those goods which are the objects of desire, are procured by labour; and they may be multiplied, not in one country alone, but in many, almost without any assignable limit, if we are disposed to bestow the labour necessary to obtain them.

In speaking then of commodities, of their exchangeable value, and of the laws which regulate their relative prices, we mean always such commodities only as can be increased in quantity by the exertion of human industry, and on the production of which competition operates without restraint.

In the early stages of society, the exchangeable value of these commodities, or the rule which determines how much of one shall be given in exchange for another, depends almost exclusively on the comparative quantity of labour expended on each.

"The real price of every thing," says Adam Smith, "what every thing really costs to the man who wants to acquire it, is the toil and trouble of acquiring it. What every thing is really worth to the man who has acquired it, and who wants to dispose of it, or exchange it for something else, is the toil and trouble which it can save to himself, and which it can impose upon other people." "Labour was the first price—the original purchase-money that was paid for all things." Again, "in that early and rude state of society, which precedes both the accumulation of stock and the appropriation of land, the proportion between the quantities of labour necessary for acquiring different objects seems to be the only circumstance which can afford any rule for exchanging them for one another. If among a nation of hunters, for example, it usually cost twice the labour to kill a beaver which it does to kill a deer, one beaver should naturally exchange for, or be worth two deer. It is natural that what is usually the produce of two days', or two hours' labour, should be worth double of what is usually the produce of one day's, or one hour's labour."

That this is really the foundation of the exchangeable value of all things, excepting those which cannot be increased by human industry, is a doctrine of the utmost importance in political economy; for from no source do so many errors, and so much difference of opinion in that science proceed, as from the vague ideas which are attached to the word value.

If the quantity of labour realized in commodities, regulate their exchangeable value, every increase of the quantity of labour must augment the value of that commodity on which it. is exercised, as every diminution must lower it.

Adam Smith, who so accurately defined the original source of exchangeable value, and who was bound in consistency to maintain, that all things became more or less valuable in proportion as more or less labour was bestowed on their production, has himself erected another standard measure of value, and speaks of things being more or less valuable in proportion as they will exchange for more or less of this standard measure. Sometimes he speaks of corn, at other times of labour, as a standard measure; not the quantity of labour bestowed on the production of any object, but the quantity which it can command in the market: as if these were two equivalent expressions, and as if because a man's labour had become doubly efficient, and he could therefore produce twice the quantity of a commodity, he would necessarily receive twice the former quantity in exchange for it.

If this indeed were true, if the reward of the labourer were always in proportion to what he produced, the quantity of labour bestowed on a commodity, and the quantity of labour which that commodity would purchase, would be equal, and either might accurately measure the variations of other things: but they are not equal; the first is under many circumstances an invariable standard, indicating correctly the variations of other things; the latter is subject to as many fluctuations as the commodities compared with it. Adam Smith, after most ably showing the insufficiency of a variable medium, such as gold and silver, for the purpose of determining the varying value of other things, has himself, by fixing on corn or labour, chosen a medium no less variable.

## Section II

*Labour of different qualities differently rewarded. This no cause of variation in the relative value of commodities.*

In speaking, however, of labour, as being the foundation of all value, and the relative quantity of labour as almost exclusively determining the relative value of commodities, I must not be supposed to be inattentive to the different qualities of labour, and the difficulty of comparing an hour's or a day's labour, in one employment, with the same duration of labour in another. The estimation in which different qualities of labour are held, comes soon to be adjusted in the market with sufficient precision for all practical purposes, and depends much on the comparative skill of the labourer, and intensity of the labour performed. The scale, when once formed, is liable to little variation. If a day's labour of a working jeweller be more valuable than a day's labour of a common labourer, it has long ago been adjusted, and placed in its proper position in the scale of value.

In comparing therefore the value of the same commodity, at different periods of time, the consideration of the comparative skill and intensity of labour, required for that particular commodity, needs scarcely to be attended to, as it operates equally at both periods. One description of labour at one time is compared with the same description of labour at another; if a tenth, a fifth, or a fourth, has been added or taken away, an effect proportioned to the cause will be produced on the relative value of the commodity.

If a piece of cloth be now of the value of two pieces of linen, and if, in ten years hence, the ordinary value of a piece of cloth should be four pieces of linen, we may safely conclude, that either more labour is required to make the cloth, or less to make the linen, or that both causes have operated.

As the inquiry to which I wish to draw the reader's attention, relates to the effect of the variations in the relative value of commodities, and not in their absolute value, it will be of little importance to examine into the comparative degree of estimation in which the different kinds of human labour are held. We may fairly conclude, that whatever inequality there might originally have been in them, whatever the ingenuity, skill, or time necessary for the acquirement of one species of manual dexterity more than another, it continues nearly the same from one generation to another; or at least, that the variation is very inconsiderable from year to year, and therefore, can have little effect, for short periods, on the relative value of commodities.

According to Adam Smith "the proportion between the different rates both of wages and profit in the different employments of labour and stock, seems not to be much affected, as has already been observed, by the riches or poverty, the advancing, stationary, or declining state of the society. Such revolutions in the public welfare, though they affect the general rates both of wages and profit, must in the end affect them equally in all different employments. The proportion between them therefore must remain the same, and cannot well be altered, at least for any considerable time, by any such revolutions."

## Section III

*Not only the labour applied immediately to commodities affect their value, but the labour also which is bestowed on the implements, tools, and buildings, with which such labour is assisted.*

Even in that early state to which Adam Smith refers, some capital, though possibly made and accumulated by the hunter himself, would be necessary to enable him to kill his game. Without some weapon, neither the beaver nor the deer could be destroyed, and therefore the value of these animals would be regulated, not solely by the time and labour necessary to their destruction, but also by the time and labour necessary for providing the hunter's capital, the weapon, by the aid of which their destruction was effected.

Suppose the weapon necessary to kill the beaver, was constructed with much more labour than that necessary to kill the deer, on account of the greater difficulty of approaching near to the former animal, and the consequent necessity of its being more true to its mark; one beaver would naturally be of more value than two deer, and precisely for this reason, that more labour would, on the whole, be necessary to its destruction. Or suppose that the same quantity of labour was necessary to make both weapons, but that they were of very unequal durability; of the durable implement only a small portion of its value would be transferred to the commodity, a much greater portion of the value of the less durable implement would be realized in the commodity which it contributed to produce.

All the implements necessary to kill the beaver and deer might belong to one class of men, and the labour employed in their destruction might be furnished by another class; still, their comparative prices would be in proportion to the actual labour bestowed, both on the formation of the capital, and on the destruction of the animals. Under different circumstances of plenty or scarcity of capital, as compared with labour, under different circumstances of plenty or scarcity of the food and necessaries essential to the support of men, those who furnished an equal value of capital for either one employment or for the other, might have a half, a fourth, or an eighth of the produce obtained, the remainder being paid as wages to those who furnished the labour; yet this division could not affect the relative value of these commodities, since whether the profits of capital were greater

61

or less, whether they were 50, 20, or 10 per cent. or whether the wages of labour were high or low, they would operate equally on both employments.

If we suppose the occupations of the society extended, that some provide canoes and tackle necessary for fishing, others the seed and rude machinery first used in agriculture, still the same principle would hold true, that the exchangeable value of the commodities produced would be in proportion to the labour bestowed on their production; not on their immediate production only, but on all those implements or machines required to give effect to the particular labour to which they were applied.

## Section IV

*The principle that the quantity of labour bestowed on the production of commodities regulates their relative value, considerably modified by the employment of machinery and other fixed and durable capital.*

In the former section we have supposed the implements and weapons necessary to kill the deer and salmon, to be equally durable, and to be the result of the same quantity of labour, and we have seen that the variations in the relative value of deer and salmon depended solely on the varying quantities of labour necessary to obtain them, but in every state of society, the tools, implements, buildings, and machinery employed in different trades may be of various degrees of durability, and may require different portions of labour to produce them. The proportions, too, in which the capital that is to support labour, and the capital that is invested in tools, machinery and buildings, may be variously combined. This difference in the degree of durability of fixed capital, and this variety in the proportions in which the two sorts of capital may be combined, introduce another cause, besides the greater or less quantity of labour necessary to produce commodities, for the variations in their relative value this cause is the rise or fall in the value of labour.

The food and clothing consumed by the labourer, the buildings in which he works, the implements with which his labour is assisted, are all of a perishable nature. There is however a vast difference in the time for which these different capitals will endure: a steam-engine will last longer than a ship, a ship than the clothing of the labourer, and the clothing of the labourer longer than the food which he consumes.

According as capital is rapidly perishable, and requires to be frequently reproduced, or is of slow consumption, it is classed under the heads of circulating, or of fixed capital. A brewer, whose buildings and machinery are valuable and durable, is said to employ a large portion of fixed capital: on the contrary, a shoemaker, whose capital is chiefly employed in the payment of wages, which are expended on food and clothing, commodities more perishable than buildings and machinery, is said to employ a large proportion of his capital as circulating capital.

It is also to be observed that the circulating capital may circulate, or be returned to its employer, in very unequal times. The wheat bought by a farmer to sow is comparatively a fixed capital to the wheat purchased by a baker to make into loaves. One leaves it in the ground, and can obtain no return for a year; the other can get it ground into flour, sell it as bread to his customers, and have his capital free to renew the same, or commence any other employment in a week.

Two trades then may employ the same amount of capital; but it may be very differently divided with respect to the portion which is fixed, and that which is circulating.

In one trade very little capital may be employed as circulating capital, that is to say in the support of labour—it may be principally invested in machinery, implements, buildings, &c. capital of a comparatively fixed and durable character. In another trade the same amount of capital may be used, but it may be chiefly employed in the support of labour, and very little may be invested in implements, machines, and buildings. A rise in the wages of labour cannot fail to affect unequally, commodities produced under such different circumstances.

Again two manufacturers may employ the same amount of fixed, and the same amount of circulating capital; but the durability of their fixed capitals may be very unequal. One may have steam-engines of the value of 10,000$l$., the other, ships of the same value.

If men employed no machinery in production but labour only, and were all the same length of time before they brought their commodities to market, the exchangeable value of their goods would be precisely in proportion to the quantity of labour employed.

If they employed fixed capital of the same value and of the same durability, then, too, the value of the commodities produced would be the same, and they would vary with the greater or less quantity of labour employed on their production.

But although commodities produced under similar circumstances, would not vary with respect to each other, from any cause but an addition or diminution of the quantity of labour necessary to produce one or other of them, yet compared with others not produced with the same proportionate quantity of fixed capital, they would vary from the other cause also which I have before mentioned, namely, a rise in the value of labour, although neither more nor less labour were employed in the production of either of them. Barley and oats would continue to bear the same relation to each other under any variation of wages. Cotton goods and cloth would do the same, if they also were produced under circumstances precisely similar to each other, but yet with a rise or fall of wages, barley might be more or less valuable compared with cotton goods, and oats compared with cloth.

Suppose two men employ one hundred men each for a year in the construction of two machines, and another man employs the same number of men in cultivating corn, each of the machines at the end of the year will be of the same value as the corn, for they will each be produced by the same quantity of labour. Suppose one of the owners of one of the machines to employ it, with the assistance of one hundred men, the following year in making cloth, and the owner of the other machine to employ his also, with the assistance likewise of one hundred men, in making cotton goods, while the farmer continues to employ one hundred men as before in the cultivation of corn. During the second year they will all have employed the same quantity of labour, but the goods and machine together of the clothier, and also of the cotton manufacturer, will be the result of the labour of two hundred men, employed for a year; or, rather, of the labour of one hundred men for two years; whereas the corn will be produced by the labour of one hundred men for one year, consequently if the corn be of the value of 500*l*. the machine and cloth of the clothier together, ought to be of the value of 1000*l*. and the machine and cotton goods of the cotton manufacturer, ought to be also of twice the value of the corn. But they will be of more than twice the value of the corn, for the profit on the clothier's and cotton manufacturer's capital for the first year has been added to their capitals, while that of the farmer has been expended and enjoyed. On account then of the different degrees of durability of their capitals, or, which is the same thing, on account of the time which must elapse before one set of commodities can be brought to market, they will be valuable, not exactly in proportion to the quantity of labour bestowed on them,—they will not be as two to one, but something more, to compensate for the greater length of time which must elapse before the most valuable can be brought to market.

## CHAPTER VII

### ON FOREIGN TRADE

Under a system of perfectly free commerce, each country naturally devotes its capital and labour to such employments as are most beneficial to each. This pursuit of individual advantage is admirably connected with the universal good of the whole. By stimulating industry, by rewarding ingenuity, and by using most efficaciously the peculiar powers bestowed by nature, it distributes labour most effectively and most economically: while, by increasing the general mass of productions, it diffuses general benefit, and binds together by one common tie of interest and intercourse, the universal society of nations throughout the civilized world. It is this principle which determines that wine shall be made in France and Portugal, that corn shall be grown in America and Poland, and that hardware and other goods shall be manufactured in England.

In one and the same country, profits are, generally speaking, always on the same level; or differ only as the employment of capital may be more or less secure and agreeable. It is not so between different countries. If the profits of capital employed in Yorkshire, should exceed those of capital employed in London, capital would speedily move from London to Yorkshire, and an equality of profits would be effected; but if in consequence of the diminished rate of production in the lands of England, from the increase of capital and population, wages should rise, and profits fall, it would not follow that capital and population would necessarily move from England to Holland, or Spain, or Russia, where profits might be higher.

If Portugal had no commercial connexion with other countries, instead of employing a great part of her capital and industry in the production of wines, with which she purchases for her own use the cloth and hardware of other countries, she would be obliged to devote a part of that capital to the manufacture of those commodities, which she would thus obtain probably inferior in quality as well as quantity.

The quantity of wine which she shall give in exchange for the cloth of England, is not determined by the respective quantities of labour devoted to the production of each, as it would be, if both commodities were manufactured in England, or both in Portugal.

England may be so circumstanced, that to produce the cloth may require the labour of 100 men for one year; and if she attempted to make the wine, it might require the labour of 120 men for the same time. England would therefore find it her interest to import wine, and to purchase it by the exportation of cloth.

To produce the wine in Portugal, might require only the labour of 80 men for one year, and to produce the cloth in the same country, might require the labour of 90 men for the same time. It would therefore be advantageous for her to export wine in exchange for cloth. This exchange might even take place, notwithstanding that the commodity imported by Portugal could be produced there with less labour than in England. Though she could make the cloth with the labour of 90 men, she would import it from a country where it required the labour of 100 men to produce it, because it would be advantageous to her rather to employ her capital in the production of wine, for which she would obtain more cloth from England, than she could produce by diverting a portion of her capital from the cultivation of vines to the manufacture of cloth.

Thus England would give the produce of the labour of 100 men, for the produce of the labour of 80. Such an exchange could not take place between the individuals of the same country. The labour of 100 Englishmen cannot be given for that of 80 Englishmen, but the produce of the labour of 100 Englishmen may be given for the produce of the labour of 80 Portuguese, 60 Russians, or 120 East Indians. The difference in this respect, between a single country and many, is easily accounted for, by considering the difficulty with which capital moves from one country to another, to seek a more profitable employment, and the activity with which it invariably passes from one province to another in the same country.

It would undoubtedly be advantageous to the capitalists of England, and to the consumers in both countries, that under such circumstances, the wine and the cloth should both be made in Portugal, and therefore that the capital and labour of England employed in making cloth, should be removed to Portugal for that purpose. In that case, the relative value of these commodities would be regulated by the same principle, as if one were the produce of Yorkshire, and the other of London: and in every other case, if capital freely flowed towards those countries where it could be most profitably employed, there could be no difference in the rate of profit, and no other difference in the real or labour price of commodities, than the additional quantity of labour required to convey them to the various markets where they were to be sold.

Experience, however, shews, that the fancied or real insecurity of capital, when not under the immediate control of its owner, together with the natural disinclination which every man has to quit the country of his birth and connexions, and intrust himself with all his habits fixed, to a strange government and new laws, check the emigration of capital. These feelings, which I should be sorry to see weakened, induce most men of property to be satisfied with a low rate of profits in their own country, rather than seek a more advantageous employment for their wealth in foreign nations.

Gold and silver having been chosen for the general medium of circulation, they are, by the competition of commerce, distributed in such proportions amongst the different countries of the world, as to accommodate themselves to the natural traffic which would take place if no such metals existed, and the trade between countries were purely a trade of barter.

Thus, cloth cannot be imported into Portugal, unless it sell there for more gold than it cost in the country from which it was imported; and wine cannot be imported into England, unless it will sell for more there than it cost in Portugal. If the trade were purely a trade of barter, it could only continue whilst England could make cloth so cheap as to obtain a greater quantity of wine with a given quantity of labour, by manufacturing cloth than by growing vines; and also whilst the industry of Portugal were attended by the reverse effects. Now suppose England to discover a process for making wine, so that it should become her interest rather to grow it than import it; she would naturally divert a portion of her capital from the foreign trade to the home trade; she would cease to manufacture cloth for exportation, and would grow wine for herself. The money price of these commodities would be regulated accordingly; wine would fall here while cloth continued at its former price, and in Portugal no alteration would take place in the price of either commodity. Cloth would continue for some time to be exported from this country, because its price would continue to be higher in Portugal than here; but money instead of wine would be given in exchange for it, till the accumulation of money here, and its diminution abroad, should so operate on the relative value of cloth in the two countries, that it would cease to be profitable to export it. If the improvement in making wine were of a very important description, it might become profitable for the two countries to exchange employments; for England to make all the wine, and Portugal all the cloth consumed by them; but this could be effected only by a new distribution of the precious metals, which should raise the price of cloth in England, and lower it in Portugal. The relative price of wine would fall in England in consequence of the real advantage from the improvement of its manufacture; that is to say, its natural price would fall; the relative price of cloth would rise there from the accumulation of money.

Thus, suppose before the improvement in making wine in England, the price of wine here were 50l. per pipe, and the price of a certain quantity of cloth were 45l., whilst in

Portugal the price of the same quantity of wine was 45*l.*, and that of the same quantity of cloth 50*l.*; wine would be exported from Portugal with a profit of 5*l.* and cloth from England with a profit of the same amount.

Suppose that, after the improvement, wine falls to 45*l.* in England, the cloth continuing at the same price. Every transaction in commerce is an independent transaction. Whilst a merchant can buy cloth in England for 45*l.* and sell it with the usual profit in Portugal, he will continue to export it from England. His business is simply to purchase English cloth, and to pay for it by a bill of exchange, which he purchases with Portuguese money. It is to him of no importance what becomes of this money: he has discharged his debt by the remittance of the bill. His transaction is undoubtedly regulated by the terms on which he can obtain this bill, but they are known to him at the time; and the causes which may influence the market price of bills, or the rate of exchange, is no consideration of his.

If the markets be favourable for the exportation of wine from Portugal to England, the exporter of the wine will be a seller of a bill, which will be purchased either by the importer of the cloth, or by the person who sold him his bill; and thus without the necessity of money passing from either country, the exporters in each country will be paid for their goods. Without having any direct transaction with each other, the money paid in Portugal by the importer of cloth will be paid to the Portuguese exporter of wine; and in England by the negotiation of the same bill, the exporter of the cloth will be authorized to receive its value from the importer of wine.

But if the prices of wine were such that no wine could be exported to England, the importer of cloth would equally purchase a bill; but the price of that bill would be higher, from the knowledge which the seller of it would possess, that there was no counter bill in the market by which he could ultimately settle the transactions between the two countries; he might know that the gold or silver money which he received in exchange for his bill, must be actually exported to his correspondent in England, to enable him to pay the demand which he had authorized to be made upon him, and he might therefore charge in the price of his bill all the expenses to be incurred, together with his fair and usual profit.

If then this premium for a bill on England should be equal to the profit on importing cloth, the importation would of course cease, but if the premium on the bill were only 2 per cent., if to be enabled to pay a debt in England of 100*l.*, 102*l.* should be paid in Portugal, whilst cloth which cost 45*l.* would sell for 50*l.*, cloth would be imported, bills would be bought, and money would be exported, till the diminution of money in Portugal, and its accumulation in England, had produced such a state of prices as would make it no longer profitable to continue these transactions.

But the diminution of money in one country, and its increase in another, do not operate on the price of one commodity only, but on the prices of all, and therefore the price of wine and cloth will be both raised in England, and both lowered in Portugal. The price of cloth, from being 45*l.* in one country and 50*l.* in the other, would probably fall to 49*l.* or

48*l.* in Portugal, and rise to 46*l.* or 47*l.* in England, and not afford a sufficient profit after paying a premium for a bill to induce any merchant to import that commodity.

It is thus that the money of each country is apportioned to it in such quantities only as may be necessary to regulate a profitable trade of barter. England exported cloth in exchange for wine, because, by so doing, her industry was rendered more productive to her; she had more cloth and wine than if she had manufactured both for herself; and Portugal imported cloth and exported wine, because the industry of Portugal could be more beneficially employed for both countries in producing wine. Let there be more difficulty in England in producing cloth, or in Portugal in producing wine, or let here be more facility in England in producing wine, or in Portugal in producing cloth, and the trade must immediately cease.

No change whatever takes place in the circumstances of Portugal; but England finds that she can employ her labour more productively in the manufacture of wine, and instantly the trade of barter between the two countries changes. Not only is the exportation of wine from Portugal stopped, but a new distribution of the precious metals takes place, and her importation of cloth is also prevented.

Both countries would probably find it their interest to make their own wine and their own cloth; but this singular result would take place: in England, though wine would be cheaper, cloth would be elevated in price, more would be paid for it by the consumer; while in Portugal the consumers, both of cloth and of wine, would be able to purchase those commodities cheaper. In the country where the improvement was made, prices would be enhanced; in that where no change had taken place, but where they had been deprived of a profitable branch of foreign trade, prices would fall.

This, however, is only a seeming advantage to Portugal, for the quantity of cloth and wine together produced in that country would be diminished, while the quantity produced in England would be increased. Money would in some degree have changed its value in the two countries, it would be lowered in England and raised in Portugal. Estimated in money, the whole revenue of Portugal would be diminished; estimated in the same medium, the whole revenue of England would be increased.

Thus then it appears, that the improvement of a manufacture in any country tends to alter the distribution of the precious metals amongst the nations of the world: it tends to increase the quantity of commodities, at the same time that it raises general prices in the country where the improvement takes place.

To simplify the question, I have been supposing the trade between two countries to be confined to two commodities—to wine and cloth; but it is well known that many and various articles enter into the list of exports and imports. By the abstraction of money from one country, and the accumulation of it in another, all commodities are affected in price, and consequently encouragement is given to the exportation of many more commodities besides money, which will therefore prevent so great an effect from taking place on the value of money in the two countries as might otherwise be expected.

Beside the improvements in arts and machinery, there are various other causes which are constantly operating on the natural course of trade, and which interfere with the equilibrium, and the relative value of money. Bounties on exportation or importation, new taxes on commodities, sometimes by their direct, and at other times by their indirect operation, disturb the natural trade of barter, and produce a consequent necessity of importing or exporting money, in order that prices may be accommodated to the natural course of commerce; and this effect is produced not only in the country where the disturbing cause takes place, but, in a greater or less degree, in every country of the commercial world.

This will in some measure account for the different value of money in different countries; it will explain to us why the prices of home commodities, and those of great bulk, though of comparatively small value, are, independently of other causes, higher in those countries where manufactures flourish. Of two countries having precisely the same population, and the same quantity of land of equal fertility in cultivation, with the same knowledge too of agriculture, the prices of raw produce will be highest in that where the greater skill, and the better machinery is used in the manufacture of exportable commodities. The rate of profits will probably differ but little; for wages, or the real reward of the labourer, may be the same in both; but those wages, as well as raw produce, will be rated higher in money in that country, into which, from the advantages attending their skill and machinery, an abundance of money is imported in exchange for their goods.

Of these two countries, if one had the advantage in the manufacture of goods of one quality, and the other in the manufacture of goods of another quality, there would be no decided influx of the precious metals into either; but if the advantage very heavily preponderated in favour of either, that effect would be inevitable.

In the former part of this work, we have assumed, for the purpose of argument, that money always continued of the same value; we are now endeavouring to shew that besides the ordinary variations in the value of money, and those which are common to the whole commercial world, there are also partial variations to which money is subject in particular countries; and in fact, that the value of money is never the same in any two countries, depending as it does on relative taxation, on manufacturing skill, on the advantages of climate, natural productions, and many other causes.

Although, however, money is subject to such perpetual variations, and consequently the prices of the commodities which are common to most countries, are also subject to considerable difference, yet no effect will be produced on the rate of profits, either from the influx or efflux of money. Capital will not be increased, because the circulating medium is augmented. If the rent paid by the farmer to his landlord, and the wages to his labourers, be 20 per cent. higher in one country than another, and if at the same time the nominal value of the farmer's capital be 20 per cent. more, he will receive precisely the same rate of profits, although he should sell his raw produce 20 per cent. higher.

Profits, it cannot be too often repeated, depend on wages; not on nominal, but real wages; not on the number of pounds that may be annually paid to the labourer, but on the number of days work necessary to obtain those pounds. Wages may therefore be precisely the same in two countries; they may bear too the same proportion to rent, and to the whole produce obtained from the land, although in one of those countries the labourer should receive ten shillings per week, and in the other twelve.

In the early states of society, when manufactures have made little progress, and the produce of all countries is nearly similar, consisting of the bulky and most useful commodities, the value of money in different countries will be chiefly regulated by their distance from the mines which supply the precious metals; but as the arts and improvements of society advance, and different nations excel in particular manufactures, although distance will still enter into the calculation, the value of the precious metals will be chiefly regulated by the superiority of those manufactures.

Suppose all nations to produce corn, cattle, and coarse clothing only, and that it was by the exportation of such commodities that gold could be obtained from the countries which produced them, or from those who held them in subjection; gold would naturally be of greater exchangeable value in Poland than in England, on account of the greater expense of sending such a bulky commodity as corn the more distant voyage, and also the greater expense attending the conveying of gold to Poland.

This difference in the value of gold, or which is the same thing, this difference in the price of corn in the two countries, would exist, although the facilities of producing corn in England should far exceed those of Poland, from the greater fertility of the land, and the superiority in the skill and implements of the labourer.

If however Poland should be the first to improve her manufactures, if she should succeed in making a commodity which was generally desirable, including great value in little bulk, or if she should be exclusively blessed with some natural production, generally desirable, and not possessed by other countries, she would obtain an additional quantity of gold in exchange for this commodity, which would operate on the price of her corn, cattle, and coarse clothing. The disadvantage of distance would probably be more than compensated by the advantage of having an exportable commodity of great value, and money would be permanently of lower value in Poland than in England. If, on the contrary, the advantage of skill and machinery were possessed by England, another reason would be added to that which before existed, why gold should be less valuable in England than in Poland, and why corn, cattle, and clothing, should be at a higher price in the former country.

These I believe to be the only two causes which regulate the comparative value of money in the different countries of the world; for although taxation occasions a disturbance of the equilibrium of money, it does so by depriving the country in which it is imposed of some of the advantages attending skill, industry, and climate.

It has been my endeavour carefully to distinguish between a low value of money, and a high value of corn, or any other commodity with which money may be compared. These have been generally considered as meaning the same thing; but it is evident, that when corn rises from five to ten shillings a bushel, it may be owing either to a fall in the value of money, or to a rise in the value of corn. Thus we have seen, that from the necessity of having recourse successively to land of a worse and worse quality, in order to feed an increasing population, corn must rise in relative value to other things. If therefore money continue permanently of the same value, corn will exchange for more of such money, that is to say, it will rise in price. The same rise in the price of corn will be produced by such improvement of machinery in manufactures, as shall enable us to manufacture commodities with peculiar advantages: for the influx of money will be the consequence; it will fall in value, and therefore exchange for less corn. But the effects resulting from a high price of corn when produced by the rise in the value of corn, and when caused by a fall in the value of money, are totally different. In both cases the money price of wages will rise, but if it be in consequence of the fall in the value of money, not only wages and corn, but all other commodities will rise. If the manufacturer has more to pay for wages, he will receive more for his manufactured goods, and the rate of profits will remain unaffected. But when the rise in the price of corn is the effect of the difficulty of production, profits will fall; for the manufacturer will be obliged to pay more wages, and will not be enabled to remunerate himself by raising the price of his manufactured commodity.

Any improvement in the facility of working the mines, by which the precious metals may be produced with a less quantity of labour, will sink the value of money generally. It will then exchange for fewer commodities in all countries; but when any particular country excels in manufactures, so as to occasion an influx of money towards it, the value of money will be lower, and the prices of corn and labour will be relatively higher in that country, than in any other.

This higher value of money will not be indicated by the exchange; bills may continue to be negotiated at par, although the prices of corn and labour should be 10, 20, or 30 per cent. higher in one country than another. Under the circumstances supposed, such a difference of prices is the natural order of things, and the exchange can only be at par, when a sufficient quantity of money is introduced into the country excelling in manufactures, so as to raise the price of its corn and labour. If foreign countries should prohibit the exportation of money, and could successfully enforce obedience to such a law, they might indeed prevent the rise in the prices of the corn and labour of the manufacturing country; for such rise can only take place after the influx of the precious metals, supposing paper money not to be used; but they could not prevent the exchange from being very unfavourable to them. If England were the manufacturing country, and it were possible to prevent the importation of money, the exchange with France, Holland, and Spain, might be 5, 10, or 20 per cent. against those countries.

Whenever the current of money is forcibly stopped, and when money is prevented from settling at its just level, there are no limits to the possible variations of the exchange. The effects are similar to those which follow, when a paper money, not exchangeable for specie at the will of the holder, is forced into circulation. Such a currency is necessarily confined to the country where it is issued: it cannot, when too abundant, diffuse itself generally amongst other countries. The level of circulation is destroyed, and the exchange will inevitably be unfavourable to the country where it is excessive in quantity: just so would be the effects of a metallic circulation, if by forcible means, by laws which could not be evaded, money should be detained in a country, when the stream of trade gave it an impetus towards other countries.

When each country has precisely the quantity of money which it ought to have, money will not indeed be of the same value in each, for with respect to many commodities it may differ, 10, or even 20 per cent., but the exchange will be at par. One hundred pounds in England, or the silver which is in 100*l*., will purchase a bill of 100*l*., or an equal quantity of silver in France, Spain, or Holland.

In speaking of the exchange and the comparative value of money in different countries, we must not in the least refer to the value of money estimated in commodities, in either country. The exchange is never ascertained by estimating the comparative value of money in corn, cloth, or any commodity whatever, but by estimating the value of the currency of one country, in the currency of another.

It may also be ascertained by comparing it with some standard common to both countries. If a bill on England for 100*l*. will purchase the same quantity of goods in France or Spain, that a bill on Hamburgh for the same sum will do, the exchange between Hamburgh and England is at par; but if a bill on England for 130*l*., will purchase no more than a bill on Hamburgh for 100*l*., the exchange is 30 per cent. against England.

In England 100*l*. may purchase a bill, or the right of receiving 101*l*. in Holland, 102*l*. in France, and 105*l*. in Spain. The exchange with England is, in that case, said to be 1 per cent. against Holland, 2 per cent. against France, and 5 per cent. against Spain. It indicates that the level of currency is higher than it should be in those countries, and the comparative value of their currencies, and that of England, would be immediately restored to par, by abstracting from theirs, or by adding to that of England.

# Chapter 8

## Mill on the Workability of Socialism

John Stuart Mill (1806-1873) focused his keen analytic powers on a large number of social issues, including the workability of socialism. In the mid-nineteenth century, he took more seriously than most writers the ideas raised by social critics such as Robert Owen, Henri Saint-Simon, and Charles Fourier. These early socialists sought to reform capitalism, which they believed nurtured social discontent and upheaval by skewing the distribution of income. In 1869 Mill designed a major work on socialism, but when he died four years later, he had completed only a few chapters in rough draft form. These remnants were published for the first time in 1879 in the Fortnightly Review. As we see in the following extract from these early "chapters", Mill was enamored with the ideal of socialism, but was keenly aware of its practical difficulties.

Source:  Mill, J.S. *On Socialism*. Buffalo, NY: Prometheus Books, 2987. Pages 115-136

## The Difficulties of Socialism

Among those who call themselves Socialists, two kinds of persons may be distinguished. There are, in the first place, those whose plans for a new order of society, in which private property and individual competition are to be superseded and other motives to action substituted, are on the scale of a village community or township, and would be applied to an entire country by the multiplication of such self-acting units; of this character are the systems of Owen, of Fourier, and the more thoughtful and philosophic Socialists generally. The other class, who are more a product of the Continent than of Great Britain and may be called the revolutionary Socialists, propose to themselves a much bolder stroke. Their scheme is the management of the whole productive resources of the country by one central authority, the general government. And with this view some of them avow as their purpose that the working classes, or somebody in their behalf, should take possession of all the property of the country, and administer it for the general benefit.

Whatever be the difficulties of the first of these two forms of Socialism, the second must evidently involve the same difficulties and many more. The former, too, has the great advantage that it can be brought into operation progressively, and can prove its capabilities by trial. It can be tried first on a select population and extended to others as their education and cultivation permit. It need not, and in the natural order of things would not, become an engine of subversion until it had shown itself capable of being also a means

73

of reconstruction. It is not so with the other; the aim of that is to substitute the new rule for the old at a single stroke, and to exchange the amount of good realized under the present system, and its large possibilities of improvement, for a plunge without any preparation into the most extreme form of the problem of carrying on the whole round of the operations of social life without the motive power which has always hitherto worked the social machinery. It must be acknowledged that those who would play this game on the strength of their own private opinion, unconfirmed as yet by any experimental verification—who would forcibly deprive all who have now a comfortable physical existence of their only present means of preserving it, and would brave the frightful bloodshed and misery that would ensue if the attempt was resisted—must have a serene confidence in their own wisdom on the one hand and a recklessness of other people's sufferings on the other, which Robespierre and St. Just, hitherto the typical instances of those united attributes, scarcely came up to. Nevertheless this scheme has great elements of popularity which the more cautious and reasonable form of Socialism has not; because what it professes to do it promises to do quickly, and holds out hope to the enthusiastic of seeing the whole of their aspirations realized in their own time and at a blow.

The peculiarities, however, of the revolutionary form of Socialism will be most conveniently examined after the considerations common to both the forms have been duly weighed.

The produce of the world could not attain anything approaching to its present amount, nor support anything approaching to the present number of its inhabitants, except upon two conditions: abundant and costly machinery, buildings, and other instruments of production; and the power of undertaking long operations and waiting a considerable time for their fruits. In other words, there must be a large accumulation of capital, both fixed in the implements and buildings, and circulating, that is, employed in maintaining the laborers and their families during the time which elapses before the productive operations are completed and the products come in. This necessity depends on physical laws, and is inherent in the condition of human life; but these requisites of production, the capital, fixed and circulating, of the country (to which has to be added the land, and all that is contained in it), may either be the collective property of those who use it, or may belong to individuals; and the question is, which of these arrangements is most conducive to human happiness. What is characteristic of Socialism is the joint ownership by all the members of the community of the instruments and means of production; which carries with it the consequence that the division of the produce among the body of owners must be a public act, performed according to rules laid down by the community. Socialism by no means excludes private ownership of articles of consumption; the exclusive right of each to his or her share of the produce when received, either to enjoy, to give, or to exchange it. The land, for example, might be wholly the property of the community for agricultural and other productive purposes, and might be cultivated on their joint account, and yet the dwelling assigned to each individual or family as part of their remuneration might be as exclusively theirs, while they continued to fulfill their share of the common labors, as any one's house now is; and not the dwelling only, but any ornamental ground which the circumstances of the association allowed to be attached to the house for purposes of enjoyment. The distinctive feature of Socialism is not that all things are in common, but that production is only carried on upon the common account, and that the instruments of production are held as common property. The *practicability* then of Socialism, on the scale of Mr. Owen's or M. Founer's villages, admits of no dispute. The attempt to manage the whole production of a nation by one central organization is a totally different matter; but a mixed agricultural and manufacturing association of from two thousand to four thousand inhabitants under any tolerable circumstances of soil and climate would be easier to manage than many a joint stock company. The question to be considered is, whether this joint management is likely to be as efficient and successful as the management's of private industry by private capital. And this question has to be considered in a double aspect; the efficiency of the directing mind, or minds, and that of the simple workpeople. And in order to state this question in its simplest form, we will suppose the form of Socialism to be simple Communism, i.e., equal division of the produce among all the sharers, or, according to M. Louis Blanc's still higher standard of justice, apportionment of it according to difference of need, but without making any difference of reward according to the nature of the duty nor according to the supposed merits or services of the individual. There are other forms of Socialism, particularly Fourierism, which do, on considerations of justice or expediency, allow differences of remuneration for different kinds or degrees of service to the community; but the consideration of these may be for the present postponed.

The difference between the motive powers in the economy of society under private property and under Communism would be greatest in the case of the directing minds. Under the present system, the direction being entirely in the hands of the person or persons who own (or are personally responsible for) the capital, the whole benefit of the difference between the best administration and the worst under which the business can continue to be carried on accrues to the person or persons who control the administration: they reap the whole profit of good management except so far as their self interest or liberality induce them to share it with their subordinates; and they suffer the whole detriment of mismanagement except so far as this may cripple their subsequent power of employing labor. This strong personal motive to do their very best and utmost for the efficiency and economy of the operations, would not exist under Communism; as the managers would only receive out of the produce the same equal dividend as the other members of the association: "What would remain would be the interest common to all in so managing affairs as to make the dividend as large as possible; the incentives of public spirit, of conscience, and of the honor and credit of the managers. The force of these motives, especially when combined, is great. But it varies greatly in different persons, and is much greater for some purposes than for others. The verdict of experience, in the

75

imperfect degree of moral cultivation which mankind have yet reached, is that the motive of conscience and that of credit and reputation, even when they are of some strength, are, in the majority of cases, much stronger as restraining than as impelling forces—are more to be depended on for preventing wrong, than for calling forth the fullest energies in the pursuit of ordinary occupations. In the case of most men the only inducement which has been found sufficiently constant and unflagging to overcome the ever-present influence of indolence and love of ease, and induce men to apply themselves unrelaxingly to work for the most part in itself dull and unexciting," is the prospect of bettering their own economic condition and that of their family; and the closer the connection of every increase of exertion with a corresponding increase of its fruits, the more powerful is its motive. To suppose the contrary would be to imply that with men as they now are, duty and honor are more powerful principles of action than personal interest, not solely as to special acts and forbearance's respecting which those sentiments have been exceptionally cultivated, but in the regulation of their whole lives; which no one, I suppose, will affirm. It may be said that this inferior efficacy of public and social feelings is not inevitable—is the result of imperfect education. This I am quite ready to admit, and also that there are even now many individual exceptions to the general infirmity. But before these exceptions can grow into a majority, or even into a very large minority, much time will be required. The education of human beings is one of the most difficult of all arts, and this is one of the points in which it has hitherto been least successful; moreover improvements in general education are necessarily very gradual, because the future generation is educated by the present, and the imperfections of the teachers set an invincible limit to the degree in which they can train their pupils to be better than themselves. We must therefore expect, unless we are operating upon a select portion of the population, that personal interest will for a long time be a more effective stimulus to the most vigorous and careful conduct of the industrial business of society than motives of a higher character. It will be said that at present the greed of personal gain by its very excess counteracts its own end by the stimulus it gives to reckless and often dishonest risks. This it does, and under Communism that source of evil would generally be absent. It is probable, indeed, that enterprise either of a bad or of a good kind would be a deficient element, and that business in general would fall very much under the dominion of routine; rather, as the performance of duty in such communities has to be enforced by external sanctions, the more nearly each person's duty can be reduced to fixed rules, the easier it is to hold him to its performance. A circumstance which increases the probability of this result is the limited power which the managers would have of independent action. They would of course hold their authority from the choice of the community, by whom their function might at any time be withdrawn from them; and this would make it necessary for them, even if not so required by the constitution of the community, to obtain the general consent of the body before making any change in the established mode of carrying on the concern. The difficulty of persuading a numerous body to make a change in their accustomed mode of working, of which change the trouble is often great, and the risk more obvious to their minds than the advantage, would have a great tendency to keep things in their accustomed track. Against this it has to be set, that choice by the persons who are directly interested in the success of the work, and who have practical knowledge and opportunities of judgment, might be expected on the average to produce managers of greater skill than the chances of birth, which now so often determine who shall be the owner of the capital. This may be true; and though it may be replied that the capitalist by inheritance can also, like the community, appoint a manager more capable than himself, this would only place him on the same level of advantage as the community, not on a higher level. But it must be said on the other side that under the Communist system the persons most qualified for the management would be likely very often to hang back from undertaking it. At present the manager, even if he be a hired servant, has a very much larger remuneration than the other persons concerned in the business; and there are open to his ambition higher social positions to which his function of manager is a stepping-stone. On the Communist system none of these advantages would be possessed by him; he could obtain only the same dividend out of the produce of the community's labor as any other member of it; he would no longer have the chance of raising himself from a receiver of wages into the class of capitalists; and while he could be in no way better off than any other laborer, his responsibilities and anxieties would be so much greater that a large proportion of mankind would be likely to prefer the less onerous position. This difficulty was foreseen by Plato as an objection to the system proposed in his Republic of community of goods among a governing class; and the motive on which he relied for inducing the fit persons to take on themselves, in the absence of all the ordinary inducements, the cares and labors of government, was the fear of being governed by worse men. This, in truth, is the motive which would have to be in the main depended upon; the persons most competent to the management would be prompted to undertake the office to prevent it from falling into less competent hands. And the motive would probably be effectual at times when there was an impression that by incompetent management the affairs of the community were going to ruin, or even only decidedly deteriorating. But this motive could not, as a rule, expect to be called into action by the less stringent inducement of merely promoting improvement; unless in the case of inventors or schemers eager to try some device from which they hoped for great and immediate fruits; and persons of this kind are very often unfitted by over-sanguine temper and imperfect judgment for the general conduct of affairs, while even when fitted for it they are precisely the kind of persons against whom the average man is apt to entertain a prejudice, and they would often be unable to overcome the preliminary difficulty of persuading the community both to adopt their project and to accept them as managers. Communistic management would thus be, in all probability, less favorable than private management to that striking out of new paths and making immediate sacrifices for distant and uncertain advantages, which, though seldom unattended with risk, is generally indispensable to great improvements in the economic condition of mankind, and even to keeping up the existing state in the face of a continual increase of the number of mouths to be fed.

We have thus far taken account only of the operation of motives upon the managing minds of the association. Let us now consider how the case stands in regard to the ordinary workers.

These, under Communism, would have no interest, except their share of the general interest, in doing their work honestly and energetically. But in this respect matters would be no worse than they now are in regard to the great majority of the producing classes. These, being paid by fixed wages, are so far from having any direct interest of their own in the efficiency of their work, that they have not even that share in the general interest which every worker would have in the Communistic organization. Accordingly, the inefficiency of hired labor, the imperfect manner in which it calls forth the real capabilities of the laborers, is matter of common remark. It is true that a character for being a good workman is far from being without its value, as it tends to give him a preference in employment, and sometimes obtains for him higher wages. There are also possibilities of rising to the position of foreman, or other subordinate administrative posts, which are not only more highly paid than ordinary labor, but sometimes open the way to ulterior advantages. But on the other side is to be set that under Communism the general sentiment of the community, composed of the comrades under whose eyes each person works, would be sure to be in favor of good and hard working, and unfavorable to laziness, carelessness, and waste. In the present system not only is this not the case, but the public opinion of the workman class often acts in the very opposite direction: the rules of some trade societies actually forbid their members to exceed a certain standard of efficiency, lest they should diminish the number of laborers required for the work; and for the same reason they often violently resist contrivances for economizing labor. The change from this to a state in which every person would have an interest in rendering every other person as industrious, skillful, and careful as possible (which would be the case under Communism), would be a change very much for the better.

It is, however, to be considered that the principal defects of the present system in respect to the efficiency of labor may be corrected, and the chief advantages of Communism in that respect may be obtained, by arrangements compatible with private property and individual competition. Considerable improvement is already obtained by piece-work, in the kinds of labor which admit of it. By this the workman's personal interest is closely connected with the quantity of work he turns out—not so much with its quality, the security for which still has to depend on the employer's vigilance; neither does piece-work carry with it the public opinion of the workman class, which is often, on the contrary, strongly opposed to it, as a means of (as they think) diminishing the market for laborers. And there is really good ground for their dislike of piece-work, if, as is alleged, it is a frequent practice of employers, after using piece-work to ascertain the utmost which a good workman can do, to fix the price of piece-work so low that by doing that utmost he is not able to earn more than they would be obliged to give him as day wages for ordinary work.

But there is a far more complete remedy than piece-work for the disadvantages of hired labor, viz. what is now called industrial partnership—the admission of the whole body of laborers to a participation in the profits, by distributing among all who share in the work, in the form of a percentage on their earnings, the whole or a fixed portion of the gains after a certain remuneration has been allowed to the capitalist. This plan has been found of admirable efficacy, both in this country and abroad. It has enlisted the sentiments of the workmen employed on the side of the most careful regard by all of them to the general interest of the concern; and by its joint effect in promoting zealous exertion and checking waste, it has very materially increased the remuneration of every description of labor in the concerns in which it has been adopted. It is evident that this system admits of indefinite extension and of an indefinite increase in the share of profits assigned to the laborers, short of that which would leave to the managers less than the needful degree of personal interest in the success of the concern. It is even likely that when such arrangements become common, many of these concerns would at some period or another, on the death or retirement of the chiefs, pass, by arrangement, into the state of purely cooperative associations.

It thus appears that as far as concerns the motives of exertion in the general body, Communism has no advantage which may not be reached under private property, while as respects the managing heads it is at a considerable disadvantage. It has also some disadvantages which seem to be inherent in it, through the necessity under which it lies of deciding in a more or less arbitrary manner questions which, on the present system, decide themselves, often badly enough, but spontaneously.

It is a simple rule, and under certain aspects a just one, to give equal payment to all who share in the work. But this is a very imperfect justice unless the work also is apportioned equally. Now the many different kinds of work required in every society are very unequal in hardness and unpleasantness. To measure these against one another, so as to make quality equivalent to quantity, is so difficult that Communists generally propose that all should work by turns at every kind of labor. But this involves an almost complete sacrifice of the economic advantages of the division of employment's, advantages which are indeed frequently overestimated (or rather the counterconsiderations are underestimated) by political economists, but which are nevertheless, in the point of view of the productiveness of labor, very considerable, for the double reason that the cooperation of employment enables the work to distribute itself with some regard to the special capacities and qualifications of the worker, and also that every worker acquires greater skill and rapidity in one kind of work by confining himself to it. The arrangement, therefore, which is deemed indispensable to a just distribution would probably be a very considerable disadvantage in respect of production. But further, it is strain a very imperfect standard of justice to demand the same amount of work from every one. People

79

have unequal capacities of work, both mental and bodily, and what is a light task for one is an insupportable burden to another. It is necessary, therefore, that there should be a dispensing power, an authority competent to grant exemptions from the ordinary amount of work, and to proportion tasks in some measure to capabilities. As long as there are any lazy or selfish persons who like better to be worked for by others than to work, there will be frequent attempts to obtain exemptions by favor or fraud, and the frustration of these attempts will be an affair of considerable difficulty, and will by no means be always successful. These inconveniences would be little felt, for some time at least, in communities composed of select persons, earnestly desirous of the success of the experiment; but plans for the regeneration of society must consider average human beings, and not only them but the large residuum of persons greatly below the average m the personal and social virtues. The squabbles and ill-blood which could not fail to be engendered by the distribution of work whenever such persons have to be dealt with, would be a great abatement from the harmony and unanimity which Communists hope would be found among the members of their association. That concord would, even in the most fortunate circumstances, be much more liable to disturbance than Communists suppose. The institution provides that there shall be no quarreling about material interests; individualism is excluded from that department of affairs. But there are other departments from which no institutions can exclude it: there will still be rivalry for reputation and for personal power. When selfish ambition is excluded from the field in which, with most men, it chiefly exercises itself, that of riches and pecuniary interest, it would betake itself with greater intensity to the domain still open to it, and we may expect that the struggles for preeminence and for influence in the management would be of great bitterness when the personal passions, diverted from their ordinary channel, are driven to seek their principal gratification in that other direction. For these various reasons it is probable that a Communist association would frequently fail to exhibit the attractive picture of mutual love and unity of will and feeling which we are often told by Communists to expect, but would often be torn by dissension and not infrequently broken up by it.

Other and numerous sources of discord are inherent in the necessity which the Communist principle involves, of deciding by the general voice questions of the utmost importance to every one, which on the present system can be and are left to individuals to decide, each for his own case. As an example, take the subject of education. All Socialists are strongly impressed with the all importance of the training given to the young, not only for the reasons which apply universally, but because their demands being much greater than those of any other system upon the intelligence and morality of the individual citizen, they have even more at stake than any other societies on the excellence of their educational arrangements. Now under Communism these arrangements would have to be made for every citizen by the collective body, since individual parents, supposing them to prefer some other mode of educating their children, would have no private means of paying for it, and would be limited to what they could do by their own personal teaching and influence. But every adult member of the body would have an equal voice in determining the collective system designed for the benefit of all. Here, then, is a most fruitful source of discord in every association. All who had any opinion or preference as to the education they would desire for their own children, would have to rely for their chance of obtaining it upon the influence they could exercise in the joint decision of the community.

It is needless to specify a number of other important questions affecting the mode of employing the productive resources of the association, the conditions of social life, the relations of the body with other associations, &c., on which difference of opinion, often irreconcilable, would be likely to arise. But even the dissension's which might be expected would be a far less evil to the prospects of humanity than a delusive unanimity produced by the prostration of all individual opinions and wishes before the decree of the majority. The obstacles to human progression are always great, and require a concurrence of favorable circumstances to overcome them; but an indispensable condition of their being overcome is, that human nature should have freedom to expand spontaneously in various directions, both in thought and practice; that people should both think for themselves and try experiments for themselves, and should not resign into the hands of rulers, whether acting in the name of a few or of the majority, the business of thinking for them, and of prescribing how they shall act. But in Communist associations private life would be brought in a most unexampled degree within the dominion of public authority, and there would be less scope for the development of individual character and individual preferences than has hitherto existed among the full citizens of any state belonging to the progressive branches of the human family. Already in all societies the compression of individuality by the majority is a great and growing evil; it would probably be much greater under Communism, except so far as it might be in the power of individuals to set bounds to it by selecting to belong to a community of persons like-minded with themselves.

From these various considerations I do not seek to draw any inference against the possibility that Communistic production is capable of being at some future time the form of society best adapted to the wants and circumstances of mankind. I think that this is, and will long be, an open question, upon which fresh light will continually be obtained, both by trial of the Communistic principle under favorable circumstances, and by the improvements which will be gradually effected in the working of the existing system, that of private ownership. The one certainty is, that Communism, to be successful, requires a high standard of both moral and intellectual education in all the members of the community—moral, to qualify them for doing their part honestly and energetically in the labor of life under no inducement but their share in the general interest of the association, and their feelings of duty and sympathy towards it; intellectual, to make them capable of estimating distant interests and entering into complex considerations, sufficiently at least to be able to discriminate, in these matters, good counsel from bad. Now I reject altogether the notion that it is impossible for education and cultivation such as is implied in these things to be made the inheritance of every person in the nation; but I am convinced that it is very difficult, and that the passage to it from our present condition can only be slow. I admit the plea that in the points of moral education on which the success of Communism depends, the present state of society is demoralizing, and that only a Communistic association can effectively train mankind for Communism. It is for Communism, then, to prove, by practical experiment, its power of giving this training. Experiments alone can show whether there is as yet in any portion of the population a sufficiently high level of moral cultivation to make Communism succeed, and to give to the next generation among themselves the education necessary to keep up that high level permanently. If Communist associations show that they can be durable and prosperous, they will multiply, and will probably be adopted by successive portions of the population of the more advanced countries as they become morally fitted for that mode of life. But to force unprepared populations into Communist societies, even if a political revolution gave the power to make such an attempt, would end in disappointment.

If practical trial is necessary to test the capabilities of Communism, it is no less required for those other forms of Socialism which recognize the difficulties of Communism and contrive means to surmount them. The principal of these is Fourierism, a system which, if only as a specimen of intellectual ingenuity, is highly worthy of the attention of any student, either of society or of the human mind. There is scarcely an objection or a difficulty which Fourier did not foresee, and against which he did not make provision beforehand by self-acting contrivances, grounded, however, upon a less high principle of distributive justice than that of Communism, since he admits inequalities of distribution and individual ownership of capital, but not the arbitrary disposal of it. The great problem which he grapples with is how to make labor attractive, since, if this could be done, the principal difficulty of Socialism would be overcome. He maintains that no kind of useful labor is necessarily or universally repugnant, unless either excessive in amount or devoid of the stimulus of companionship and emulation, or regarded by mankind with contempt. The workers in a Fourierist village are to class themselves spontaneously in groups, each group undertaking a different kind of work, and the same person may be a member not only of one group but of any number; a certain minimum having first been set apart for the subsistence of every member of the community, whether capable or not of labor, the society divides the remainder of the produce among the different groups, in such shares as it finds attract to each the amount of labor required, and no more; if there is too great a run upon particular groups it is a sign that those groups are over-remunerated relatively to others; if any are neglected their remuneration must be made higher. The share of produce assigned to each group is divided in fixed proportions among three elements—labor, capital, and talent; the part assigned to talent being rewarded by the suffrages of the group itself, and it is hoped that among the variety of human capacities all, or nearly all, will be qualified to excel in some group or other. The remuneration for capital is to be such as is found sufficient to induce savings from individual consumption, in order to increase the common stock to such point as is desired. The number and ingenuity of the contrivances for meeting minor difficulties, and getting rid of minor inconveniences, is very remarkable. By means of these various provisions it is the expectation of Fourierists that the personal inducements to exertion for the public interest, instead of being taken away, would be made much greater than at present, since every increase of the service rendered would be much more certain of leading to increase of reward than it is now, when accidents of position have so much influence. The efficiency of labor, they therefore expect, would be unexampled, while the saving of labor would be prodigious, by diverting to useful occupations that which is now wasted on things useless or hurtful, and by dispensing with the vast number of superfluous distributors, the buying and selling for the whole community being managed by a single agency. The free choice of individuals as to their manner of life would be no further interfered with than would be necessary for gaining the full advantages of cooperation in the industrial operations. Al-together, the picture of a Fourierist community is both attractive in itself and requires less from common humanity than any other known system of Socialism; and it is much to be desired that the scheme should have that fair trial which alone can test the workableness of any new scheme of social life.[1]

The result of our review of the various difficulties of Socialism has led us to the conclusion that the various schemes for managing the productive resources of the country by public instead of private agency have a case for a trial, and some of them may eventually establish their claims to preference over the existing order of things, but that they are at present workable only by the *élite* of mankind, and have yet to prove their power of training mankind at large to the state of improvement which they presuppose. Far more, of course, may this be said of the more ambitious plan which aims at taking possession of the whole land and capital of the country, and beginning at once to administer it on the public account. Apart from all consideration of injustice to the present possessors, the very idea of conducting the whole industry of a country by direction from a single center is so obviously chimerical, that nobody ventures to propose any mode in which it should be done; and it can hardly be doubted that if the revolutionary Socialists attained their immediate object, and actually had the whole property of the country at their disposal, they would find no other practicable mode of exercising their power over it than that of dividing it into portions, each to be made over to the administration of a small Socialist community. The problem of management, which we have seen to be so difficult even to a select population well prepared beforehand, would be thrown down to be solved as best it could by aggregations united only by locality, or taken indiscriminately from the population, including all the malefactors, all the widlest and most vicious, the most incapable of steady industry, forethought, or self-control, and a majority who, though not equally degraded, are yet, in the opinion of Socialists themselves, as far as regards the qualities essential for the success of Socialism, profoundly demoralized by the existing state of society. It is saying but little to say that the introduction of Socialism under such conditions could have no effect but disastrous failure, and its apostles could have only the consolation that the order of society as it now exists would have perished first, and all who benefit by it would be involved in the common ruin—a consolation which to some of them would probably be real, for if appearances can be trusted the animating principle of too many of the revolutionary Socialists is hate; a very excusable hatred of existing evils, which would vent itself by putting an end to the present system at all costs even to those who suffer by it, in the hope that out of chaos would arise a better Cosmos, and in the impatience of desperation respecting any more gradual improvement. They are unaware that chaos is the very most unfavorable position for setting out in the construction of a Cosmos, and that many ages of conflict, violence, and tyrannical oppression of the weak by the strong must intervene; they know not that they would plunge mankind into the state of nature so forcibly described by Hobbes (*Leviathan*, Part I. ch. xiii.), where every man is an enemy to every man:

> In such condition there is no place for industry, because the fruit thereof is uncertain, and consequently no culture of the earth, no navigation, no use of the commodities that may be imported by sea, no commodious building, no instruments of moving and removing such things as require such force, no knowledge of the face of the earth, no account of time, no arts, no letters, no society; and, which is worst of all, continual fear and danger of violent death; and the life of man solitary, poor, nasty, brutish, and short.

If the poorest and most wretched members of a so-called civilized society are in as bad a condition as every one would be in that worst form of barbarism produced by the dissolution of civilized life, it does not follow that the way to raise them would be to reduce all others to the same miserable state. On the contrary, it is by the aid of the first who have risen that so many others have escaped from the general lot, and it is only by better organization of the same process that it may be hoped in time to succeed in raising the remainder.

# Chapter 9

## Chadwick on Competition

Edwin Chadwick (1800-1890) was one of the two or three most influential policymakers of nineteenth-century England. He and Nassau Senior were primarily responsible for the Report which led to the restructuring of the Poor Law in 1834 along the lines that economists had been urging for years. Chadwick spent twenty years as a British civil servant, becoming best known for his *Report on the Sanitary Condition of the Labouring Population* (1842), which laid the foundations for the modern public health movement. But he was a difficult man to deal with, and he was eventually pensioned off by the government in 1854.

A born reformer and a domineering personality, Chadwick was eager to stick his interventionist thumb into practically every major economic "pie". As a disciple of Jeremy Bentham (he served as secretary and assistant to Bentham during the last two years of the latter's life), Chadwick pushed the Benthamite principle of "the greatest good for the greatest number" to the limit. His Benthamite zeal was displayed often in various reform measures, including important social issues such as sanitation and crime. Chadwick greatly enriched the Benthamite paradigm with his administrative principle of "competition for the field," which is roughly equivalent to the modern notion of franchising. He sought to apply this principle to government bureaucracies (e.g., administration of prisons), the regulation of "natural monopolies" (water utilities), and even to the markets for funerals and beer!

The excerpts below reveal Chadwick's statement of the principle of *competition for the field* and his proposed applications of this principle to water and gas service in London and Paris, on the one hand, and to the distribution of the two staples of the British worker's diet—bread and beer—on the other. Pay particular attention to Chadwick's frequent resort to statistics. He had a passion for collecting "facts," and constantly sought to weave them into his arguments.

Source: Chadwick, Edwin. "Results of Different Principles of Legislation and Administration in Europe: Of Competition for the Field, as Compared with Competition within the Field of Service," *Royal Statistical Society Journal*, vol. 22 (1859), pp. 384-388; 408-420.

*II.—Economic Principle of regulated Competition for a Field, as opposed to Competition within a Field of Service, defined and exemplified in Legislation on the Railway service of England and the Continent.*

From 1838 to 1841, whilst examining the sanitary conditions of town populations, I found urban districts in England, where there are two or three sets of water-pipes carried through streets which might be as well or better supplied under one establishment, and competitions ending in strict monopolies, bad and deficient supplies at high charges to the public, with low dividends to the shareholders, and an almost impracticability of improvement in their separate condition without augmenting the already excessive charges of the ratepayers or further reducing the low returns to the capitalists. These competitions are what I then designated as competitions "within the field of service." As opposed to that form of competition, I proposed, as an administered principle, competition "for the field," that is to say, that the whole field of service should be put up on behalf of the public for competition,—on the only condition on which efficiency, as well as the utmost cheapness, was practicable, namely, the possession, by one capital or by one establishment, of the entire field, which could be most efficiently and economically administered by one, with full securities towards the public for the performance of the requisite service during a given period. The principle was, upon due consideration, extensively adopted and advocated by permanent public officers, commissioners and disinterested public investigators for the regulation of enterprises in railways, then at their commencement; but the views chiefly advocated by speculators and persons who profit by multiplied conflicts -who gain whosoever else lose—were adopted by Parliament. The principle was, however, upon independent consideration, adopted by the continental administrators and legislators, and the results stand out in wide and undeniable contrast of legislative and administrative ability and integrity;—in France, for example, in a much more responsible and more regular service for the public at lower fares, with higher-priced materials, with dearer fuel, poorer, thinner, and less active population, and lower elements of traffic; and yet, with an average return of from seven to nine per cent. to the original shareholders of the lines worked by Companies. In England we have a clashing, immensely more dangerous, unsatisfactory, and generally less responsible service to the public, fares, as contrasted with the continental fares, generally one-third higher, with fuel, iron, and machinery cheaper, and population and traffic more active; yet with only an average return of 3.60 per cent. to the original shareholders, with extensive ruin to them—with gigantic fortunes to the promoters of conflicts. In France, the original shareholders have, moreover, the elements of security and further improvement to their property, whilst the French public have in reversion, on the termination of the present concessions, the prospect of further reductions of fares and increased facilities for intercommunication, or a new source of revenue, derivable from past economy in reduction of the general taxation of the country. In England, the greater mass of original shareholders have before them elements of further depreciation, and loss, and even ruin, by the bounty afforded by the practicability of cheaper constructions and by competitive extensions, that are not to be averted by the patchings of quarrels or by any combinations of their respective directories,—whilst the public have the main arteries of communication—which ought with sound legislation to be as cheap and free as any in the world—clogged with inconveniences and even with delays as well with high charges, amounting to between six and seven millions per annum in excess at the present time, of what a sound administrative principle would have insured. The maladministration which has incurred the excessive outlays—which maintains nearly a hundred separate chief and independent establishments, at the expense of the shareholders, and to the inconvenience and loss of the public in working, seeks to impose these excessive charges upon the public by high fares, and does so in defiance of the experience thus enunciated by an observer of railway administration, that "There is hardly an exception to the rule, that a high fare produces a low amount of traffic and stunts its growth, while a low or moderate fare collects a larger amount of traffic and fosters growth."

### III.—Legislation on the service of the Supply of Water in London and of Gas at Paris.

To the matter of these statements, the answers I usually meet with are, first, that but for the unregulated competition and the original expenses of English Railways, we should have had none at all; and secondly and impatiently, that what has been done cannot now be undone; to which I reply that I do not admit the charge implied in the first answer, that a large and corrupt expenditure for obtaining Parliamentary sanction, is an essential and unavoidable condition of representative institutions; and as to the second objection, I have now to refer to the evidence of some experience proving that much of the existing evil may be undone, and much further impending mischief to such properties, as well as to the public, may be averted, by means of the administrative principle which I have proposed. In analogous cases of the mischievous operation, to the public as well as to capitalists, of competitions permitted or encouraged "within the field of supply," my colleagues on several commissions could find no other remedy. For example, London in itself we found the field of service for a supply of Water, to which I have already adverted, divided amongst seven separate companies and establishments, of which six were originally competing within the field of supply, with two and three sets of pipes down many of the same streets, but which had become multiform monopolies, doling out supplies of water of inferior and often unwholesome quality, insufficient in quantity, although positively nearly three-fifths of it ran to waste during the intermittent periods of service. We found, although the fact was attempted to be denied, that fully 100,000*l*. per annum might be saved by a consolidation of establishments, which sum, capitalised, would hare formed a fund for procuring a superior supply from entirely new sources, soft and pure, instead of hard and impure. It was our duty in this and similar instances, to submit what in the matters referred to us appeared to be the efficient remedies, whatsoever might be the interests opposed to their being carried, of which we could not be unaware. The administrative principle appeared to be beyond the time; and the loud reclamations chiefly of persons interested in separate establishments prevailed against the principle. Since then, as much money as would have sufficed to have obtained supplies of soft water of the highest purity has been expended by the separate companies in the partial improvement of a supply which is hard, essentially inferior in quality, consisting to a great extent, in times of rain, of ditch-delivered water, the surface washing of lands under increasing cultivation and high manuring; unsatisfactory in the mode of delivery, and at heavy charges to the consumers, with unsafe returns to the shareholders. Whilst I was in Paris in 1855, serving as one of the international jurors at the Great Exhibition, I was requested by the Society of Arts to act as one of a special committee appointed on the occasion of the visit at the instance of the president, his Royal Highness the Prince Consort, for the purpose of testing the principles upon which the acknowledged vast improvements lately made in the French metropolis have been carried on, and of considering how far they may with advantage be applied to our circumstances at home. My special attention was directed by the other Englishmen, as well as by my own interests, from the circumstances I have stated, to the principles of the administrative means by which the improvements had been effected in Paris. I found that the attention of the municipality had been directed to a case closely analogous to the water supply of London, namely, of the supplies of gas by seven independent gas companies, when, upon competent and disinterested examination, directed by the government in behalf of the people, the supplies were found to be bad, and the charges upon the actual cost of production of a really good gas to the consumers excessive. A consolidation had been effected precisely on the principle we had recommended for the improvement of the water supply for London; the service had been, in effect, as far as circumstances permitted, put up to competition for the whole field, and the consolidation of all the establishments had been effected under the best available direction, with the result of a considerable improvement of the quality of the gas supplied, a reduction of 30 per cent. upon the previous cost to the private consumers, of 40 per cent. to the public consumers, arising from reductions of establishment charges, and an improvement of 24 per cent. in the value of the shareholders' property.

In respect to one case of a competition of two Gas companies within a field of supply in the North of England, I had evidence that, whereas the prime cost of the manufacture of gas by those separate companies was more than 3s. per 1,000 cubic feet, the result of a competition for the whole field of supply by one establishment instead of two, was its being made at a prime cost of about 1s. 9d. per 1,000 cubic feet. It was out of the saving of a like difference that the results described at Paris were achieved.

.   .   .   .   .   .   .   .   .   .   .   .   .   .   .   .   .   .   .   .   .

The political economists to whom I have submitted cases such as I have described, have expressed concurrent opinions upon them, that the earlier politico-economical doctrines as to competition must now receive considerable modifications. The waste and possible saving of capital, indeed, admit of as little dispute as do cases of the waste of mechanical power, or the direction of the means of economy. To the questions sometimes put me, where I would stop in the application of my principle, I am at present only prepared to answer, "where waste stops;" which must be a matter of inquiry in each case involving the question where the application of the principle needs authoritative intervention, or where it must be left to voluntary means guided by an advanced intelligence. The economical question I have raised, will be found to be in reality not one for the restriction, but one for the enlargement *of* the freedom of competition; the present practice of competition within the field, being like what might be called "the freedom of racing," with small and poor horses, necessarily as it were doubly weighted with establishment charges, whilst the principle of competition for the field may be said to be one of the most free competitions possible, by horses of the greatest power, with the lightest proportion of weight for the attainment of the object of competition,— the maximum of speed, or the best service at the lowest charge. For the better understanding of the requisite modifications of economic doctrine in these respects, as well as for a better appreciation of the large moral and social bearings of the question, it appears to me to be requisite that I should describe the condition of two other fields of service, the one for the supply of bread, the other for the supply of beer.

### VIII.—*On the conditions of Competition in respect to the Manufacture and Distribution of Bread in London and Paris; —Co-operation for the Distribution of Flour.*

I recognise as a fact of common experience, that where a single tradesman is permitted to have the entire and unconditional possession of a field of service, as in remote rural districts, he generally becomes indolent, slow, unaccommodating, and too often insolent, reckless of public inconvenience, and unprogressive. To check these evils, competition of a second is no doubt requisite; and where the two combine, the intrusion of a third. But experience should be consulted, and the public intelligence must be exercised against bounding on a competition, which consideration would show involves palpable waste,—as where two or three capitals may suffice for the performance of a service moderately well, the intrusion of a fourth, fifth, or sixth competing capital eventually lends to its being performed immoderately ill.

In the service of the Baker, for example, in London, the profit in the production, and distribution of bread is, under ordinary circumstances, about twelve shillings per sack of flour, making 94 four-pound loaves, being nearly one penny three farthings per loaf. A field of supply or sale of twelve or fourteen sacks a week, according to local circumstances, may be assumed to be a "living profit" for a respectable baker in a moderate way of business in London, to pay the rent and taxes of a 60*l.* or 80*l.* house and shop, with its bakehouse. With the same bakehouse and shop, and nearly the same fixed establishment charges, he might produce and distribute double the quantity; but from this he is generally precluded by a competitor. Upon fields of supply so occupied with double capitals other competitors break in, until the share of the field is reduced, often to the distribution of six sacks a week, and sometimes to four sacks each, or to an occupation by four capitals of a field in which competition would be better maintained by two. The sanitary condition of the small bakers and competitors in towns, whether masters or journeymen, is most wretched. The bakehouses are confined, miserable and unwholesome. The little master to pay his rent, lets off the upper portions of the house, and crowds himself and family in the lower apartments. The small capitalist who enters into this sort of competition is frequently a man of small understanding, and of the smallest skill in working of his material, except when, under the pressure of his necessities, his ingenuity is excited in adulterating it. He is obliged to obtain his flour on credit, and is supplied with that of the worst quality.

Under the ordinary circumstances of the competitor, within the reduced fields, he is almost compelled to extort from the public his excessive establishment charges by cheating, by adulterations, by short weights, by bribing servants, and by overcharges as to the quantities. Fines may be inflicted, but the necessities being pressing and continued, the frauds and evasions are continued. The only chance of relief for the public will, I apprehend, be found to be in removal of the producer's necessities and temptations by creating widened fields of supply and corresponding production on a larger scale.

It must be admitted, however, that experience of the contracts for the supply of poor law unions and for large public establishments in England, show that the enlargement of the field of service does not alone suffice as a complete security at the least, under the existing conditions. So difficult was it found to obtain good biscuit for the Navy, that it became absolutely necessary to establish governmental bakeries, a measure which was attended with entire success, both in the purity and economy of the product; and the experience of the Army contracts for provisions, shows that resort must be had to original production at a security. At Birmingham the quality of the bread supplied under the highest competition of numerous small capitals had become so bad that a private company was set up, on small shares, for baking bread, and having the good fortune, for a joint stock company, of getting a good practical management, pure bread was made and sold at a penny a loaf cheaper than by the numerous small bakers; and the company gaining a wide field of supply, a good profit was divided amongst the shareholders. In time, the principle of unity of management on a large scale prevailed, the shares of the company were bought up by one manufacturer, who had another large manufacturer as a competitor within the field. The result of this modified competition for the larger field was, that

Birmingham was supplied much cheaper and better with bread than any of the adjacent towns.

From the difficulty of obtaining unadulterated bread in London and elsewhere, private families are driven, much to their inconvenience, to bake for themselves; but their object is extensively defeated by the difficulty of obtaining unadulterated flour. At the meeting at Birmingham of the Association for the Advancement of Social Science, a paper containing highly important, economical and social facts, was read by Mr. John Holmes, of Leeds, on "The Moral and Economic advantages of cooperation in the Provision of Food." To meet the difficulty of obtaining unadulterated flour, cooperative associations, which were in reality joint stock companies, were formed, in 1*l.* shares, first and most successfully at Rochdale, in 1894, and then at Leeds, in 1847, by the more intelligent persons of the wage class. At Rochdale the capital of one association amounts to 14,000*l.*, inclusive of a mill, and the business done by them, with a good profit, amounts to 90,000*l.* per annum. Their profit is gained chiefly by the saving of establishment charges of numerous small capitalists, of whom it is calculated that eighty have been superseded by the one society, having less than half the number of places of subdistribution conducted by salaried servants, and by performing the service of distribution at little more than one and a quarter per cent. at the central or wholesale establishment, and two and a-half per cent. at the retail branches;—whilst private trades do not effect the chief distribution at less than 5 per cent., and the subdistribution at less than 15 or 20 per cent. or even more. They have, from their complete success, been led to extend the operations of joint stock stores, to meat and groceries, with the like success. In speaking of the results of the Leeds Flour Mill Society, Mr. Holmes says, "if 20,000 people will agree at once to give their orders for flour, and will find the requisite capital, then all expense of catering for a business is saved and all risk avoided. Capital can be adapted to requirement, and the machinery can be exactly fitted to supply. No power need be wasted, and no disadvantage accrue from the want of means. No traveler need be paid to seek orders, no cost of law in recovering bad debts, and above all, no loss from debts being incurred. In one district near the Leeds mill it has been shewn that the shops for provisions have no relation to the number of the consumers, and it has followed that of twenty persons beginning in these shops, fifteen have lost their all and more, for five who have succeeded to live. All failure is loss, to the public as well as to the private trader."

But the Birmingham example of the manufacture and distribution of bread on a large scale and other instances which may be cited appear to be in advance of those of extended distributions of flour, because in the large scale, the saving out of the waste incidental to the home baking, is sufficient to allow the bread to be made and distributed to them for nothing beyond the prime cost of the materials. M. de Fawtier shews that in France the public bread making is really eleven per cent. cheaper than the domestic bread making, allowing 4 per cent. as the value of the domestic labour, but not allowing for the domestic mischances of burned bread, ill-fermented, sodden, and spoiled bread; yet in France, the art of domestic bread making is commonly in advance of England. In France, too, there have been late improvements in the construction of the larger ovens, which further reduce the cost of fuel one-third. In the common practice of baking, in the kneading of the dough in England, the journeymen are stripped to the waist, and in consequence of the severity of the labour, and the excessive heat of the bakery, profuse perspiration is induced, and this is unavoidably mixed up with the material. Moreover the journeyman baker is afflicted with a skin disease peculiar to his occupation. In the government bakeries 450 pounds of dough is mixed up in four minutes, and kneaded in six minutes by machinery, and the improved machine labour performs at 5*d*. per cwt., including wages, with wear and tear of utensils, what previously cost 1*s*. 5*d*. I am assured that at Carlisle, where some bakeries on a large scale have been long carried on, and the work is enabled by the scale to be performed by machinery, the workmen are better paid than in the common bakeries, and are put in a good sanitary condition, and the product is superior in quality, as well as cheaper.

In France the principle of competition for the field, and a considerably improved production is effected by the authoritative extension of the field of competition and supply. In Paris the total number of Bakers in proportion to the population is restricted to nearly one-third that of London; the establishments are consequently on a larger scale; the art of baking is in advance, and the rate of production of better bread is on the average one penny a loaf cheaper than in London, which it may well be with reduced establishment charges and really more powerful competition. Dr. Ure states it is proved, indeed, that in Paris the baker's charge on the four pound loaf is a half-penny, whilst in London it is about a penny three farthings. M. de Payen, a Member of the Institute, has examined the practice of bread making in England, as compared with that in France, and reports, that the proceeding on the same basis as to the price of flour, the price of bread, which is pure in Paris, is as 6 against 7 in London, for bread which, on analysis, he found to be generally adulterated. Mr. F. O. Ward has examined the system of bread making in France, as compared with that in England, and concurs with M. Payen as to the public advantage of the principle of regulated competition for the field. The bakers with whom I have spoken in England on the economy of their trade are unanimous in their declaration that the public might be better and cheaper supplied by one-half their present number.

Mr. F. O. Ward informs me that, in Paris, the bakers of the *banlieue,* or suburbs, who hare never been under the regulation as to number by which the bakers of Paris within the walls are governed, have multiplied to about three times the number (relatively to the population they supply) of their Parisian brethren:—the increase bringing them up, curiously enough, to about the same excessive proportion as prevails in London; thus showing how in economical statistics the same laws in operation bring about everywhere the same results. The suburban bakers of Paris, Mr. Ward states, petitioned some years ago, as well in their own interest as in that of the public, to have their numbers reduced and placed under permanent restriction. In this singular document these bakers show the disadvantage under which they labour in consequence of this freedom to multiply at random. They set forth for a period of years the annual excess of bankruptcies among the bakers of the *banlieue,* above the average occurring among their Parisian brethren; and on other tables contrasted columns show how much more frequently shops change hands in the suburbs than in the city from the ruin of their proprietors. They further establish that the average quality of the suburban bread, made under free competition, is inferior to that of the bread made under regulated competition in Paris—the struggling bakers of the *banlieue* being driven to eke out their scanty profit by using inferior flour, and too often by having recourse to adulteration. They show how the poverty of a majority of the suburban bakers place them at the mercy of the great millers, who first get the poorer bakers a little into their debt, and then oblige them to accept inferior flour at a price beyond its value; an extortion of which the baker is only the first victim, and by which the consumers of the deteriorated bread, i. e., the suburban population, are the ultimate sufferers. They offer to find among themselves the money required to buy up and close the redundant establishments, and they declare themselves ready to submit to the restriction of price imposed on their Parisian brethren, provided they can be secured against the intolerable evils of excessive multiplication, so injurious to the consumer as well as to the producer. It is rare, as Mr. Ward observes, to see two economical systems at work in such close proximity, and with such sharply contrasted results; and it is probably rarer still to find the victims of unregulated economical freedom conscious of its pernicious influence on their own usefulness and happiness, and petitioning for regulated freedom as the only true remedy for their misfortunes. Bread in Brussels with unregulated competition was dearer and worse in quality than in Paris. In the poorer quarters of Brussels the small shops for retailing bread literally swarmed. To meet the evil a manufactory of bread on a large scale was established, which produced better bread at a lower price than the petty bakers could turn out, and it is stated to be prospering well. In France there are fiscal and other regulations requiring the bakers to keep reserves of flour, etc., to which economical objections may attach, but they are quite beside the principle propounded in the regulation of competition. Experience everywhere shews, that whilst the extension of the field of production, reduces the temptations and the means to falsification, and inferior production, the unlimited reduction of the field augments and almost necessitates them, so much so, that it has become a popular aphorism applicable to the particular branch of industry, that "an empty sack can never stand upright," whilst a full one may. Breaking the service in question into fragments, the large moral and legislative error is committed of putting sinister interest against duty, under conditions, which it will be shewn, also, in respect to another branch of service, make such interests too strong for private morals, for the law, and public administration. To give a conception of the extent of the bearing of the economical question, I may state that some years ago I had occasion to make what I term an economic analysis of a four-pound loaf that is to say, how much of the cost of production, of transport, of distribution, there was in it, when I found, that at the prices, and the rents of the time, averaging in England 25*s.* per acre, the rent in the four-pound loaf was about three farthings, whilst the cost of distribution was more than three-halfpence. On the like economical analysis of the cost of a pound of meat to the consumer the charge to him for distribution appeared to bear the like proportion, i.e., double the rent in the price of the commodity to the consumer. It appeared, generally, that the cost of distributing the produce of the soil was double the rental of the soil. It appeared that, by the extension of the field of the service, and the saving of the charges of unnecessary establishments and labour, the service of distribution might be greatly improved, and the expense reduced to less than one half; or, in other words, the result was indicated of a possible aggregate saving to the community equal to the whole rental of the land—equal to the whole of the general taxation of the country.

### IX.—On the Moral and Social Evils from Competition within the Field exemplified in the Distribution of Beer.

In no branch of production and trade will the effects of false principles of economy be found, on competent examination, to be more strikingly manifest than in the production and distribution of Beer. In respect to its production, it will be found that, on the scale of the great public breweries, by superior art and scientific appliances,—in getting out a greater quantity of extractive matter, in the avoidance of waste, a saving is achieved which may be estimated as high as 16 per cent. on the raw material as against the home brewer. By the powerful competition of large capitals only a part of the saving so derived is obtained as profit by the manufacturing capitalist. The householder who buys his beer direct from the large brewers, at the large brewers' wholesale prices, may be said to get his brewing done for him for less than nothing—for less than the saving from the previous waste in his home brewing. But in the present grossly neglected condition, of the great bulk of the wage class,—neglected as to education and training, they are unfit to be entrusted with the commodity in bulk. Nor is this unfitness confined to beer. There is with ill-trained classes so much waste, even of bread and groceries when they get them in bulk, as to make the charge of retailing them a charge for a service of economy. It would often be destructive to give to such classes a week's rations at once. The respectable publican, who performs the service of distribution over a fair field, and doles the beer out, pint by pint, amongst a population of such habits, as against their free access to the barrel of beer in the house, prevents large pernicious waste, and renders the service of an economist; and when he does not allow scores to be run up, but requires immediate payment, he administers a moral check which is entitled to consideration. The respectable licensed *victualler*, the hosteler, the innkeeper, with his "tap" for the wage class, may not be interested in any innovation upon the old-accustomed habits of the population, or in rigid temperance movements, according to our notions;—but with a fair trade he is in no need to labour to stimulate consumption, and he has a decided interest against intemperance,—for the drunkard annoys the bulk of his regular customers, disturbs his business, by quarrels, brings in the police, keeps the house open until late, abridges the family's rest, and is really a nuisance. The most desirable and practicable advance for the promotion of temperance would appear to be the consolidation of the business of the coffee-shop keeper with that of the publican, to make him more of the ancient hosteller and victualler, that he may withdraw custom from the modern gin-shop keeper. With the more full sale for beverages, there is the less temptation for their adulteration. When, however, the field of service, which may be occupied in fair competition by two establishments, is by an increased competition occupied by three, four, five, or six competitors within the field, then the conditions are wholly and injuriously altered. As in the competitions within the field for the supply of bread, the ordinary profits will not suffice to bear the disproportionate establishment charges on limited areas or restricted custom, and those charges are extorted from the customer by frauds, less by short measures than by reducing the quality of the beverage, and giving fictitious strength and intoxicating power, by adulterations. (*Vide* Report of the Commons Committee on Public-houses.) The lower class of competitors frequently compete in depraved stimuli to consumption, to riot and intoxication. "I recollect the time," says a respectable witness, Mr. Stinton, the Chairman of the United Towns Licensed Victuallers' Association, "when the licensed victualler was master of his house. I know when he used to say to a working man, 'Now, you have had enough, you go to work'; but he dare not say so now. There are, perhaps, two beer-houses, one on each side of him, and if he said that, the man would say, 'What does it matter to you, if you are paid? if you do not serve me or trust me I can go next door.' The licensed victualler is bound to do this, and  sacrifice the working man's family, from no other cause than the  beer trade; it has brought gin palaces into existence again." " I recollect a case in which I said 'I will not allow cards in my tap room,' and the consequence was that the men said, 'Well, there is a beer-house very near, and if you do not allow it, we will go to that house.' Bad language was being used, and my house was cleared. I lost all my custom for a time, and I was obliged to  allow cards to regain it, in spite of the law." The statements which were brought before me as a Commissioner of Inquiry, as to the frequent depravity of this competition would appear almost incredible. "It's odd," said one of these competitors, a beer-shop keeper in an agricultural district, "if I don't beat, for I  provide my customers with a girl and a fiddle." But this fellow was shamed by another competitor, who had girls dancing naked for his customers. The customers of the licensed victualler's tap, or of the inn, were under the possible check of "master," or of "master's friends," the parlour customers; but in the common level of the beer-shop, in the bye-lanes, or hedgerows, where the poorer competitors get cheap tenements, every restraint is thrown off, and vice revels, with no effectual check, against the full operation of the maleficent interests which a false political economy and empirical legislation allows to be created. I apprehend that the respectable publicans would themselves concur in conclusions similar to those adopted by the competing bakers of the suburbs of Paris.

Ignorant legislation, upon false principles of economy, has in this great branch of service as in others, grievously aggravated all the evils sought to be remedied. Intending to improve the quality of the chief beverage of the wage classes, it has made it worse for them. Intending to increase their domestic comforts, it has diminished them, and occasioned destitution and pauperism an army of active workers for their improvement, consisting of benevolent country gentlemen, magistrates, parochial clergymen, educationists, and social reformers, were making strong head against the peculiar vice and failing of the ill-trained Anglo-Saxon population—an unregulated and excessive appetite for intoxicating beverage which makes high and fluctuating wages almost synonymous with ruinous excess, and were getting them into habits of temperance, thrift, and domestic comfort, when their labours were frustrated by that most unhappy measure, the Beer Act, which is justly pronounced by the Committee of the House of Lords (of 1850) to be "in itself an evil of the first magnitude, not only by increasing the temptations to excess which are thus presented at every step, but by driving houses, even those under the direct control of magistrates, as well as others originally respectable, to practices for the purposes of attracting custom which are degrading to their own character and most injurious to morality and order."

The perceptions of the bakers of the *banlieue* of Paris, as to the means of preventing the sinister exercise of the power of large dealers or producers, stand out in marked contrast to those of the Committee of the House of Commons on public-houses. That Committee, disregarding the evil effects everywhere manifest from competitions within the field, actually proposed to extend them still further, to all persons of good character, i.e., to all persons not convicted of any offence,—as if the Committee had not had widely displayed in the evidence the working of such competitions in subjecting the competitors to degrading influences, destructive of any good characters exposed to them I as if it were not proved that that sort of competition, by subdividing the field of supply, and by making and keeping the half of the competitors poor, drives them into debt and makes them more dependent on the large producers or the great brewers, whilst it impairs the just and salutary powers of those same large brewers to protect the commodity from adulteration for the sake of their own character, if not for the sake of the consumers!

. . . . . . . . . . . . . . . . . . .

It remains to be described on some future opportunity, how much bad morality, anti-social feelings, and painful sense of individual insecurity, pervading and corrupting all society, and extending to the Commons House itself, have their remedies in the advance of correct economic science and sound legislative and administrative principle; the facts cited may serve to show that the advance of economic science will not be by hypothetical assumptions, as to what will be done in the face of experience of what is not done, but by well examined and complete collections of facts as to past experience on which to found safe practical rules for future guidance.

# Chapter 10

## Marx and Engels on the Nature of Communism

Karl Marx (1818-1883), like some other important economists of the nineteenth and twentieth centuries, did not consider himself merely an economist, pure and simple. His conception of "historical materialism" is really an attempt to unite all social sciences into a single science of society. Although he did not totally succeed in this quest, one measure of his *relative* success is the fact that his ideas affected many other social sciences, e.g., anthropology, history, sociology, psychology, etc. Still, his greatest work, *Capital*, is first and foremost an analysis of economic relations and institutions. For Marx, there are no universal economic laws that are valid in every historical epoch. Each mode of production has its own specific economic laws which become irrelevant when the general social framework changes. Marx's economics, therefore, focused almost exclusively on the capitalist mode of production.

In the *Communist Manifesto*, excerpted here, Marx and Engels combined to present a social blueprint of the post-capitalist society. It is as close as Marx ever came to specifying his vision of a better society. The *Manifesto* is a political document as well as an economic one, for although it describes the economic features of capitalism, it also justifies the aims of the Communist Party: to form the proletariat into a class; to overthrow the bourgeois; and to grasp political power. Marx's venom for the bourgeoisie literally oozes through these pages. But it is also interesting to note that despite Marx's reputation as a revolutionary, he concludes with a proclamation of *gradualism*. He and Engels write, for example: "The proletariat will use its political supremacy to wrest, *by degrees*, all capital from the bourgeoisie, to centralize all instruments of production in the hands of the State..., and to increase the total of productive forces as rapidly as possible." Their ten-point program, unveiled at the very last, may therefore be seen as a blueprint for creeping socialism rather a revolutionary call to arms.

Source:   Karl Marx: Essential Writings, edited by Fredric L. Bender. New York: Harper Torchbooks, 1972. Pages 240-263

# 25. The Manifesto

This selection comprises the first two parts of *The Manifesto of the Communist Party,* written by Marx and Engels in January, 1848. It remains the classic popular expression of their program and must be counted as among the handful of most influential books ever published. For our purpose it illustrates Marx's position on the development and significance of modern industry and of the historical roles played by the bourgeoisie and the proletariat. One should carefully note the dialectical relationship described as holding between these two classes, for a great deal of Marx's political argument depends upon the thesis that as capitalism develops so too must the proletariat necessarily develop along with it. The second part of the *Manifesto*, concerned with the program of the infant Communist party of Germany in 1848, has served as a model for all subsequent Communist movements.

A SPECTER is haunting Europe—the specter of Communism. All the Powers of old Europe have entered into a holy alliance to exorcise this specter: Pope and Czar, Metternich and Guizot, French Radicals and German police spies.

Where is the party in opposition that has not been decried as Communistic by its opponents in power? Where the Opposition that has not hurled back the branding reproach of Communism, against the more advanced opposition parties, as well as against its reactionary adversaries?

Two things result from this fact.

I. Communism is already acknowledged by all European Powers to be itself a Power.

II. It is high time that Communists should openly, in the face of the whole world, publish their views, their aims, their tendencies, and meet this nursery tale of the Specter of Communism with a Manifesto of the party itself.

To this end, Communists of various nationalities have assembled in London, and sketched the following Manifesto, to be published in the English, French, German, Italian, Flemish and Danish languages.

---

From The Manifesto of the Communist Party, trans. By Samuel Moore (Moscow: Foreign Languages Publishing House, n.d.).

# I
# Bourgeois and Proletarians

The history of all hitherto existing society is the history of class struggles.

Freeman and slave, patrician and plebeian, lord and serf, guild-master and journeyman, in a word, oppressor and oppressed, stood in constant opposition to one another, carried on an uninterrupted, now hidden, now open fight, a fight that each time ended, either in a revolutionary reconstitution of society at large, or in the common ruin of the contending classes.

In the earlier epochs of history, we find almost everywhere a complicated arrangement of society into various orders, a manifold gradation of social rank. In ancient Rome we have patricians, knights, plebeians, slaves; in the Middle Ages, feudal lords, vassals, guild-masters, journeymen, apprentices, serfs; in almost all of these classes, again, subordinate gradations. The modern bourgeois society that has sprouted from the ruins of feudal society has not done away with class antagonisms. It has but established new classes, new conditions of oppression, new forms of struggle in place of the old ones.

Our epoch, the epoch of the bourgeoisie, possesses, however, this distinctive feature: it has simplified the class antagonisms. Society as a whole is more and more splitting up into two great hostile camps, into two great classes directly facing each other: Bourgeoisie and Proletariat.

From the serfs of the Middle Ages sprang the chartered burghers of the earliest towns. From these burgesses the first elements of the bourgeoisie were developed.

The discovery of America, the rounding of the Cape, opened up fresh ground for the rising bourgeoisie. The East Indian and Chinese markets, the colonization of America, trade with the colonies, the increase in the means of exchange and in commodities generally, gave to commerce, to navigation, to industry, an impulse never before known, and thereby, to the revolutionary element in the tottering feudal society, a rapid development.

The feudal system of industry, under which industrial production was monopolized by closed guilds, now no longer sufficed for the growing wants of the new markets. The manufacturing system took its place. The guild-masters were pushed on one side by the manufacturing middle class; division of labor between the different corporate guilds vanished in the face of division of labor in each single workshop.

Meantime the markets kept ever growing, the demand ever rising. Even manufacture no longer sufficed. Thereupon, steam and machinery revolutionized industrial production. The place of manufacture was taken by the giant, Modern Industry, the place of the industrial middle class, by industrial millionaires, the leaders of whole industrial armies, the modern bourgeois.

Modern industry has established the world market, for which the discovery of America paved the way. This market has given an immense development to commerce, to navigation, to communication by land. This development has, in its turn, reacted on the extension of industry; and in proportion as industry, commerce, navigation, railways extended, in the same proportion the bourgeoisie developed, increased its capital, and pushed into the background every class handed down from the Middle Ages.

We see, therefore, how the modern bourgeoisie is itself the product of a long course of development, of a series of revolutions in the modes of production and of exchange.

Each step in the development of the bourgeoisie was accompanied by a corresponding political advance of that class. An oppressed class under the sway of the feudal nobility, an armed and self-governing association in the medieval commune; here independent urban republic (as in Italy and Germany), there taxable "third estate" of the monarchy (as in France), afterward, in the period of manufacture proper, serving either the semifeudal or the absolute monarchy as a counterpoise against the nobility, and, in fact, cornerstone of the great monarchies in general, the bourgeoisie has at last, since the establishment of Modern Industry and of the world market, conquered for itself, in the modern representative State, exclusive political sway. The executive of the modern State is but a committee for managing the common affairs of the whole bourgeoisie.

The bourgeoisie, historically, has played a most revolutionary part.

The bourgeoisie, wherever it has got the upper hand, has put an end to all feudal, patriarchal, idyllic relations. It has pitilessly torn asunder the motley feudal ties that bound man to his "natural superiors," and has left remaining no other nexus between man and man than naked self-interest, than callous "cash payment." It has drowned the most heavenly ecstasies of religious fervor, of chivalrous enthusiasm, of philistine sentimentalism, in the icy water of egotistical calculation. It has resolved personal worth into exchange value, and in place of the numberless indefeasible chartered freedoms, has set up that single, unconscionable freedom—Free Trade. In one word, for exploitation, veiled by religious and political illusions, it has substituted naked, shameless, direct, brutal exploitation.

The bourgeoisie has stripped of its halo every occupation hitherto honored and looked up to with reverent awe. It has converted the physician, the lawyer, the priest, the poet, the man of science, into its paid wage laborers.

The bourgeoisie has torn away from the family its sentimental veil, and has reduced the family relation to a mere money relation.

The bourgeoisie has disclosed how it came to pass that the brutal display of vigor in the Middle Ages, which Reactionists so much admire, found its fitting complement in the most slothful indolence. It has been the first to show what man's activity can bring about. It has accomplished wonders far surpassing Egyptian pyramids, Roman aqueducts, and Gothic cathedrals; it has conducted expeditions that put in the shade all former Exoduses of nations and crusades.

The bourgeoisie cannot exist without constantly revolutionizing the instruments of production, and thereby the relations of production, and with them the whole relations of society. Conservation of the old modes of production in unaltered form was, on the contrary, the first condition of existence for all earlier industrial classes. Constant revolutionizing of production, uninterrupted disturbance of all social conditions, everlasting uncertainty and agitation distinguish the bourgeois epoch from all earlier ones. All fixed, fast-frozen relations, with their train of ancient and venerable prejudices and opinions are swept away, all new-formed ones become antiquated before they can ossify.

All that is solid melts into air, all that is holy is profaned, and man is at last compelled to face with sober senses his real conditions of life, and his relations with his kind.

The need of a constantly expanding market for its products chases the bourgeoisie over the whole surface of the globe. It must nestle everywhere, settle everywhere, establish connections everywhere.

The bourgeoisie has through its exploitation of the world market given a cosmopolitan character to production and consumption in every country. To the great chagrin of Reactionists, it has drawn from under the feet of industry the national ground on which it stood. All old-established national industries have been destroyed or are daily being destroyed. They are dislodged by new industries, whose introduction becomes a life and death question for all civilized nations, by industries that no longer work up indigenous raw material, but raw material drawn from the remotest zones; industries whose products are consumed, not only at home, but in every quarter of the globe. In place of the old wants, satisfied by the productions of the country, we find new wants, requiring for their satisfaction the products of distant lands and climes. In place of the old local and national seclusion and self-sufficiency, we have intercourse in every direction, universal interdependence of nations. And as in material, so also in intellectual production. The intellectual creations of individual nations become common property. National one-sidedness and narrow-mindedness become more and more impossible, and from the numerous national and local literature's, there arises a world literature.

The bourgeoisie, by the rapid improvement of all instruments of production, by the immensely facilitated means of communication, draws all, even the most barbarian, nations into civilization. The cheap prices of its commodities are the heavy artillery with which it batters down all Chinese walls, with which it forces the barbarians' intensely obstinate hatred of foreigners to capitulate. It compels all nations, on pain of extinction, to adopt the bourgeois mode of production; it compels them to introduce what it calls civilization into their midst, i.e., to become bourgeois themselves. In one word, it creates a world after its own image.

The bourgeoisie has subjected the country to the rule of the towns. It has created enormous cities, has greatly increased the urban population as compared with the rural, and has thus rescued a considerable part of the population from the idiocy of rural life. Just as it has made the country dependent on the towns, so it has made barbarian and semibarbarian countries dependent on the civilized ones, nations of peasants on nations of bourgeois, the East on the West.

The bourgeoisie keeps more and more doing away with the scattered state of the population, of the means of production, and of property. It has agglomerated population, centralized means of production, and has concentrated property in a few hands. The necessary consequence of this was political centralization. Independent, or but loosely connected, provinces with separate interests, laws, governments and systems of taxation, became lumped together into one nation, with one government, one code of laws, one national class-interest, one frontier and one customs tariff.

The bourgeoisie, during its rule of scarce one hundred years, has created more massive and more colossal productive forces than have all preceding generations together. Subjection of Nature's forces to man, machinery, application of chemistry to industry and agriculture, steam navigation, railways, electric telegraphs, clearing of whole continents for cultivation, canalization of rivers, whole populations conjured out of the ground— what earlier century had even a presentiment that such productive forces slumbered in the lap of social labor?

We see then: the means of production and of exchange, on whose foundation the bourgeoisie built itself up, were generated in feudal society. At a certain stage in the development of these means of production and of exchange, the conditions under which feudal society produced and exchanged, the feudal organization of agriculture and manufacturing industry, in one word, the feudal relations of property became no longer compatible with the already developed productive forces; they became so many fetters. They had to be burst asunder; they were burst asunder.

Into their place stepped free competition, accompanied by a social and political constitution adapted to it, and by the economical and political sway of the bourgeois class.

A similar movement is going on before our own eyes. Modern bourgeois society with its relations of production, of exchange and of property, a society that has conjured up such gigantic means of production and of exchange, is like the sorcerer, who is no longer able to control the powers of the nether world whom he has called up by his spells. For many a decade past, the history of industry and commerce is but the history of the revolt of modern productive forces against modern conditions of production, against the property relations that are the conditions for the existence of the bourgeoisie and of its rule. It is enough to mention the commercial crises that by their periodical return put on its trial, each time more threateningly, the existence of the entire bourgeois society. In these crises a great part not only of the existing products, but also the previously created productive forces, are periodically destroyed. In these crises there breaks out an epidemic that, in all earlier epochs, would have seemed an absurdity—the epidemic of overproduction. Society suddenly finds itself put back into a state of momentary barbarism; it appears as if a famine, a universal war of devastation had cut off the supply of every means of subsistence; industry and commerce seem to be destroyed; and why? Because there is too much civilization, too much means of subsistence, too much industry, too much commerce. The productive forces at the disposal of society no longer tend to further the development of the conditions of bourgeois property; on the contrary, they have become too powerful for these conditions, by which they are fettered, and so soon as they overcome these fetters, they bring disorder into the whole of bourgeois society, endanger the existence of bourgeois property. The conditions of bourgeois society are too narrow to comprise the wealth created by them. And how does the bourgeoisie get over these crises? On the one hand by enforced destruction of a mass of productive forces; on the other, by the conquest of new markets, and by the more thorough exploitation of the old ones. That is to say, by paving the way for more extensive and more destructive crises, and by diminishing the means whereby crises are prevented.

The weapons with which the bourgeoisie felled feudalism to the ground are now turned against the bourgeoisie itself.

But not only has the bourgeoisie forged the weapons that bring death to itself; it has also called into existence the men who are to wield those weapons—the modern working class—the proletarians.

In proportion as the bourgeoisie, i.e., capital, is developed, in the same proportion is the proletariat, the modern working class, developed—a class of laborers, who live only so long as they find work, and who find work only so long as their labor increases capital. These laborers, who must sell themselves piecemeal, are a commodity, like every other article of commerce, and are consequently exposed to all the vicissitudes of competition, to all the fluctuations of the market.

Owing to the extensive use of machinery and to division of labor, the work of the proletarians has lost all individual character, and, consequently, all charm for the workman. He becomes an appendage of the machine, and it is only the most simple, most monotonous, and most easily acquired knack that is required of him. Hence, the cost of production of a workman is restricted, almost entirely, to the means of subsistence that he requires for his maintenance, and for the propagation of his race. But the price of a commodity, and therefore also of labor, is equal to its cost of production. In proportion, therefore, as the repulsiveness of the work increases, the wage decreases. Nay more, in proportion as the use of machinery and division of labor increases, in the same proportion the burden of toil also increases, whether by prolongation of the working hours, by increase of the work exacted in a given time or by increased speed of the machinery, etc.

Modern industry has converted the little workshop of the patriarchal master into the great factory of the industrial capitalist. Masses of laborers, crowded into the factory, are organized like soldiers. As privates of the industrial array they are placed under the command of a perfect hierarchy of officers and sergeants. Not only are they slaves of the bourgeois class, and of the bourgeois State; they are daily and hourly enslaved by the machine, by the overlooker, and, above all, by the individual bourgeois manufacturer himself. The more openly this despotism proclaims gain to be its end and aim, the more petty, the more hateful and the more embittering it is.

The less the skill and exertion of strength implied in manual labor, in other words, the more modern industry becomes developed, the more is the labor of men superseded by that of women. Differences of age and sex have no longer any distinctive social validity for the working class. All are instruments of labor, more or less expensive to use, according to their age and sex.

No sooner is the exploitation of the laborer by the manufacturer, so far, at an end, that he receives his wages in cash, than he is set upon by the other portions of the bourgeoisie, the landlord, the shopkeeper, the pawnbroker, etc.

The lower strata of the middle class—the small tradespeople, shopkeepers, and retired tradesmen generally, the handicraftsmen and peasants—all these sink gradually into the proletariat, partly because their diminutive capital does not suffice for the scale on which Modern Industry is carried on, and is swamped in the competition with the large capitalists, partly because their specialized skill is rendered worthless by new methods of production. Thus the proletariat is recruited from all classes of the population.

The proletariat goes through various stages of development. With its birth begins its struggle with the bourgeoisie. At first the contest is carried on by individual laborers, then by the workpeople of a factory, then by the operatives of one trade, in one locality, against the individual bourgeois who directly exploits them. They direct their attacks not against the bourgeois conditions of production, but against the instruments of production themselves; they destroy imported wares that compete with their labor, they smash to pieces machinery, they set factories ablaze, they seek to restore by force the vanished status of the workman of the Middle Ages.

At this stage the laborers still form an incoherent mass scattered over the whole country, and broken up by their mutual competition. If anywhere they unite to form more compact bodies, this is not yet the consequence of their own active union, but of the union of the bourgeoisie, which class, in order to attain its own political ends, is compelled to set the whole proletariat in motion, and is moreover yet, for a time, able to do so. At this stage, therefore, the proletarians do not fight their enemies, but the enemies of their enemies, the remnants of absolute monarchy, the landowners, the nonindustrial bourgeois, the petty bourgeoisie. Thus the whole historical movement is concentrated in the hands of the bourgeoisie; every victory so obtained is a victory for the bourgeoisie.

But with the development of industry the proletariat not only increases in number; it becomes concentrated in greater masses, its strength grows, and it feels that strength more. The various interests and conditions of life within the ranks of the proletariat are more and more equalized, in proportion as machinery obliterates all distinctions of labor, and nearly everywhere reduces wages to the same low level. The growing competition among the bourgeois, and the resulting commercial crises, make the wages of the workers ever more fluctuating. The unceasing improvement of machinery, ever more rapidly developing, makes their livelihood more and more precarious; the collisions between individual workmen and individual bourgeois take more and more the character of collisions between two classes. Thereupon the workers begin to form combinations (Trades' Unions) against the bourgeois; they club together in order to keep up the rate of wages; they found permanent associations in order to make provision beforehand for these occasional revolts. Here and there the contest breaks out into riots.

Now and then the workers are victorious, but only for a time. The real fruit of their battles lies, not in the immediate result, but in the ever-expanding union of the workers. This union is helped on by the improved means of communication that are created by modern industry and that place the workers of different localities in contact with one another. It was just this contact that was needed to centralize the numerous local struggles, all of the same character, into one national struggle between classes. But every class struggle is a political struggle. And that union, to attain which the burghers of the Middle Ages, with their miserable highways, required centuries, the modern proletarians thanks to railways, achieve in a few years.

This organization of the proletarians into a class, and consequently into a political party, is continually being upset again by the competition between the workers themselves. But it ever rises up again, stronger, firmer, mightier. It compels legislative recognition of particular interests of the workers, by taking advantage of the divisions among the bourgeoisie itself. Thus the ten-hours' bill in England was carried.

Altogether collisions between the classes of the old society further, in many ways, the course of development of the proletariat. The bourgeoisie finds itself involved in a constant battle. At first with the aristocracy; later on, with those portions of the bourgeoisie itself, whose interests have become antagonistic to the progress of industry; at all times, with the bourgeoisie of foreign countries. In all these battles it sees itself compelled to appeal to the proletariat, to ask for its help, and thus, to drag it into the political arena. The bourgeoisie itself, therefore, supplies the proletariat with its own elements of political and general education, in other words, it furnishes the proletariat with weapons for fighting the bourgeoisie.

Further, as we have already seen, entire sections of the ruling classes are, by the advance of industry, precipitated into the proletariat, or are at least threatened in their conditions of existence. These also supply the proletariat with fresh elements of enlightenment and progress.

Finally, in times when the class struggle nears the decisive hour, the process of dissolution going on within the ruling class, in fact within the whole range of old society, assumes such a violent, glaring character that a small section of the ruling class cuts itself adrift, and joins the revolutionary class, the class that holds the future in its hands. Just as, therefore, at an earlier period, a section of the nobility went over to the bourgeoisie, so now a portion of the bourgeoisie goes over to the proletariat, and in particular, a portion of the bourgeois ideologists, who have raised themselves to the level of comprehending theoretically the historical movement as a whole.

Of all the classes that stand face to face with the bourgeoisie today, the proletariat alone is a really revolutionary class. The other classes decay and finally disappear in the face of modern industry; the proletariat is its special and essential product.

The lower middle class, the small manufacturer, the shopkeeper, the artisan, the peasant, all these fight against the bourgeoisie, to save from extinction their existence as fractions of the middle class. They are therefore not revolutionary, but conservative. Nay more, they are reactionary, for they try to roll back the wheel of history. If by chance they are revolutionary, they are so only in view of their impending transfer into the proletariat, they thus defend not their present, but their future interests, they desert their own standpoint to place themselves at that of the proletariat.

The "dangerous class," the social scum, that passively rotting mass thrown off by the lowest layers of old society, may, here and there, be swept into the movement by a proletarian revolution; its conditions of life, however, prepare it far more for the part of a bribed tool of reactionary intrigue.

In the conditions of the proletariat, those of old society at large are already virtually swamped. The proletarian is without property; his relation to his wife and children has no longer anything in common with the bourgeois family relations; modern industrial labor, modern subjection to capital, the same in England as in France, in America as in Germany, has stripped him of every trace of national character. Law, morality, religion, are to him so many bourgeois prejudices, behind which lurk in ambush just as many bourgeois interests.

All the preceding classes that got the upper hand sought to fortify their already acquired status by subjecting society at large to their conditions of appropriation. The proletarians cannot become masters of the productive forces of society, except by abolishing their own previous mode of appropriation, and thereby also every other previous mode of appropriation. They have nothing of their own to secure and to fortify; their mission is to destroy all previous securities for, and insurance's of, individual property.

All previous historical movements were movements of minorities, or in the interest of minorities. The proletarian movement is the self-conscious, independent movement of the immense majority, in the interest of the immense majority. The proletariat, the lowest stratum of our present society, cannot stir, cannot raise itself up, without the whole superincumbent strata of official society being sprung into the air.

Though not in substance, yet in form, the struggle of the proletariat with the bourgeoisie is at first a national struggle. The proletariat of each country must, of course, first of all settle matters with its own bourgeoisie.

In depicting the most general phases of the development of the proletariat, we traced the more or less veiled civil war, raging within existing society, up to the point where that war breaks out into open revolution, and where the violent overthrow of the bourgeoisie lays the foundation for the sway of the proletariat.

Hitherto, every form of society has been based, as we have already seen, on the antagonism of oppressing and oppressed classes. But in order to oppress a class, certain conditions must be assured to it under which it can, at least, continue its slavish existence. The serf, in the period of serfdom, raised himself to membership in the commune, just as the petty bourgeois, under the yoke of feudal absolutism, managed to develop into a bourgeois. The modern laborer, on the contrary, instead of rising with the progress of industry, sinks deeper and deeper below the conditions of existence of his own class. He becomes a pauper, and pauperism develops more rapidly than population and wealth. And here it becomes evident that the bourgeoisie is unfit any longer to be the ruling class in society, and to impose its conditions of existence upon society as an overriding law. It is unfit to rule because it is incompetent to assure an existence to its slave within his slavery, because it cannot help letting him sink into such a state, that it has to feed him, instead of being fed by him. Society can no longer live under this bourgeoisie, in other words, its existence is no longer compatible with society.

The essential condition for the existence, and for the sway of the bourgeois class, is the formation and augmentation of capital; the condition for capital is wage labor. Wage labor rests exclusively on competition between the laborers. The advance of industry, whose involuntary promoter is the bourgeoisie, replaces the isolation of the laborers, due to competition, by their revolutionary combination, due to association. The development of Modern Industry, therefore, cuts from under its feet the very foundation on which the bourgeoisie produces and appropriates products. What the bourgeoisie, therefore, produces, above all, is its own gravediggers. Its fall and the victory of the proletariat are equally inevitable.

# II
# Proletarians and Communists

In what relation do the Communists stand to the proletarians as a whole?

The Communists do not form a separate party opposed to other working-class parties.

They have no interests separate and apart from those of the proletariat as a whole.

They do not set up any sectarian principles of their own, by which to shape and mold the proletarian movement.

The Communists are distinguished from the other working-class parties by this only: 1. In the national struggles of the proletarians of the different countries, they point out and bring to the front the common interests of the entire proletariat, independently of all nationality. 2. In the various stages of development which the struggle of the working class against the bourgeoisie has to pass through, they always and everywhere represent the interests of the movement as a whole.

The Communists, therefore, are on the one hand, practically, the most advanced and resolute section of the working-class parties of every country, that section which pushes forward all others; on the other hand, theoretically, they have over the great mass of the proletariat the advantage of clearly understanding the line of march, the conditions, and the ultimate general results of the proletarian movement.

The immediate aim of the Communists is the same as that of all the other proletarian parties: formation of the proletariat into a class, overthrow of the bourgeois supremacy, conquest of political power by the proletariat.

The theoretical conclusions of the Communists are in no way based on ideas or principles that have been invented, or discovered, by this or that would-be universal reformer.

They merely express, in general terms, actual relations springing from an existing class struggle, from a historical movement going on under our very eyes. The abolition of existing property relations is not at all a distinctive feature of Communism.

All property relations in the past have continually been subject to historical change consequent upon the change in historical conditions.

The French Revolution, for example, abolished feudal property in favor of bourgeois property.

The distinguishing feature of Communism is not the abolition of property generally, but the abolition of bourgeois property. But modern bourgeois private property is the final and most complete expression of the system of producing and appropriating products, that is based on class antagonisms, on the exploitation of the many by the few.

In this sense, the theory of the Communists may be summed up in the single sentence: Abolition of private property.

We Communists have been reproached with the desire of abolishing the right of personally acquiring property as the fruit of a man's own labor, which property is alleged to be the groundwork of all personal freedom, activity and independence.

Hard-won, self-acquired, self-earned property! Do you mean the property of the petty artisan and of the small peasant, a form of property that preceded the bourgeois form? There is no need to abolish that; the development of industry has to a great extent already destroyed it, and is still destroying it daily.

Or do you mean modern bourgeois private property?

But does wage labor create any property for the laborer? Not a bit. It creates capital, i.e., that kind of property which exploits wage labor, and which cannot increase except upon condition of begetting a new supply of wage labor for fresh exploitation. Property, in its present form, is based on the antagonism of capital and wage labor. Let us examine both sides of this antagonism.

To be a capitalist is to have not only a purely personal, but a social *status* in production. Capital is a collective product, and only by the united action of many members, nay, in the last resort, only by the united action of all members of society, can it be set in motion.

Capital is, therefore, not a personal, it is a social power.

When, therefore, capital is converted into common property, into the property of all members of society, personal property is not thereby transformed into social property. It is only the social character of the property that is changed. It loses its class character.

Let us now take wage labor.

The average price of wage labor is the minimum wage, i.e., that quantum of the means of subsistence, which is absolutely requisite to keep the laborer in bare existence as a laborer. What, therefore, the wage laborer appropriates by means of his labor, merely suffices to prolong and reproduce a bare existence. We by no means intend to abolish this personal appropriation of the products of labor, an appropriation that is made for the maintenance and reproduction of human life, and that leaves no surplus wherewith to command the labor of others. All that we want to do away with is the miserable character of this appropriation, under which the laborer lives merely to increase capital, and is allowed to live only in so far as the interest of the ruling class requires it.

In bourgeois society, living labor is but a means to increase accumulated labor. In Communist society, accumulated labor is but a means to widen, to enrich, to promote the existence of the laborer.

In bourgeois society, therefore, the past dominates the present; in Communist society, the present dominates the past. In bourgeois society capital is independent and has individuality, while the living person is dependent and has no individuality.

And the abolition of this state of things is called by the bourgeois, abolition of individuality and freedom! And rightly so. The abolition of bourgeois individuality, bourgeois independence, and bourgeois freedom is undoubtedly aimed at.

By freedom is meant, under the present bourgeois conditions of production, free trade, free selling and buying.

But if selling and buying disappears, free selling and buying disappears also. This talk about free selling and buying, and all the other "brave words" of our bourgeoisie about freedom in general, have a meaning, if any, only in contrast with restricted selling and buying, with the fettered traders of the Middle Ages, but have no meaning when opposed to the Communistic abolition of buying and selling, of the bourgeois conditions of production, and of the bourgeoisie itself.

You are horrified at our intending to do away with private property. But in your existing society, private property is already done away with for nine-tenths of the population; its existence for the few is solely due to its nonexistence in the hands of those nine-tenths. You reproach us, therefore, with intending to do away with a form of property, the necessary condition for whose existence is the nonexistence of any property for the immense majority of society.

In one word, you reproach us with intending to do away with your property. Precisely so; that is just what we intend.

From the moment when labor can no longer be converted into capital, money, or rent, into a social power capable of being monopolized, i.e., from the moment when individual property can no longer be transformed into bourgeois property, into capital, from that moment, you say, individuality vanishes.

You must, therefore, confess that by "individual" you mean no other person than the bourgeois, than the middle-class owner of property. This person must, indeed, be swept out of the way, and made impossible.

Communism deprives no man of the power to appropriate the products of society; all that it does is to deprive him of the power to subjugate the labor of others by means of such appropriation.

It has been objected that upon the abolition of private property all work will cease, and universal laziness will overtake us.

According to this, bourgeois society ought long ago to have gone to the dogs through sheer idleness; for those of its members who work acquire nothing, and those who acquire anything do not work. The whole of this objection is but another expression of the tautology: that there can no longer be any wage labor when there is no longer any capital.

All objections urged against the Communistic mode of producing and appropriating material products, have, in the same way, been urged against the Communistic modes of producing and appropriating intellectual products. Just as, to the bourgeois, the disappearance of class property is the disappearance of production itself, so the disappearance of class culture is to him identical with the disappearance of all culture.

That culture, the loss of which he laments, is, for the enormous majority, a mere training to act as a machine.

But don't wrangle with us so long as you apply, to our intended abolition of bourgeois property, the standard of your bourgeois notions of freedom, culture, law, etc. Your very ideas are but the outgrowth of the conditions of your bourgeois production and bourgeois property, just as your jurisprudence is but the will of your class made into a law for all, a will whose essential character and direction are determined by the economical conditions of existence of your class.

The selfish misconception that induces you to transform into eternal laws of nature and of reason, the social forms springing from your present mode of production and form of property-historical relations that rise and disappear in the progress of production—this misconception you share with every ruling class that has preceded you. What you see clearly in the case of ancient property, what you admit in the case of feudal property, you are of course forbidden to admit in the case of your own bourgeois form of property.

Abolition of the family! Even the most radical flare up at this infamous proposal of the Communists.

On what foundation is the present family, the bourgeois family, based? On capital, on private gain. In its completely developed form this family exists only among the bourgeoisie. But this state of things finds its complement in the practical absence of the family among the proletarians, and in public prostitution.

The bourgeois family will vanish as a matter of course when its complement vanishes, and both will vanish with the vanishing of capital.

Do you charge us with wanting to stop the exploitation of children by their parents? To this crime we plead guilty.

But, you will say, we destroy the most hallowed of relations, when we replace home education by social.

And your education! Is not that also social, and determined by the social conditions under which you educate, by the intervention, direct or indirect, of society, by means of schools, etc.? The Communists have not invented the intervention of society in education; they do but seek to alter the character of that intervention, and to rescue education from the influence of the ruling class.

The bourgeois clap-trap about the family and education, about the hallowed correlation of parent and child, becomes all the more disgusting, the more, by the action of Modern Industry, all family ties among the proletarians are torn asunder, and their children transformed into simple articles of commerce and instruments of labor.

But you Communists would introduce community of women, screams the whole bourgeoisie in chorus.

The bourgeois sees in his wife a mere instrument of production. He hears that the instruments of production are to be exploited in common, and, naturally, can come to no other conclusion than that the lot of being common to all will likewise fall to the women.

He has not even a suspicion that the real point aimed at is to do away with the status of women as mere instruments of production.

For the rest, nothing is more ridiculous than the virtuous indignation of our bourgeois at the community of women which, they pretend, is to be openly and officially established by the Communists. The Communists have no need to introduce community of women; it has existed almost from time immemorial.

Our bourgeois, not content with having the wives and daughters of their proletarians at their disposal, not to speak of common prostitutes, take the greatest pleasure in seducing each other's wives.

Bourgeois marriage is in reality a system of wives in common and thus, at the most, what the Communists might possibly be reproached with, is that they desire to introduce, in substitution for a hypocritically concealed, an openly legalized community of women. For the rest, it is self-evident that the abolition of the present system of production must bring with it the abolition of the community of women springing from that system, i.e., of prostitution both public and private.

The Communists are further reproached with desiring to abolish countries and nationality.

The working men have no country. We cannot take from them what they have not got. Since the proletariat must first of all acquire political supremacy, must rise to be the leading class of the nation, must constitute itself *the* nation, it is, so far, itself national, though not in the bourgeois sense of the word.

National differences and antagonisms between peoples are daily more and more vanishing, owing to the development of the bourgeoisie, to freedom of commerce, to the world market, to uniformity in the mode of production and in the conditions of life corresponding thereto.

The supremacy of the proletariat will cause them to vanish still faster. United action, of the leading civilized countries at least, is one of the first conditions for the emancipation of the proletariat.

In proportion as the exploitation of one individual by another is put an end to, the exploitation of one nation by another will also be put an end to. In proportion as the antagonism between classes within the nation vanishes, the hostility of one nation to another will come to an end.

The charges against Communism made from a religious, a philosophical, and, generally, from an ideological standpoint, are not deserving of serious examination.

Does it require deep intuition to comprehend that man's ideas, views and conceptions, in one word, man's consciousness, changes with every change in the conditions of his material existence, in his social relations and in his social life?

What else does the history of ideas prove, than that intellectual production changes its character in proportion as material production is changed? The ruling ideas of each age have ever been the ideas of its ruling class.

When people speak of ideas that revolutionize society, they do but express the fact that within the old society, the elements of a new one have been created, and that the dissolution of the old ideas keeps even pace with the dissolution of the old conditions of existence.

When the ancient world was in its last throes, the ancient religions were overcome by Christianity. When Christian ideas succumbed in the eighteenth century to rationalist ideas, feudal society fought its death battle with the then revolutionary bourgeoisie. The ideas of religious liberty and freedom of conscience merely gave expression to the sway of free competition within the domain of knowledge.

"Undoubtedly," it will be said, "religious, moral, philosophical and juridical ideas have been modified in the course of historical development. But religion, morality, philosophy, political science, and law constantly survived this change."

"There are, besides, eternal truths, such as Freedom, Justice, etc., that are common to all states of society. But Communism abolishes eternal truths, it abolishes all religion, and all morality, instead of constituting them on a new basis; it therefore acts in contradiction to all past historical experience."

What does this accusation reduce itself to? The history of all past society has consisted in the development of class antagonisms, antagonisms that assumed different forms at different epochs.

But whatever form they may have taken, one fact is common to all past ages, viz., the exploitation of one part of society by the other. No wonder, then, that the social consciousness of past ages, despite all the multiplicity and variety it displays, moves within certain common forms, or general ideas, which cannot completely vanish except with the total disappearance of class antagonisms.

The Communist revolution is the most radical rupture with traditional property relations; no wonder that its development involves the most radical rupture with traditional ideas.

But let us have done with the bourgeois objections to Communism.

We have seen above that the first step in the revolution by the working class is to raise the proletariat to the position of ruling class, to win the battle of democracy.

The proletariat will use its political supremacy to wrest, by degrees, all capital from the bourgeoisie, to centralize all instruments of production in the hands of the State, i.e., of the proletariat organized as the ruling class; and to increase the total of productive forces as rapidly as possible.

Of course, in the beginning, this cannot be effected except by means of despotic inroads on the rights of property, and on the conditions of bourgeois production; by means of measures, therefore, which appear economically insufficient and untenable, but which, in the course of the movement, outstrip themselves, necessitate further inroads upon the old social order, and are unavoidable as a means of entirely revolutionizing the mode of production.

These measures will of course be different in different countries.

Nevertheless in the most advanced countries, the following will be pretty generally applicable.

1. Abolition of property in land and application of all rents of land to public purposes.
2. A heavy progressive or graduated income tax.
3. Abolition of all right of inheritance.
4. Confiscation of the property of all emigrants and rebels.
5. Centralization of credit in the hands of the State, by means of a national bank with State capital and an exclusive monopoly.
6. Centralization of the means of communication and transport in the hands of the State.
7. Extension of factories and instruments of production owned by the State; the bringing into cultivation of wastelands, and the improvement of the soil generally in accordance with a common plan.
8. Equal liability of all to labor. Establishment of industrial armies, especially for agriculture.
9. Combination of agriculture with manufacturing industries; gradual abolition of the distinction between town and country, by a more equable distribution of the population over the country.
10. Free education for all children in public schools. Abolition of children's factory labor in its present form. Combination of education with industrial production, etc., etc.

When, in the course of development, class distinctions have disappeared, and all production has been concentrated in the hands of a vast association of the whole nation, the public power will lose its political character. Political power, properly so called, is merely the organized power of one class for oppressing another. If the proletariat during its contest with the bourgeoisie is compelled, by the force of circumstances, to organize itself as a class, if, by means of a revolution, it makes itself the ruling class, and, as such, sweeps away by force the old conditions of production, then it will, along with these conditions, have swept away the conditions for the existence of class antagonisms and of classes generally, and will thereby have abolished its own supremacy as a class.

In place of the old bourgeois society, with its classes and class antagonisms, we shall have an association in which the free development of each is the condition for the free development of all.

# Chapter 11

# Cournot on Mathematical Method and Demand Theory

Augustin Cournot (1801-1877), published *his Researches into the Mathematical Principles of the Theory of Wealth* in 1838, ten years before the appearance of John Stuart Mill's *Principles of Political Economy.* Cournot's book was a substantial departure from the concerns of classical economics, and hence was originally greeted with suspicion and disdain. Almost totally neglected by economists for the next forty years, Cournot's work eventually influenced two giants of neoclassical economics-- Léon Walras and Alfred Marshall. Thus the ultimate vindication of Cournot's ideas came about only after his death.

In his *Researches*, excerpted here, Cournot set forth his theoretical concerns and showed how he intended to apply the forms and symbols of mathematical analysis to them. But Cournot thought that mathematics was more than a mere "shorthand" language for expressing economic relationships. He also thought of mathematics as an "engine" of analysis, capable of discovering important economic principles and filling in gaps in existing knowledge. The *Researches* is one of the earliest explicit pleas for *positive* economics, i.e., arguments that are framed in a way to be either verified or rejected on the basis of statistical evidence. Can you ascertain why it is that Cournot rejected utility as a foundation for his demand curve?

Source: *Researches into the Mathematical Principles of the Theory of Wealth*, by
Augustin Cournot, trans. N. T. Bacon. Homewood, IL: Richard D. Irwin, Inc.,
1963. Pages 1-13; 36-43.

## PREFACE

The science known as Political Economy, which for a century has so much interested thinkers, is today more generally diffused than ever before. It shares with politics proper the attention of the great journals, which are today the most important means of spreading information; but the public is so tired of theories and systems that now the demand is for so-called "positive" matter, *i.e.*, in political economy, custom-house abstracts, statistical documents, and government reports, such as will throw the light of experience on the important questions which are being agitated before the country, and which so greatly interest all classes of society.

I make no objection to this tendency; it is good, and in accord with the laws which govern the development of all branches of science. I will only observe that theory ought not to be confounded with systems, although in the infancy of all sciences the instinct of system necessarily attempts to outline theories. I will add that theory should always have some part, small though it may be, in the development of a science; and that, to a man of my profession in particular, more than to any other, it should be permissible to consider from an exclusively theoretical standpoint, a subject of general interest which has so many different sides.

But the title of this work sets forth not only theoretical researchers; it shows also that I intend to apply to them the forms and symbols of mathematical analysis. This is a plan likely, I confess, to draw on me at the outset the condemnation of theorists of repute. With one accord they have set themselves against the use of mathematical forms, and it will doubtless be difficult to overcome to-day a prejudice which thinkers, like Smith and other more modern writers, have contributed to strengthen. The reasons for this prejudice seem to be, on the one hand, the false point of view from which theory has been regarded by the small number of those who have thought of applying mathematics to it; and, on the other hand, the false notion which has been formed of this analysis by men otherwise judicious and well versed in the subject of Political Economy, but to whom the mathematical sciences are unfamiliar.

The attempts which have been made in this direction have remained very little known, and I have been able to learn only the titles of them, except one, *Les Principes de l'Économie Politique,* by *Canard,* a small work published in the year X [of the French Republic, A.D. 1801], and crowned by the *Insitut.* The pretended principles are so radically at fault, and the application of them is so erroneous, that the approval of a distinguished body of men was unable to preserve the work from oblivion. It is easy to see why essays of this nature should not incline such economists as Say and Ricardo to algebra.

I have said that most authors who have devoted themselves to political economy seem also to have had a wrong idea of the nature of the applications of mathematical analysis to the theory of wealth. They imagined that the use of symbols and formulas could only lead to numerical calculation and, as it was clearly perceived that the subject was not suited to such a numerical determination of values by means of theory alone, the conclusion was drawn that the mathematical apparatus if not liable to lead to erroneous results, was at least idle and pedantic. But those skilled in mathematical analysis know that its object is not simply to calculate numbers but that it is also employed to find the relations between magnitudes which cannot be expressed in numbers and between functions whose law is not capable of algebraic expression. Thus the theory of probabilities furnishes a demonstration of very important propositions, although, without the help of experience, it is impossible to give numerical values for contingent events, except in questions of mere curiosity, such as arise from certain games of chance. Thus, also, theoretical Mechanics furnishes to practical Mechanics general theorems of most useful application, although in almost all cases recourse to experience is necessary for the numerical results which practice requires.

The employment of mathematical symbols is perfectly natural when the relations between magnitudes are under discussion; and even if they are not rigorously necessary, it would hardly be reasonable to reject them, because they are not equally familiar to all readers and because they have sometimes been wrongly used, if they are able to facilitate the exposition of problems, to render it more concise, to open the way to more extended developments, and to avoid the digressions of vague argumentation.

There are authors, like Smith and Say, who, in writing on Political Economy, have preserved all the beauties of a purely literary style; but there are others, like Ricardo, who, when treating the most abstract questions, or when seeking great accuracy, have not been able to avoid algebra, and have only disguised it under arithmetical calculation of tiresome length. Any one who understands algebraic notation, reads at a glance in an equation results reached arithmetically only with great labor and pains.

I propose to show in this essay that the solution of the general questions which arise from the theory of wealth, depends essentially not on elementary algebra, but on that branch of analysis which comprises arbitrary functions, which are merely restricted to satisfying certain conditions. As only very simple conditions will he considered, the first principles of the differential and integral calculus suffice for understanding this little treatise. Also, although I fear that it may appear too abstruse to most people who have a liking for these topics, I hardly dare to hope that it will deserve the attention of professional mathematicians, except as they may discover in it the germ of questions more worthy of their powers.

But there is a large class of men, and, thanks to a famous school, especially in France, who, after thorough mathematical training, have directed their attention to applications of those sciences which particularly interest society. Theories of the wealth of the community must attract their attention; and in considering them they are sure to feel, as I have felt, the need of rendering determinate by symbols familiar to them, an analysis which is generally indeterminate and often obscure, in authors who have thought fit to confine themselves to the resources of ordinary language. In thinking that they may be led by their reflections to enter upon this path, I hope that my book may be of some use to them, and may lessen their labor.

In the remarks on the first notions of competition and the mutual relations of producers, they may possibly notice certain relations, which are very curious from a purely abstract standpoint without reference to proposed applications.

I have not set out to make a complete and dogmatic treatise on Political Economy; I have put aside questions, to which mathematical analysis cannot apply, and those which seem to me entirely cleared up already. I have assumed that this book will only fall into the hands of readers who are familiar with what is found in the most ordinary books on those topics.

I am far from having thought of writing in support of any system, and from joining the banners of any party; I believe that there is an immense step in passing from theory to governmental applications; I believe that theory loses none of its value in thus remaining preserved from contact with impassioned polemics; and I believe, if this essay is of any practical value, it will be chiefly in making clear how far we are from being able to solve, with full knowledge of the case, a multitude of questions which are boldly decided every day.

## Chapter I

### OF VALUE IN EXCHANGE OR OF WEALTH IN GENERAL

The Teutonic root *Rik* or *Reich,* which has passed into all the Romance languages, vaguely expressed a relation of superiority, of strength, or of powers *Los ricos hombres is* still used in Spain for distinguished noblemen and eminent men, and such is also the force of the words *riches hommes* in the French of de Joinville. The idea which the word *wealth* presents to us today, and which is relative to our state of civilization, could not have been grasped by men of Teutonic stock, either at the epoch of the Conquest, or even at much later periods, when the feudal law existed in full vigor. Property, power, the distinctions between masters, servants and slaves, abundance, and poverty, rights and privileges, all these are found among the most savage tribes, and seem to flow necessarily from the natural laws which preside over aggregations of individuals and of families; but such an idea of wealth as we draw from our advanced state of civilization, and such as is necessary to give rise to a theory, can only be slowly developed as a consequence of the progress of commercial relations, and of the gradual reaction of those relations on civil institutions.

A shepherd is in possession of a vast pasture ground, and no one can disturb him with impunity; but it would be vain for him to think of exchanging it for something which he might prefer; there is nothing in existing habits and customs to make such an exchange possible; this man is a landholder, but he is not rich.

The same shepherd has cattle and milk in abundance; he can provide for a numerous retinue of servants and slaves; he maintains a generous hospitality towards poor dependents; but he is neither able to accumulate his products, nor to exchange them for objects of luxury which do no exist; this man has power, authority, the enjoyments which belong to his position, but he has not wealth.

It is inconceivable that men should live for a considerable time near together without effecting an exchange of goods and services; but from this natural, and we may even say instinctive, action, it is a long step to the abstract idea of value *in exchange,* which supposes that the objects to which such value is attributed *are in commercial circulation;* *i.e.* that it is always possible to find means to exchange them for other objects of equal value. The things, then, to which the state of commercial relations and civil institutions permits a value in exchange to be attached, are those which in the language of to-day are characterized by the word *wealth;* and to form an intelligible theory we ought to absolutely identify the sense of the word *wealth* with that which is presented to us by the words *exchangeable values.*

Under this conception, *wealth* has doubtless only an abstract existence; for, strictly speaking, of all the things on which we set a price, or to which we attribute a value in exchange, there are none always exchangeable at will for any other commodity of equal price or value. In the act of exchange, as in the transmission of power by machinery, there is friction to be overcome, losses which must be borne, and limits which cannot be exceeded. The proprietor of a great forest is only rich on condition of managing his lumbering with prudence, and of not glutting the market with his lumber; the owner of a valuable picture gallery may spend his life in the vain attempt to find purchasers; while, on the other hand, in the neighborhood of a city the conversion of a sack of grain into money will only require the time necessary to carry it to the grain market; and at great commercial centers a stock of coffee can always be sold on the exchange.

The extension of commerce and the development of commercial facilities tend to bring the actual condition of affairs nearer and nearer to this order of abstract conceptions, on which alone theoretical calculations can be based, in the same way as the skillful engineer approaches nearer to theoretical conditions by diminishing friction through polished bearings and accurate gearing. In this way nations are said to make progress in the commercial or mercantile system. These two expressions are etymologically equivalent, but one is now taken in a good and the other in a bad sense, as is generally the case, according to Bentham, with the names of things that involve advantages and evils of a moral order.

We will not take up either these advantages or these evils. The progress of nations in the commercial system is a fact in the face of which all discussion of its desirability becomes idle; our part is to observe, and not to criticize, the irresistible laws of nature. Whatever man can measure, calculate, and systematize, ultimately becomes the object of measurement, calculation, and system. Wherever fixed relations can replace indeterminate, the substitution finally takes place. It is thus that the sciences and all human institutions are organized. The use of coin, which has been handed down to us from remote antiquity, has powerfully aided the progress of commercial organization, as the art of making glass helped many discoveries in astronomy and physics; but commercial organization is not essentially bound to the use of the monetary metals. All means are good which tend to facilitate exchange, to fix value in exchange; and there is reason to believe that in the further development of this organization the monetary metals will play a part of gradually diminishing importance.

The abstract idea of *wealth* or of *value in exchange,* a definite idea, and consequently susceptible of rigorous treatment in combinations, must be carefully distinguished from the accessory ideas of utility, scarcity, and suitability to the needs and enjoyments of mankind, which the word *wealth* still suggests in common speech. These ideas are variable, and by nature indeterminate, and consequently ill suited for the foundation of a scientific theory. The division of economists into schools, and the war waged between practical men and theorists, have arisen in large measure from the ambiguity of the word *wealth* in ordinary speech, and the confusion which has continued to obtain between the fixed, definite idea or *value in exchange,* and the ideas of utility which every one estimates in his own way, because there is no fixed standard for the utility of things.[*]

It has sometimes happened that a publisher, having in store an unsalable stock of some work, useful and sought after by connoisseurs, but of which too many copies were originally printed in view of the class of readers for whom it was intended, has sacrificed and destroyed two-thirds of the number, expecting to derive more profit from the remainder than from the entire edition.

There is no doubt that there might be a book of which it would be easier to sell a thousand copies at sixty francs, than three thousand at twenty francs. Calculating in this way, the Dutch Company is said to have caused the destruction in the islands of the Sound of a part of the precious spices of which it had a monopoly. Here is a complete destruction of objects to which the word *wealth* is applied because they are both sought after, and not easily obtainable. Here is a miserly, selfish act, evidently opposed to the interests of society; and yet it is nevertheless evident that this sordid act, this actual destruction, is a real creation of *wealth* in the commercial sense of the word. The publisher's inventory will rightly show a greater value for his assets; and after the copies have left his hands, either wholly or in part, if each individual should draw up his inventory in commercial fashion, and if all these partial inventories could be collated to form a general inventory or balance sheet of the wealth in circulation, an increase would be found in the sum of these items of wealth.

On the contrary, suppose that only fifty copies exist of a curious book, and that this scarcity carries up the price at auction to three hundred francs a copy. A publisher reprints this book in an edition of a thousand copies, of which each will be worth five francs, and which will bring down the other copies to the same price from the exaggerated value which their extreme scarcity had caused. The 1050 copies will therefore only enter for 5250 francs into the sum of wealth which can be inventoried, and this sum will thus have suffered a loss of 9750 francs. The decrease will be even more considerable if (as should be the case) the value of the raw materials is considered, from which the reprints were made, and which existed prior to the reprinting. Here is an industrial operation, a material production, useful to the publisher who undertook it, useful to those whose products and labor it employed, useful even to the public if the book contains valuable information, and

---

[*] By this we do not intend that there is neither truth nor error in opinions on the utility of things; we only mean that generally neither the truth nor the error is capable of proof; that these are questions of valuation, and not soluble by calculation, nor by logical argument.

which is nevertheless a real destruction of wealth, in the abstract and commercial meaning of the term.

The rise and fall of exchange show perpetual oscillations in values, or in the abstract wealth in circulation, without intervention of actual production or destruction of the physical objects to which, in the concrete sense, the term *wealth is* applicable.

It has been long remarked, and justly, that commerce, properly so called, *i.e.* the transportation of raw materials or finished products, from one market to another, by adding to the worth of the objects transported, creates value or wealth in just the same way as the labor of the miner who extracts metals from the bowels of the earth, or the workman who adapts them to our needs. What ought to have been added, and what we shall have occasion to develop, is that commerce may also be a cause of destruction of values, even while making profits for the merchants who carry it on, and even when in every one's eyes it is a benefit to the countries which it connects in commercial intercourse.

A fashion, a whim, or a chance occurrence may cause a creation or annihilation of values without notable influence on what is regarded as public utility or the general welfare; it can even come about that a destruction of wealth may be salutary, and an increase detrimental. If chemists should solve the problem of making diamonds, jewelers and the ladies who own sets of jewelry would suffer heavy losses; the general mass of wealth capable of circulation would experience a notable decrease, and yet I can hardly think that any sensible man would be tempted to consider it a public calamity, even though he might regret the individual losses involved. On the contrary, if the taste for diamonds should decline, if wealthy people should stop devoting an important part of their fortunes to this idle vanity, and if, in consequence, the value of diamonds in commerce should decrease, wise men would gladly commend this new departure of fashion.

When any event, accounted favorable to a country, as improving the condition of the majority of its inhabitants (for what other basis can be taken to estimate utility?), has nevertheless for its first effect the diminution of the mass of values in circulation, we are tempted to suppose that this event conceals the germ of an increase in the general wealth by means of its remote consequences, and that it will in this way turn out to the advantage of the country. Experience unquestionably shows that this is true in most cases, since, in general, an incontestable improvement in the condition of the people has kept pace with an equally incontestable increase in the sum total of wealth in circulation. But in consequence of the impossibility of following up analytically all the consequences of such complex relations, theory is unable to explain why this usually happens and is still less able to demonstrate that it must always continue to occur. Let us avoid confounding what is in the domain of accurate reasoning with what is the object of a more or less happy guess; what is rational with what is empirical. It is enough to have to guard against errors in logic on the first score; let us avoid encountering passionate declamations and insoluble questions on the other.

From a standpoint of mere etymology, whatever appertains to the organization of society belongs to the field of Political Economy; but it has become customary to use this last term in a sense much more restricted and by so much less precise. The Political Economist, being occupied principally with the material wants of mankind, only considers social institutions as far as they favor or interfere with labor, thrift, commerce, and population; and as far as they affect the subdivision between the members of society of the gifts of nature and the rewards of labor.

This subject is still far too vast to be properly grasped by any one man. It affords inexhaustible material for unripe systems and slow investigations. How can we abstract the moral influences which enter into all these questions and which are entirely incapable of measurement? How are we to compare what may be called the material welfare of the Alpine shepherd with that of the Spanish idler or of the Manchester workingman; the convent alms with the poor-rates; the drudgery of the farm with that of the workshop; the pleasures and expenditures of a Norman noble in his feudal manor, with the pleasures and expenditures of his far-away descendant in a house in London or on a tour through Europe?

If we compare one nation with another, by what invariable tokens shall we determine the progress or decay of their prosperity? Shall it be according to population? In that ease China would far excel Europe. According to the abundance of coin? The example of Spain, mistress of the Peruvian mines, turned the world away from this gross error long ago, and, in fact, before even the first crude notions of the true role of coin were developed. According to business activity? Then inland peoples would be very unfortunate compared with those whom proximity to the sea invites to a mercantile career. According to the high price of goods or of wages? Then some miserable island would surpass the most smiling and fertile countries. According to the pecuniary value of what economists call the annual product? A year when this value increases greatly may easily be one of great distress for the greatest number. According to the actual quantity of this product reckoned in the appropriate unit for each kind of goods? But the kinds of goods produced and the relative proportions are different for each country. How can comparisons be made in this respect? According to the rate of movement up or down whether of population or of annual product? Provided that the reckoning covers a sufficient time this is, to be sure, the least equivocal symptom of the welfare or misery of society; but how can this symptom help us except to recognize accomplished facts, and facts which have been produced, not only by economic causes in the ordinary meaning of the words, but also by the simultaneous cooperation of a multitude of moral causes.

We are far from wishing to depreciate the philanthropic efforts of those who seek to throw some light on social economy. It is characteristic only of narrow minds to decry medical science because physiological phenomena cannot be evaluated as accurately as the planetary movements. Political Economy is the hygiene and pathology of the social system. It recognizes as its guide experience or rather observation; but sometimes the sagacity of a superior mind can even anticipate the results of experience. We only seek to make clear, that Political Economy fails to make progress by theory, towards its noble object of the improvement of the lot of mankind, either because the relations which it has to deal with are not reducible to fixed terms, or because these relations are much too complicated for our powers of combination and analysis.

On the other hand, as the abstract idea of wealth according to our conception constitutes a perfectly determinate relation, like all precise conceptions it can become the object of theoretical deductions, and if these deductions are sufficiently numerous and seem important enough to be collected into a system, it will presumably be advantageous to present this system by itself, except for such applications as it may seem proper to make to those branches of Political Economy with which the theory of wealth is ultimately connected. It will be useful to distinguish what admits of abstract demonstration from what allows only of a questionable opinion.

The Theory of Wealth, according to the idea we are trying to give, would doubtless only be an idle speculation, if the abstract idea of *wealth* or *value in exchange,* on which it is founded, were too far from corresponding with the actual objects which make up wealth in the existing social status. The same would be true of hydrostatics if the character of ordinary fluids should be too far removed from the hypothesis of perfect fluidity. However, as we have already said, the influence of a progressive civilization constantly tends to bring actual and variable relations nearer and nearer to the absolute relation, which we attain to from abstract considerations. In such matters everything becomes more and more easily valued, and consequently more easily measured. The steps towards finding a market resolve themselves into brokerage, losses of time into discounts, chances of loss into insurance charges, and so on. The progress of the gregarious tendency and of the institutions related to it, and the modifications which have taken place in our civil institutions, all cooperate towards this mobility, which we would neither apologize for nor detract from, but on which the application of theory to social facts is founded.

## Chapter IV

### *OF THE LAW OF DEMAND*

To lay the foundations of the theory of exchangeable values, we shall not accompany most speculative writers back to the cradle of the human race; we shall undertake to explain neither the origin of property nor that of exchange or division of labor. All this doubtless belongs to the history of mankind, but it has no influence on a theory which could only become applicable at a very advanced state of civilization, at a period when (to use the language of mathematicians) the influence of the *initial* conditions is entirely gone.

We shall invoke but a single axiom, or, if you prefer, make but a single hypothesis, *i.e.* that each one seeks to derive the greatest possible value from his goods or his labor. But to deduce the rational consequences of this principle, we shall endeavor to establish better than has been the case the elements of the data which observation alone can furnish. Unfortunately, this fundamental point is one which theorists, almost with one accord, have presented to us, we will not say falsely, but in a manner which is really meaningless.

It has been said almost unanimously that "the price of goods is in the inverse ratio of the quantity offered, and in the direct ratio of the quantity demanded." It has never been considered that the statistics necessary for accurate numerical estimation might be lacking, whether of the quantity offered or of the quantity demanded, and that this might prevent deducing from this principle general consequences capable of useful application. But wherein does the principle itself consist ? Does it mean that in case a double quantity of any article is offered for sale, the price will fall one-half? Then it should be more simply expressed, and it should only be said that the price is in the inverse ratio of the quantity offered. But the principle thus made intelligible would be false; for, in general, that 100 units of an article have been sold at 20 francs is no reason that 200 units would sell at 10 francs in the same lapse of time and under the same circumstances. Sometimes less would be marketed; often much more.

Furthermore, what is meant by the quantity demanded? Undoubtedly it is not that which is actually marketed at the demand of buyers, for then the generally absurd consequence would result from the pretended principle, that the more of an article is marketed the dearer it is. If by demand only a vague desire of possession of the article is understood, without reference to the *limited price* which every buyer supposes in his demand, there is scarcely an article for which the demand cannot be considered indefinite; but if the price is to he considered at which each buyer is willing to buy, and the price at which each seller is willing to sell, what becomes of the pretended principle ? It is not, we repeat, an erroneous proposition—it is a proposition devoid of meaning. Consequently all those who have united to proclaim it have likewise united to make no use of it. Let us try to adhere to less sterile principles.

The cheaper an article is, the greater ordinarily is the demand for it. The sales or the demand (for to us these two words are synonymous, and we do not see for what reason theory need take account of any demand which does not result in a sale) the sales or the demand generally, we say, increases when the price decreases.

We add the word *generally* as a corrective; there are, in fact, some objects of whim and luxury which are only desirable on account of their rarity and of the high price which is the consequence thereof. If any one should succeed in carrying out cheaply the crystallization of carbon, and in producing for one franc the diamond which to-day is worth a thousand, it would not be astonishing if diamonds should cease to be used in sets of jewelry, and should disappear as articles of commerce. In this case a great fall in price would almost annihilate the demand. But objects of this nature play so unimportant a part in social economy that it is not necessary to bear in mind the restriction of which we speak.

The demand might be in the inverse ratio of the price; ordinarily it increases or decreases in much more rapid proportion—an observation especially applicable to most manufactured products. On the contrary, at other times the variation of the demand is less rapid; which appears (a very singular thing) to be equally applicable both to the most necessary things and to the most superfluous. The price of violins or of astronomical telescopes might fall one-half and yet probably the demand would not double; for this demand is fixed by the number of those who cultivate the art or science to which these instruments belong; who have the disposition requisite and the leisure to cultivate them and the means to pay teachers and to meet the other necessary expenses, in consequence of which the price of the instruments is only a secondary question. On the contrary, firewood, which is one of the most useful articles, could probably double in price, from the progress of clearing land or increase in population, long before the annual consumption of fuel should be halved; as a large number of consumers are disposed to cut down other expenses rather than go along without firewood.

Let us admit therefore that the sales or the annual demand $D$ is, for each article, a particular function $F(p)$ of the price $p$ of such article. To know the form of this function would be to know what we call *the law of demand* or *of sales*. It depends evidently on the kind of utility of the article, on the nature of the services it can render or the enjoyments it can procure, on the habits and customs of the people, on the average wealth, and on the scale on which wealth is distributed.

Since so many moral causes capable of neither enumeration nor measurement affect the law of demand, it is plain that we should no more expect this law to be expressible by an algebraic formula than the law of mortality, and all the laws whose determination enters into the field of statistics, or what is called social arithmetic. Observation must therefore be depended on for furnishing the means of drawing up between proper limits a table of the corresponding values of $D$ and $p$; after which, by the well-known methods of interpolation or by graphic processes, an empirical formula or a curve can be made to represent the function in question; and the solution of problems can be pushed as far as numerical applications.

But even if this object were unattainable (on account of the difficulty of obtaining observations of sufficient number and accuracy, and also on account of the progressive variations which the law of demand must undergo in a country which has not yet reached a practically stationary condition), it would be nevertheless not improper to introduce the unknown law of demand into analytical combinations, by means of an indeterminate symbol; for it is well known that one of the most important functions of analysis consists precisely in assigning determinate relations between quantities to which numerical values and even algebraic forms are absolutely unassignable.

Unknown functions may none the less possess properties or general characteristics which are known; as, for instance, to be indefinitely increasing or decreasing, or periodical, or only real between certain limits. Nevertheless such data, however imperfect they may seem, by reason of their very generality and by means of analytical symbols, may lead up to relations equally general which would have been difficult to discover without this help. Thus without knowing the law of decrease of the capillary forces, and starting solely from the principle that these forces are inappreciable at appreciable distances, mathematicians have demonstrated the general laws of the phenomena of capillarity, and these laws have been confirmed by observation.

On the other hand, by showing what determinate relations exist between unknown quantities, analysis reduces these unknown quantities to the smallest possible number, and guides the observer to the best observations for discovering their values. It reduces and coordinates statistical documents; and it diminishes the labor of statisticians at the same time that it throws light on them.

For instance, it is impossible *a priori* to assign an algebraic form to the law of mortality; it is equally impossible to formulate the function expressing the subdivision of population by ages in a stationary population; but these two functions arc connected by so simple a relation, that, as soon as statistics have permitted the construction of a table of mortality, it will be possible, without recourse to new observations, to deduce from this table one expressing the proportion of the various ages in the midst of a stationary population, or even of a population for which the annual excess of deaths over births is known.

Who doubts that in the field of social economy there is a mass of figures thus mutually connected by assignable relations, by means of which the easiest to determine empirically might be chosen, so as to deduce all the others from it by means of theory?

We will assume that the function $F(p)$, which expresses the law of demand or of the market, is a *continuous* function, i.e. a function which does not pass suddenly from one value to another, but which takes in passing all intermediate values. It might be otherwise if the number of consumers were very limited: thus in a certain household the same quantity of firewood will possibly be used whether wood costs 10 francs or 15 francs the stere, and the consumption may suddenly be diminished if the price of the stere rises above the latter figure. But the wider the market extends, and the more the combinations of needs, of fortunes, or even of caprices, are varied among consumers, the closer the function $F(p)$ will come to varying with $p$ in a continuous manner. However little may be the variation of $p$, there will be some consumers so placed that the slight rise or fall of the article will affect their consumptions, and will lead them to deprive themselves in some way or to reduce their manufacturing output, or to substitute something else for the article that has grown dearer, as, for instance, coal for wood or anthracite for soft coal. Thus the "exchange " is a thermometer which shows by very slight variations of rates the fleeting variations in the estimate of the chances which affect government bonds, variations which are not a sufficient motive for buying or selling to most of those who have their fortunes invested in such bonds.

If the function $F(p)$ *is* continuous, it will have the property common to all functions of this nature, and on which so many important applications of mathematical analysis are based: *the variations of the demand will be sensibly proportional to the variations in price so long as these last are small fractions of the original price.* Moreover, these variations will be of opposite signs, *i.e.* an increase in price will correspond with a diminution of the demand.

Suppose that in a country like France the consumption of sugar is 100 million kilograms when the price is 2 francs a kilogram, and that it has been observed to drop to 99 millions when the price reached 2 francs 10 centimes. Without considerable error, the consumption which would correspond to a price of 2 francs 20 centimes can be valued at 98 millions, and the consumption corresponding to a price of 1 franc 90 centimes at 101 millions. It is plain how much this principle, which is only the mathematical consequence of the continuity of functions, can facilitate applications of theory, either by simplifying analytical expressions of the laws which govern the movement of values, or in reducing the number of data to be borrowed from experience, if the theory becomes sufficiently developed to lend itself to numerical determinations.

Let us not forget that, strictly speaking, the principle just enunciated admits of exceptions, because a continuous function may have interruptions of continuity in some points of its course; but just as friction wears down roughness and softens outlines, so the wear of commerce tends to suppress these exceptional cases, at the same time that commercial machinery moderates variations in prices and tends to maintain them between limits which facilitate the application of theory.

To define with accuracy the quantity $D$, or the function $F(p)$ which is the expression of it, we have supposed that $D$ represented the quantity sold *annually* throughout the extent of the country or of the market under consideration. In fact, the year is the natural unit of time, especially for researches having any connection with social economy. All the wants of mankind are reproduced during this term, and all the resources which mankind obtains from nature and by labor. Nevertheless, the price of an article may vary notably in the course of a year, and, strictly speaking, the law of demand may also vary in the same interval, if the country experiences a movement of progress or decadence. For greater accuracy, therefore, in the expression $F(p)$, $p$ must be held to denote the annual average price, and the curve which represents function $F$ to be in itself an average of all the curves which would represent this function at different times of the year. But this extreme accuracy is only necessary in case it is proposed to go on to numerical applications, and it is superfluous for researches which only seek to obtain a general expression of average results, independent of periodical oscillations.

Since the function $F(p)$ *is* continuous, the function $pF(p)$, which expresses the total value of the quantity annually sold [total revenue], must be continuous also. This function would equal zero if $p$ equals zero, since the consumption of any article remains finite even on the hypothesis that it is absolutely free; or, in other words, it is theoretically always possible to assign the symbol $p$ a value so small that the product $pF(p)$ will vary imperceptibly from zero. The function $pF(p)$ disappears also when $p$ becomes infinite, or, in other words, theoretically a value can always be assigned to $p$ so great that the demand for the article and the production of it would cease. Since the function $pF(p)$ at first increases, and then decreases as $p$ increases, there is therefore a value of $p$ which makes this function a maximum, and which is given by the equation,

(1)        $F(p) + pF'(p) = 0,$

in which $F'$, according to Lagrange's notation, denotes the differential coefficient of function $F$.

We may admit that it is impossible to determine the function $F(p)$ empirically for each article, but it is by no means the case that the same obstacles prevent the approximate determination of the value of $p$ which satisfies equation (1) or which renders the product $pF(p)$ a maximum. The construction of a table, where these values could be found, would be the work best calculated for preparing for the practical and rigorous solution of questions relating to the theory of wealth.

# Chapter 12

# Menger on Economics as an Organic Science

Carl Menger (1840-1920) has a dual distinction in the history of economic thought. Along with Jevons and Walras, he was one of the pioneers of neoclassical economics. He was also the founder of the Austrian School of economics, which was distinctive, even within the neoclassical approach. As a journalist prior to entering academe, Menger observed that existing economic theories did not satisfactorily explain current economic events, so he sought to work out the laws of economics for himself. The result was two major works in economics--one, his *Principles of Economics* (1871), a major contribution to economic theory; the other, his *Investigations into the Method of the Social Sciences with Special Reference to Economics* (1883), a major contribution to economic method. On the strength of his first book, Menger obtained a teaching post at the University of Vienna, which he held for three decades. The following excerpt is taken from his second book, which is essentially a defense of economic theory against the criticism of those who favored historical rather than theoretical methods of analysis.

One of the criticisms against economic theory was the charge that pure theory ignored the development and change of economic life, i.e., it failed to take account of the *organic* nature of real economic phenomena. In his attempt to answer this criticism, Menger supplied a viewpoint that was typically Austrian, namely that many welfare-enhancing institutions come into being as a result of the *unintended* consequences of human behavior. In the passages below, Menger shows how institutions such as money, law, language, markets, and the state itself come into being without a common will directed toward establishing them. Thus, organic development in social science is not the result of conscious planning, but the unconscious result of human action directed toward other, more personal (self-interested) ends. In the process, Menger offers a brief theory of how such institutions develop. This theory, which stresses the discovery and transmission of new information through imitation, provided the basis for Hayek's (Chapter 20) new developments in the next century.

Source: Menger, Carl. *Investigations into the Method of the Social Sciences with Special Reference to Economics*, trans. F. J. Nock. New York: New York University Press, 1985. Pages 129-138; 144-147;152-159.

# BOOK 3
## The Organic Understanding of Social Phenomena

## Chapter 1

The Analogy Between Social Phenomena and Natural Organisms; Its Limits, and the Methodological Points of View for Social Research Resulting Therefrom

---

### § 1. The theory of the analogy between social phenomena and natural organisms.

There exists a certain similarity between natural organisms and a series of structures of social life, both in respect to their function and to their origin.

In natural organisms we can observe a complexity almost incalculable in detail, and especially a great variety of their parts (single organs). All this variety, however, is helpful in the preservation, development, and the propagation of the organisms as *units.* Each part of them has its specific function in respect to this result. The disturbance of this function, according to its intensity or the significance of the organ concerned, results in a more or less intensive disturbance of the function of the whole organism, or of the other organs. Conversely a disturbance of the connection of the organs forming a higher unit has a similar reaction on the nature and the function of the individual organs. The normal function and development of the unit of an organism are thus conditioned by those of its parts; the latter in turn are conditioned by the connection of the parts to form a higher unit; and finally the normal function and development of each single organ are conditioned by those of the remaining organs.

We can make an observation similar in many respects in reference to a series of social phenomena in general and human economy in particular. Here, too, in numerous instances, phenomena present themselves to us, the parts of which are helpful in the preservation, the normal functioning, and the development of the unit, even conditioning these. Their normal nature and normal function in turn are conditioned and influenced by the function of the unit, and in such a way that the unit cannot be imagined in its normal appearance and function without some essential part or other. Nor, conversely, can such a part be imagined in its normal nature and function when separated from the unit. It is obvious that we have here a certain analogy between the *nature and the function* of natural organisms on the one hand and social structures on the other.

The same is true with respect to the *origin* of a series of social phenomena. Natural organisms almost without exception exhibit, when closely observed, a really admirable functionality of all parts with respect to the whole, a functionality which is not, however, the result of human *calculation,* but of a *natural* process. Similarly we can observe in numerous social institutions a strikingly apparent functionality with respect to the whole. But with closer consideration they still do not prove to be the result of an *intention aimed at this purpose,* i.e., the result of an agreement of members of society or of positive legislation. They, too, present themselves to us rather as "natural" products (in a certain sense), as *unintended results of historical development.* One needs, e.g., only to think of the phenomenon of money, an institution which to so great a measure serves the welfare of society, and yet in most nations, by far, is by no means the result of an agreement directed at its establishment as a social institution, or of positive legislation, but is the unintended product of historical development. One needs only to think of law, of language, of the origin of markets, the origin of communities and of states, etc.

Now if social phenomena and natural organisms exhibit analogies with respect to their nature, their origin, and their function, it is at once clear that this fact cannot remain without influence on the method of research in the field of the social sciences in general and economics in particular.

*Anatomy* is the science of the empirical forms of organisms and the structure of their parts (the organs); *physiology* is the theoretical science which apprises us of the vital phenomena of organisms and the functions of their parts (organs) with respect to the preservation and development of the organisms in their totality. Now if state, society, economy, etc., are conceived of as organisms, or as structures analogous to them, the notion of following directions of research in the realm of social phenomena similar to those followed in the realm of organic nature readily suggests itself. The above analogy leads to the idea of theoretical social sciences analogous to those which are the result of theoretical research in the realm of the physico-organic world, to the conception of an *anatomy* and *physiology* of "social organisms" of state, society, economy, etc.

---

## § 2. The limits of the justification of the analogy between natural organisms and social phenomena.

The widespread dissemination which the previously mentioned, so-called organic, way of looking at social structures in the social science literature of all nations has enjoyed is at any rate an eloquent proof that, in the two respects stressed above, a striking, even if perhaps superficial, similarity exists between social phenomena and natural organisms.

Nonetheless, only that complete prejudice of preconceived opinion which sacrifices interest in all other aspects of the objects of scientific observation for interest in particular individual aspects could fail to recognize two things:

*First, that only a part of social phenomena exhibit an analogy to natural organisms.*

A large number of social structures are not the result of a natural process, in whatever sense this may be thought of. They are the result of a purposeful activity of humans directed toward their establishment and development (the result of the agreement of the members of society or of positive legislation). Social phenomena of this type, too, usually exhibit a purposefulness of their parts with respect to the whole. But this is not the consequence of a natural "organic" process, but *the result of human calculation which makes a multiplicity of means serve one end.* Thus we cannot properly speak of an "organic" nature or origin of these social phenomena which, even if an analogy does come into question, are not analogous to *organisms* but to *mechanisms.*

*Second, that the analogy* between social phenomena and natural organisms, even where it comes into question according to the previous discussion, is not *a complete one, comprising all aspects of the nature of the phenomena concerned.* Rather, it is merely one which is limited to the factors stressed in the previous section, and even in this respect it is an inexact one.

This holds true first of the analogy which is supposed to exist between the two groups of phenomena under discussion here with regard to the normal nature and the normal function of the whole being conditioned by the parts and of the parts by the whole. There is a view that the parts of a whole and the whole itself are mutually *cause* and *effect* simultaneously (that a *mutual causation* takes place), a view which has frequently taken root in the organic orientation of social research. It is a view so vague and inadequate for our laws of thinking that we will scarcely err if we designate it as eloquent testimony that our age in many respects still lacks a deeper understanding of the nature of natural organisms as well as of that of social phenomena. The above analogy, therefore, is by no means one which is based upon a full insight into the nature of the phenomena under discussion here, but upon the vague feeling of a certain similarity of the function of natural organisms and that of a part of social structures. It is clear that an analogy of this kind cannot be a satisfactory basis for an orientation of research striving for the deepest understanding of social phenomena.

To a much greater extent this is true of the analogy which is assumed between the *origin* of the two groups of phenomena under discussion here, an analogy which has led to the greatest variety of theories about the *"organic origin"* of social phenomena. Here the inadmissibility of the analogy is obvious.

*Natural* organisms are composed of elements which serve the function of the unit in a thoroughly mechanical way. They are the result of purely causal processes, of the mechanical play of natural forces. The so-called social organisms, on the contrary, simply cannot be viewed and interpreted as the product of purely mechanical force effects. They are, rather, the result of human efforts, the efforts of thinking, feeling, acting human beings. Thus, if we can speak at all of an "organic origin" of social structures, or, more correctly, of a part of these, this can merely refer to one circumstance. This is that some social phenomena are the results of a *common* will directed toward their establishment (agreement, positive legislation, etc.), while others are the unintended result of human efforts aimed at attaining essentially *individual* goals (the unintended results of these). In the first case social phenomena result from the *common will* directed toward their establishment (they are its *intended* products). In the second case social phenomena come about as the unintended result of individual human efforts (pursuing *individual interests*)

132

without a *common will* directed toward their establishment. Only this circumstance, recognized up to now only very imperfectly (but by no means, for instance, an objectively based, strict analogy to the natural organisms!), gave occasion to designate the cause of the last mentioned social phenomena (resulting *unintentionally)* as "original," "natural," or even "organic," in contrast to the cause of those mentioned first (established intentionally, by the common will).

The so-called "organic" origin of a part of social phenomena, that process of forming social structures which we designate with this expression, thus truly *exhibits essential* differences from the process to which natural organisms owe their origin. For these differences are not of the type that can also be perceived between natural organisms. The difference in the above respect turns out, rather, to be a fundamental one, like that between mechanical force and human will, between the results of mechanical force effect and purposeful activity of the individual human.

Also that part of the social structures in reference to which the analogy with natural organisms comes in question at all exhibits this analogy, therefore, only in certain respects. Even in these respects it only exhibits an analogy which must be designated in part as vague, in part really as extremely superficial and inexact.

## § 3. The methodological principles resulting for social research from the incompleteness of the analogy between social phenomena and natural organisms.

If the analogy between social phenomena and natural organisms were a perfect one, as is assumed on the part of a number of social philosophers, if social structures were really organisms, then this circumstance would without doubt be of decisive significance for the methodology of the social sciences. The methods of those natural sciences which are concerned with research in the organic world, anatomy and physiology in particular, would then, of course, at the same time be those of the social sciences in general and of economics in particular.

The circumstance that the above analogy refers to only a portion of social phenomena and furthermore is in respect to these a merely partial and superficial one excludes a priori the above logical consequence. The basic theoretical principles resulting from the preceding investigations are, rather, the following:

1. The so-called organic understanding of social phenomena can first and foremost be adequate for only a portion of them, in any case, namely for those which present themselves to us not as the result of agreement, of legislation, of the common will in general. *The organic view cannot be a universal means of consideration;* the organic understanding of social phenomena cannot be the universal goal of theoretical research in the field of the latter. Rather, for the understanding of social phenomena in their entirety the *pragmatic* interpretation is, in any case, just as indispensable as the "organic."

2. Even where social phenomena do not refer back to a pragmatic origin, the analogy between them and natural organisms is not a universal one comprising the totality of their nature. It is, rather, one which refers merely to certain aspects of their nature (their function and their origin), and therefore the organic interpretation per se cannot alone provide us with an all-round understanding of them. For this, rather, still other orientations of theoretical research are necessary which have no relation at all to the so-called organic view of social phenomena.

The theoretical social sciences have to present to us the general nature and the general connection of social phenomena at large and of social phenomena in particular fields (e.g., in the economic field). They fulfill this task among other ways by making us understand partial social phenomena in their meaning and function for the whole of social structures. The problem under discussion here comprises, however, the totality of the tasks of theoretical social sciences just as little as the analogous problem in the realm of natural organisms comprises the totality of the scientific tasks in the field of natural research. Even if the justification of the so-called organic orientation of research in the above sense is acknowledged, nonetheless the determination of the laws of the coexistence and succession of social phenomena *in general* remains the task of the theoretical social sciences. The determination of the laws of their reciprocal conditioning remains just a special branch of social research.

3. But even in those respects in which the analogies discussed here seem to be present when viewed superficially, they are not strict ones. Above all they are not based on a clear insight into the nature of social phenomena on the one hand and of natural organisms on the other. They accordingly cannot be the basis of a methodology of the social sciences in general, nor even one of any special orientations of social research. The mechanical application of the methods of anatomy and of physiology to the social sciences is therefore not permissible even within the narrow limits indicated above.

The so-called "organic" interpretation could at any rate be adequate only for a part of social phenomena, and only in consideration of certain aspects of their nature. Also, in this consideration it must not simply be borrowed from the natural sciences, but must be the result of independent investigation into the nature of social phenomena and the special aims of research in the realm of the latter. The method of the social sciences in general and of political economy in particular cannot at all be a physiological or an anatomical one. But even where it is a matter of sociological problems which have a certain superficial similarity to those of physiology and anatomy, it cannot be a method simply borrowed from physiology or anatomy, but only a *sociological* one in the strictest understanding of this word. The application of the results of physiological and anatomical research by analogy to political economy is, however, such nonsense that no one trained methodologically would even consider it worthy of a serious refutation.

The above errors are obviously no different from those of a physiologist or anatomist who wants to apply the laws and methods of economics uncritically to his science or who wants to interpret the functions of the human body by the economic theories prevailing at the moment: for instance, the circulation of the blood by one of the prevailing theories of the circulation of money or the traffic in goods; digestion by one of the prevailing theories of the consumption of goods; the nervous system by a description of telegraphy; the function of the individual organs of the human body by the function of the various social classes, etc. Our physiologists and anatomists in the field of economy deserve the same reproach to which a natural scientist of the "economic orientation" would expose himself with all serious professional contemporaries. Anyone who is acquainted with the state of the natural sciences, which even today is extremely imperfect as far as they have reference to the to organic world, really cannot help noticing the humor in the effort, often practiced with an expenditure of incredible ingenuity, to explain the unknown by what is not infrequently still more unknown.

Thus there seems to be no doubt that play with analogies between natural organisms and social phenomena, and especially the mechanical application of research results in one realm of phenomena to sciences which are supposed to open up a theoretical understanding of other realms of the empirical world, is a methodological procedure which scarcely deserves a serious refutation. Yet I should still not like in any way to deny the value of certain analogies between natural organisms and social phenomena for certain purposes of *presentation*. Analogy in the above sense, as method of *research, is* an unscientific aberration. As means for *presentation* it still may prove useful for certain purposes and certain stages of knowledge of social phenomena. The best minds have not infrequently attempted to explain the nature of social phenomena to their contemporaries by means of comparisons with organic structures. That was particularly true in epochs in which such procedure was still more foreign to the mind of the people than in our days. It remains to be seen whether such images have not already become obsolete, at least for purposes of scientific presentation, with the present-day development of the social sciences. But they definitely are to be rejected where what is supposed to be only a means of presentation appears as a means of research and the analogy is drawn not only where it corresponds to real conditions, but really becomes a principle and a universal trend of research. Also for the adherents of this orientation the author of *Inquiry into the Nature and Causes of the Wealth of Nations* has an excellent word: and with whom, on that account, the analogy, which in other writers gives occasion to a few ingenious similitudes, became the great hinge upon which everything turned.

## Chapter 2

## The Theoretical Understanding of Those Social Phenomena Which Are Not a Product of Agreement or of Positive Legislation, but Are Unintended Results of Historical Development.

### § 2. The various orientations of theoretical research which are the consequence of viewing social phenomena as "organic" structures

There are a number of social phenomena which are products of the agreement of members of society, or of positive legislation, results of the purposeful common activity of society thought of as a separate active subject. These are social phenomena, in connection with which there can properly be no thought of an "organic" origin in any admissible sense. Here the interpretation appropriate to the real state of affairs is the *pragmatic* one the explanation of the nature and origin of social phenomena from the intentions, opinions, and available instrumentalities of human social unions or their rulers.

............................................................

Another portion of them, however, is not the result of agreement of members of society or of legislation, as we have already explained. Language, religion, law, even the state itself, and, to mention a few economic social phenomena, the phenomena of markets, of competition, of money, and numerous other social structures are already met with in epochs of history where we cannot properly speak of a purposeful activity of the community as such directed at establishing them. Nor can we speak of such activity on the part of the rulers. We are confronted here with the appearance of social institutions which to a high degree serve the welfare of society. Indeed, they are not infrequently of vital significance for the latter and yet are not the result of communal social activity. It is here that we meet a noteworthy, perhaps the most noteworthy, problem of the social sciences:

*How can it be that institutions which serve the common welfare and are extremely significant for its development come into being without a* **common will** *directed toward establishing them?*

............................................................

The remark is hardly needed that the problem of the origin of unintentionally created social structures and that of the formation of those economic phenomena that we have just mentioned exhibit an extremely close relationship. Law, language, the state, money, markets, all these social structures in their various empirical forms and in their constant change are to no small extent the unintended result of social development. The prices of goods, interest rates, ground rents, wages, and a thousand other phenomena of social life in general and of economy in particular exhibit exactly the same peculiarity. Also, understanding of them cannot be "pragmatic" in the cases considered here. It must be analogous to the understanding of unintentionally created social institutions. The solution of the most important problems of the theoretical social sciences in general and of theoretical economics in particular is thus closely connected with the question of theoretically understanding the origin and change of "organically" created social structures.

............................................................

136

## § 4. The exact (atomistic) understanding of the origin of the social structures which are the unintended result of social development.

I will first present the theory of the origin of the social structures under discussion here by way of a few examples, that of the genesis of money, of states, of markets, etc., and thus by the genesis of social institutions which serve social interests to a high degree and the first origins of which in the great majority of cases can in no way be traced back to positive laws or other expressions of intentional common will.

(a) *The origin of money.*

In the markets of nearly all nations which have advanced to the barter stage in their economic culture certain goods are gradually accepted in barter by everyone in return for wares brought to market. Initially, according to varying conditions, these are heads of cattle, hides, cowrie shells, cocoa beans, tea tiles, etc.; with advancing culture they are metals in the uncoined state, then in the coined state. They are, indeed, accepted even by people who have no immediate need for these goods or have already covered this need sufficiently. In a word, in trade markets certain wares emerge from the sphere of all the others and become means of barter, "money" in the broadest sense of the word. This is a phenomenon that from the beginning social philosophers have had the greatest difficulties in understanding. That in a market an item is readily turned over by its owner for another that seems more useful to him is a phenomenon which is clear to the meanest understanding. But that in a market anyone who offers goods for sale is ready to turn these over for a definite other item, that is, according to varying conditions, for cattle, cocoa beans, certain amounts by weight of copper or silver, even when he has no direct need for these goods or has completely satisfied his possible need for them, while he nevertheless rejects certain other goods under the same presupposition—this is a paradoxical procedure. It is so contradictory to the sense of the individual oriented simply to his own interest, that we must not be astonished when it seemed really mysterious even to so excellent a thinker as Savigny and its explanation by individual human interests appeared impossible to him.

The problem which science has to solve here consists in the explanation of a *social* phenomenon, of a homogeneous way of acting on the part of the members of a community for which public motives are recognizable, but for which in the concrete case individual motives are hard to discern.

The idea of tracing these back to an agreement or to a legislative act was fairly obvious, especially with respect to the later coin form of money. Plato thought money was "an *agreed upon* token for barter," and Aristotle said that money came about through *agreement,* not by nature, but by law. The jurist Paulus and with few exceptions the medieval theoreticians on coined money down to the economists of our day are of a similar opinion.

It would be an error to reject the opinion as wrong in principle, for history actually offers us examples that certain wares have been declared money by law. To be sure, it must not be overlooked that in most of these cases the legal stipulation demonstrably had the purpose not so much of introducing a certain item as money, but rather the acknowledgment of an item which had already become money. Nonetheless, it is certain that the institution of money, like other social institutions, can be introduced by agreement or legislation, especially when new communities are formed from the elements of an old culture, e.g., in colonies. Moreover, there is no doubt that the further development of such institutions takes place as a rule in the latter way in times of higher economic culture. Therefore the above opinion has its partial justification.

It is otherwise with the understanding of the social institution discussed here when it can by no means be historically viewed as the result of legislative activity, that is, when we see that money developed from the economic conditions of a nation without such activity, "primevally," or, as others express it, "organically." Here the above, pragmatic approach is at any rate inadmissible, and the task of science is to make us understand the institution of money by presenting the process by which, as economic culture advances, a definite item or a number of items leaves the sphere of the remaining goods and becomes money, without express agreement of people and without legislative acts. This is to pose the question of how certain items turn into goods which are accepted by everyone in exchange for the goods offered for sale to him, even when he has no need for them.

The explanation of this phenomenon is given by the following considerations. As long as mere barter prevails in a nation economic individuals naturally first pursue one aim in their barterings. They exchange their excess only for goods for which they have an immediate need and reject those that they do not need at all or with which they are sufficiently supplied. For somebody who is bringing his excess to market to be able to get in exchange the goods he desires he must not only find somebody who needs his wares but also somebody who offers for sale the goods desired. This is the circumstance that presents so many obstacles to traffic when pure barter prevails and limits it to the narrowest confines.

In this state of affairs itself there lay a very effective means to do away with this untoward circumstance which is such a burden on the traffic in goods. Each individual could easily observe that there was a greater demand in the market for certain wares, namely those which fitted a very general need, than there was for others. Accordingly, among the competitors for these goods he more easily found those who offered for sale certain goods desired by him than if he went to market with less marketable wares. Thus everyone in a nomadic tribe knows from his own experience that, when he brings cattle to the market, he will more easily find among the many who try to get these goods by barter those who offer the goods he wants than if he brought another item that has only a small circle of takers. Thus every individual who brought to the market items of slight marketability in the above sense had the obvious idea of exchanging them not only for the goods he needed, but also, when these were not directly available, for others. These others were ones which he, to be sure, did not need at the moment, but which were more marketable than his. By this he did not, of course, directly attain the final goal of his planned economic operation (procuring by exchange the goods *he* needed!), but he approached it essentially. The economic interest of the economic individuals, therefore, with increased knowledge of their *individual* interests, without any agreement, without legislative compulsion, *even without any consideration of public interest,* leads them to turn over their wares for more marketable ones, even if they do not need the latter for their immediate consumer needs. Among the latter, however, as is readily evident, they again select those which are most easily and most economically suited to the function of a means of barter. Thus there appears before us under the powerful influence of custom the phenomenon to be observed everywhere with advancing economic culture that a certain number of goods are accepted in exchange by everybody. These are, with respect to time and place, the most marketable, the most easily transported, the most durable, the most easily divisible. They can, therefore, be exchanged for any other item. They are goods which our predecessors called *Geld,* from *gelten,* i.e., to perform, to "pay."

The great significance that *custom* has for the genesis of money is directly clear from the consideration of the just described process by which certain goods become money. The exchange of less marketable wares for those of greater marketability, durability, divisibility, etc., is in the interest of every *single* economic individual. But the actual closing of such an exchange operation presupposes the knowledge of this interest on the part of those economic subjects who for the sake of the above characteristics are to accept in barter for their wares an item which per se is perhaps utterly useless to them. This knowledge will never arise simultaneously with all members of a national group. Rather, at first only a number of economic subjects will recognize the advantage accruing to them. This happens because they accept in exchange other more marketable wares for their own where a direct barter of their wares for useful goods is not possible or is highly uncertain. This is an advantage *which is per se independent of the general acknowledgment of an item as money,* since such an exchange always and under all circumstances brings the economic individual considerably closer to *his* ultimate aim, the procuring of useful goods that *he* needs. But, as is well known, there is no better means to enlighten people about their economic interests than their perceiving the economic successes of those who put the right means to work for attaining them. Therefore it is also clear that nothing may have favored the genesis of money as much as the receiving of eminently marketable goods for all other goods, which had been practiced for quite a long time on the part of the most perspicacious and ablest economic subjects for their own economic advantage. Thus practice and custom have certainly contributed not a little to making the temporarily most marketable wares the ones which are received in exchange for their wares not only by many economic individuals, but ultimately by all.

Money, an institution serving the common good in the most outstanding sense of the word, can thus, as we saw, come into being legislatively, like other social institutions. But this is no more the only way than it is the most original way that money developed. This is rather to be sought in the process described above, the nature of which would be explained only imperfectly if we wanted to call it "organic," or if we wanted to designate money as something "primeval," "original," etc. It is clear, rather, that the origin of money can truly be brought to our full understanding only by our learning to understand the *social* institution discussed here as the unintended result, as the unplanned outcome of specifically *individual* efforts of members of a society.

(b) *The origin of a number of other social institutions in general and economy in particular.*

A similar statement holds true for the *origin of the state.* No unprejudiced person can doubt that under favorable conditions the basis for a community capable of development can be laid by the agreement of a number of people with a territory at their disposal. Nor can it reasonably be doubted that from the natural conditions of power in the family new states capable of development could be established by individual rulers or groups of them, even without the agreement of all subjects of the new state. The theory, according to which that social structure which we call the state will simply arise "organically," is thus one-sided, at any rate. Just as erroneous, indeed to a still greater degree unhistorical, is the theory that all states originally came into being by *an agreement directed toward establishing them* or by the conscious activity of individual rulers or groups of rulers directed toward this aim. For it can scarcely be doubted that at least in the earliest epochs of human development states developed in the following way. Family heads joined by no political bond and living side by side came to have a state community and organization even if it was undeveloped at first. They did this without special agreement, merely because they progressively recognized their *individual* interests and endeavored to pursue them (by voluntary subjection of the weaker to the protection of the stronger, by the effective aid which neighbor gave to neighbor in those cases in which the latter was to be coerced under circumstances under which the remaining inhabitants of a territory also felt threatened in their welfare, etc.). Conscious agreement and power relationships of different kinds directed toward the goal of strengthening communities as such may actually have aided this process of state formation in particular cases. The correct recognition and the activation of the *individual* interests on the part of individual family heads living side by side have certainly in other cases led to state formation even without the above influences, indeed even without any consideration of the common interest by individuals. That social structure, too, which we call the state, has been the unintended result of efforts serving individual interests, at least in its most original forms.

In the same way it might be pointed out that other social institutions, language, law, morals, but especially numerous institutions of economy, have come into being without any express agreement, without legislative compulsion, even without any consideration of public interest, merely through the impulse of *individual* interests and as a result of the activation of these interests. The organization of the traffic in goods in markets which recur periodically and are held in definite localities, the organization of society by separation of professions and the division of labor, trade customs, etc., are nothing but institutions which most eminently serve the interests of the common good and whose origin seems at first glance to be based necessarily on agreement or state power. They are, however, not the result of agreement, contract, law, or special consideration of the public interest by individuals, but the result of efforts serving individual interests.

It is clear that legislative compulsion not infrequently encroaches upon this "organic" developmental process and thus accelerates or modifies the results. The unintended genesis of social phenomena may factually be the exclusively decisive genesis for the first beginnings of social formation. In the course of social development the purposeful encroachment of public powers on social conditions becomes more and more evident. Along with the "organically" created institutions there go those which are the result of purposeful social action. Institutions which came about organically find their continuation and reorganization by means of the purposeful activity of public powers applied to social aims. The present-day system of money and markets, present-day law, the modern state, etc., offer just as many examples of institutions which are presented to us as the result of the combined effectiveness of individually and socially teleological powers, or, in other words, of "organic" and "positive" factors.

*(c) Concluding remarks.*

We might ask now about the general nature of the process to which those social phenomena owe their origin which are not the result of socially teleological factors, but are the unintended result of social movement. This is a process, which in contrast to the genesis of social phenomena by way of positive legislation, can still be designated as "organic." The answer to the above question can scarcely be in doubt any longer.

The characteristic element in the socially teleological genesis of social phenomena is in the intention of society as such directed toward establishing these phenomena, under the circumstance that they are the intended result of the common will of society, thought of as an acting subject, or of its rulers. The social phenomena of "organic" origin, on the other hand, are characterized by the fact that they present themselves to us as the unintended result of individual efforts of members of society, i.e., of efforts in pursuit of individual interests. Accordingly, in contrast to the previously characterized social structures, they are, to be sure, the unintended social result of individually teleological factors.

But in the preceding we believe we have not only presented the true nature of that process to which a large part of social phenomena owe their origin, a nature which has up to now been characterized merely by vague analogies or by meaningless phrases. We believe we have also come to another result which is important for the methodology of the social sciences.

We already alluded above to the fact that a large number of the phenomena of economy which cannot usually be viewed as "organically" created "social structures," e.g., market prices, wages, interest rates, etc., have come into existence in exactly the same way as those social institutions which we mentioned in the preceding section. For they, too, as a rule are not the result of socially teleological causes, but the unintended result of innumerable efforts of economic subjects pursuing *individual* interests. The theoretical understanding of them, the theoretical understanding of their nature and their movement can thus be attained in an exact manner only in the same way as the understanding of the above-mentioned social structures. That is, it can be attained by reducing them to their elements, to the *individual* factors of their causation, and by investigating the laws by which the complicated phenomena of human economy under discussion here are built up from these elements. This, however, as scarcely needs saying, is that method which we have characterized above as the one adequate for the exact orientation of theoretical research in the realm of social phenomena in general. The methods for the exact understanding of the origin of the "organically" created social structures and those for the solution of the main problems of exact economics are by nature identical.

# Chapter 13

## Jevons on Sunspots and Business Cycles

"I have been told repeatedly by men who have good opportunity of hearing current opinion," Jevons wrote in 1879, "that they who theorise about the relations of sun-spots, rainfall, famines, and commercial crises are supposed to be jesting, or at the best romancing. I am, of course, responsible only for a small part of what has been put forth on this subject, but so far as I am concerned in the matter, I beg leave to affirm that I never was more in earnest...". With these words Jevons launched his claim to establish what many economists, both then and now, hold to be completely fanciful--the connection between solar activity (sunspots) and business cycles. Later economists derided Jevons's theory for a number of reasons. It has been argued that it merely posits a theory of agricultural cycles, not full-fledged business cycles. Another complaint is that its validity requires an ongoing series of *exogenous* shocks to the economic system. Yet another is that it fails to show theoretically how sunspot activity (or any other exogenous disturbance) is capable of generating *endogenous* fluctuations.

Jevons's seriousness of purpose and excitement of discovery are obvious in the following excerpt. What is less obvious is the transmission mechanism through which the effect of sunspots is felt. In other places, Jevons was more illuminating on this point: sunspots affect weather patterns; weather patterns affect agricultural harvests; fluctuations in harvests alter prices; price changes affect "moods" (i.e., expectations); expectations in turn influence investment decisions, thereby multiplying the effect of the harvest cycle. When appreciated in its entirety, therefore, Jevons's idea seems less fanciful. It actually combines exogenous and endogenous variables; it encompasses more than an analysis of mere agricultural cycles; and it is not devoid of theory. What Jevons sought was the *trigger* that changed business expectations. The fact that he found it in extra-terrestrial activity may seem bizarre or "New Age" to many, but the fact that he was bent on finding the *cause* of changes in expectations underscored a clear theoretical concern.

Source:   Jevons, W. S. "Commercial Crises and Sunspots," in *Investigations in Currency and Finance*, ed. H. S. Foxwell. London: Macmillan, 1884. Pages 221-243.

## PART I

*"Thou Sun, of this great world both eye and soul."*

It is curious to notice the variety of the explanations offered by commercial writers concerning the cause of the present state of trade. Foreign competition, beer-drinking, over-production, trades-unionism, war, peace, want of gold, super-abundance of silver, Lord Beaconsfield, Sir Stafford Northcote, their extravagant expenditure, the Government policy, the Glasgow Bank directors, Mr. Edison and the electric light, are a few of the happy and consistent suggestions continually made to explain the present disastrous collapse of industry and credit.

It occurs to but few people to remember that what is happening now is but a mild repetition of what has previously happened time after time. October, 1878, is comparable with May, 1866, with November, 1857, with October, 1847, and, going yet farther back, with a somewhat similar condition of things, in 1887, in 1825-26, and even in 1815-16. The incidental circumstances of these commercial collapses have indeed been infinitely diversified. At one time the cause seemed to be the misconduct of the great firm of Overends; in 1857 there was the mutiny in India, the peace with Russia, and a commercial collapse in the United States; in 1847 occurred the Irish famine and a failure of European harvests generally, following upon the great railway mania; the crisis of 1837 succeeded an immense expansion of home trade, the establishment of joint-stock banks, and the building of multitudes of factories and other permanent works; 1825 was preceded by extravagant foreign speculations and foreign loans; 1815 was the year of the general peace. All kinds of distinct reasons can thus be given why trade should be now inflated and again depressed and collapsed. But, so long as these causes are various and disconnected, nothing emerges to explain the remarkable appearance of regularity and periodicity which characterises these events.

The periodicity of the earlier portion of the series is so remarkable that, even without the corroboration since received, it convinced scientific inquirers that there was some deep cause in action. Dr. Hyde Clarke, for instance, wrote, more than thirty years ago, a paper entitled "Physical Economy a Preliminary Inquiry into the physical Laws governing the Periods of Famines and Panics." This paper was published in the *Railway Register* for 1847, and is well worth reading. In the commencement he remarks: "We have just gone through a time of busy industry, and are come upon sorrow and ill fortune; but the same things have befallen us often within the knowledge of those now living. Of 1887, of 1827, of 1817, of 1806, of 1796, there are men among us who can remember the same things as we now see in 1847. A period of bustle, or of gambling, cut short in a trice and turned into a period of suffering and loss, is a phenomenon so often recorded, that what is most to be noticed is that it should excite any wonder." Dr. Hyde Clarke then proceeds to argue in a highly scientific spirit that events so regularly recurring cannot be attributed to accidental

causes; there must, he thinks, be some physical groundwork, and he proposed to search this out by means of a science to be called Physical Economy. In the third page of his paper he tells us that he had previously written a paper on the laws of periodical or cyclical action, printed in Herapath's "Railway Magazine" for 1838. "At this time," he says, "it was my impression that the period of speculation was a period of ten years, but I was led also to look for a period of thirteen or fourteen years.... In the course of these inquiries I looked at the astronomical periods and the meteorological theories without finding anything at all available for my purposes." A little below, Dr. Hyde Clarke continues: "Still thinking that the interval was an interval of about ten years, I was, during the present famine, led to look for a larger period, which would contain the smaller periods, and as the present famine and distress seemed particularly severe, my attention was directed to the famine so strongly felt during the French Revolution. This gave a period of about fifty-four years, with five intervals of about ten or eleven years each, which I took thus:
"1793        1804        1815        1826        1837        1847."

Dr. Hyde Clarke was by no means the only statist who adopted a theory of periodicity thirty or forty years ago. In February, 1848, Mr. J. T. Danson read a paper to the Statistical Society of London, attempting to trace a connection between periodic changes in the condition of the people and the variations occurring in the same period in the prices of the most necessary articles of food. Mr. James Wilson had published, in 1840, a separate work or large pamphlet upon "Fluctuations of Currency, Commerce, and Manufactures," in which he speaks of the frequent recurrence of periods of excitement and depression. In later years Mr. William Langton, the esteemed banker of Manchester, independently remarked the existence of the decennial cycle, saying: "These disturbances are the accompaniment of another wave, which appears to have a decennial period, and in the generation of which moral causes have no doubt an important share."

The paper in which this remark occurs is contained in *the Transactions of the Manchester Statistical Society* for 1857, and is one of the most luminous inquiries concerning commercial fluctuations anywhere to be found. In still later years Mr. John Mills, of the Manchester Statistical Society, has almost made this subject his own, insisting, however, mainly upon the mental origin of what he has aptly called the Credit Cycle.

The peculiar interest of Dr. Hyde Clarke's speculations consists in the fact that he not only remarked the cycle of ten or eleven years, but sought to explain it as due to physical causes, although he had not succeeded in discovering any similar astronomical or meteorological variation with which to connect it. Writing as he did in 1838 and 1847, this failure is not to be wondered at. His supposed period of fifty-four years is perhaps deserving of further investigation, but it is with his period of ten or eleven years that we are now concerned.

My own inquiries into this interesting subject naturally fall much posterior to those of Dr. Clarke; but, about the year 1862, I prepared two elaborate statistical diagrams, one of which exhibited in a single sheet all the accounts of the Bank of England since 1844, while the other embraced all the monthly statements I could procure of the price of corn, state of the funds, rate of discount, and number of bankruptcies in England from the year 1731 onwards. Subsequent study of these diagrams produced upon my mind a deep conviction that the events of 1815, 1825, 1836-39,1847, and 1857, exhibited a true but mysterious periodicity. There was no appearance, indeed, of like periodicity in the earlier parts of my second diagram. In the first fifteen years of this century statistical numbers were thrown into confusion by the great wars, the suspension of specie payments, and the frequent extremely high prices of corn. It must be allowed, moreover, that the statistical diagram, so far as concerns the eighteenth century, presents no appreciable trace of decennial periodicity. The recent continual discussions concerning the solar or sun-spot period much increased the interest of this matter; and in 1875 I made a laborious reduction of the data contained in Professor Thorold Rogers' admirable *History of Agriculture and Prices in England from the Year 1259.* I then believed that I had discovered the solar period in the prices of corn and various agricultural commodities, and I accordingly read a paper to that effect at the British Association at Bristol. Subsequent inquiry, however, seemed to show that periods of three, five, seven, nine, or even thirteen years would agree with Professor Rogers' data just as well as a period of eleven years; in disgust at this result I withdrew the paper from further publication. I should like, however, to be now allowed to quote the following passage from the manuscript of the paper in question:

"Before concluding I will throw out a surmise, which, though it is a mere surmise, seems worth making. It is now pretty generally allowed that the fluctuations of the money market, though often apparently due to exceptional and accidental events, such as wars, great commercial failures, unfounded panics, and so forth, yet do exhibit a remarkable tendency to recur at intervals approximating to ten or eleven years. Thus the principal commercial crises have happened in the years 1825, 1836-89, 1847, 1857, 1866, and I was almost adding 1879, so convinced do I feel that there will, within the next few years, be another great crisis. Now if there should be in or about the year 1879 a great collapse comparable with those of the years mentioned, there will have been five such occurrences in fifty-four years, giving almost exactly eleven years (10.8) as the average interval, which sufficiently approximates to 11.1, the supposed exact length of the sun-spot period, to warrant speculation as to their possible connection."

I was led to assign the then coming (that is, the now present) crisis to the year 1879, because 11.1 years added twice over to 1857, the date of the last perfectly normal crisis, or to 1847, the date of the previous one, brings the calculator to 1879. If I could have employed instead Mr. J. A. Broun's since published estimate of the sun-spot period, to be presently mentioned, namely, 10 45 years, I should have come exactly to the present year 1878. My mistake of one year was due to the meteorologist's mistake of eight months, which, as arises usually happen in October and November, was sufficient to thrown the estimate of the event into the next twelve months.

While writing my 1875 paper for the British Association, I was much embarrassed by the fact that the commercial fluctuations could with difficulty be reconciled with a period of 11.1 years. If, indeed, we start from 1825, and add 11.1 years time after time, we get 1836.1, 1847.2, 1858.3, 1869.4, 1880.5, which show a gradually increasing discrepancy from 1837, 1847, 1857, 1866 (and now 1878), the true dates of the crises. To explain this discrepancy I went so far as to form the rather fanciful hypothesis that the commercial world might be a body so mentally constituted, as Mr. John Mills must hold, as to be capable of vibrating in a period of ten years, so that it would every now and then be thrown into oscillation by physical causes having a period of eleven years. The subsequent publication, however, of Mr. J. A. Broun's inquiries tending to show that the solar period is 10.45 years, not 11.1, placed the matter in a very different light, and removed the difficulties. Thus, if we take Mr. John Mills' "Synopsis of Six Commercial Panics in the present Century," and, rejecting 1866 as an instance of a premature panic, count from 1815 to 1857, we find that four credit cycles, occupying forty-two years, give an average duration of 10.5 years, which is a remarkably close approximation to Mr. Broun's solar period. Thus encouraged, it at last occurred to me to look back into the previous century, where facts of a strongly confirmatory character at once presented themselves. Not only was there a great panic in 1793, as Dr. Hyde Clarke remarked, but there were very distinct events of a similar nature in the years 1783, 1772-73, and 1763. About these dates there can be no question, for they may all be found clearly stated on pp. 627 and 628 of the first volume of Mr. Macleod's unfinished *Dictionary of Political Economy*. Mr. Macleod gives a concise, but, I believe, correct account of these events, and as he seems to entertain no theory of periodicity, his evidence is perfectly unbiased. Yet, in the space of a few lines, he unconsciously states this periodicity, saying: "Ten years after the preceding crisis of 1763, another of a very severe nature took place in 1772, and the beginning of 1773. It extended over all the trading nations of Europe." A few lines below he goes on to state that in May, 1783, a rapid drain of bullion to the Continent set in, which greatly alarmed the Bank directors and embarrassed the merchants. The paragraph in which this occurs is headed, "The Crisis of 1783," and on turning the page we at once come on another paragraph headed, "The Crisis of 1793." Here then we have, in a few lines of a good authority concerning the history of finance, a statement of four crises occurring at almost exactly decennial intervals. It is wonderful that no writer has, so far as I know, previously pointed out the strictly periodic nature of these events; and I may add that I have several times lectured to my college classes about these crises without remarking their periodicity. It is true that we cannot, by any management of the figures, bring them into co-ordination with later crises so long as we adhere to the former estimate of the solar period. If, starting from 1857, we count back nine intervals of 11.1 years each, we get to 1757 instead of 1763; we are landed in the middle of a cycle instead of in the beginning or end; and there can be no possible doubt about the crises of 1763 and 1857. But, if we are once allowed to substitute the new estimate of Broun, which is the same as the old one of Lamont, the difficulty disappears for the average interval is 10.44 years.

This beautiful coincidence led me to look still further backwards, and to form the apparently wild notion that the great crisis, generally known as that of the South Sea Bubble, might not be an isolated and casual event, but only an early and remarkable manifestation of the commercial cycle. The South Sea Bubble is generally set down to the year 1720, and the speculations in the shares of that company did attain their climax and commence their collapse in that year. But it is perfectly well known to the historians of commerce that the general collapse of trade, which profoundly affected all the more advanced European nations, especially the Dutch, French, and English, occurred in 1721. Now, if we assume that there have been since 1721, up to 1857, thirteen commercial cycles, the average interval comes out 10.46 years; or if we consider that we are in this very month (November, 1878) passing through a normal crisis, then the interval of 157 years from 1721 to 1878 gives an average cycle of 10.466 years.

It would be impossible, however, to enlist the South Sea Bubble in our series unless there were some links to connect it with subsequent events. I have, therefore, spent much labour during the past summer in a most tedious and discouraging search among the pamphlets, magazines, and newspapers of the period, with a view to discover other decennial crises. I am free to confess that in this search I have been thoroughly biased in favour of a theory, and that the evidence which I have so far found would have no weight, if standing by itself. It is impossible in this place to state properly the facts which I possess; I can only briefly mention what I hope to establish by future more thorough inquiry.

It is remarkable to notice that the South Sea Company, which came to grief in 1720-21, was founded in 1711, just ten years before, and that on the very page (312) of Mr. Fox Bourne's *Romance of Trade* which mentions this fact the year 1701 also occurs in connection with speculation and *stock-jobs,* as the promotion of companies was then called. The occurrence of a crisis in the years 1710-12, is indeed almost established by the lists of bubble insurance companies formed in those years, as collected by Mr. Cornelius Walford, and obligingly shown to me by him.

Again, it is quite plain that about ten years after stock-jobbing had been crushed by the crisis of 1721, it reared its head again. A significant passage in *The Gentleman's Magazine* of 1739 (vol. ii., p. 361) remarks that "Stock-jobbing is grown almost epidemical. Fraud, corruption, and iniquity in great companies as much require speedy and effectual remedies, now, as in 1720. The scarcity of money and stagnation of trade in all the distant parts of England is a proof that too much of our current coin is got into the hands of a few persons." This "getting the current coin into the hands of a few people" was the favourite theory at that time to explain any slackness of trade, just as now over-production is a theme of every short-sighted politician. But the Legislature of that day thought they could remedy these things in a drastic manner, so they passed, in 1734, "An Act to prevent the infamous practice of Stock-jobbing." Mr. Walford, who has inquired into the commercial history of this time far more minutely than any other writer, remarks that "gambling in stocks and funds had broken out with considerable fervour again during the few years preceding 1734. It was the first symptom of recovery from the events of 1720."

I may add that there was in 1732 a great collapse of a society called the "Charitable Corporation for Relief of the Industrious Poor." A great many people were ruined by the unexpected deficit discovered in the funds of this kind of bank, and Parliament and the public were asked to assist the sufferers, just as they might now be asked to aid the shareholders of the City of Glasgow Bank. Thus does history repeat itself!

Whether it was that the Act of 1734 really did diminish the infamous practice of stock-jobbing, or whether the sun-spots manifested less variation than usual, it is clear that between 1732 and 1763 it is very difficult to discover anything approaching a mania or crisis. My learned and obliging correspondents at Amsterdam and Leiden, Drs. S. and W. Vissering, disclaim any knowledge of such events in the trade of Holland at that time, and my own diagram, showing the monthly bankruptcies throughout the interval, displays a flatness of a thoroughly discouraging character. Nevertheless, inquiry leads me to believe that although there really was nothing to call a crisis, mania, or panic, yet there were remarkable variations in the activity of trade and the prices of some staple commodities, such as wool and tin, sufficient to connect the earlier with the later periods. It is a matter of much regret that I have hitherto been quite unable to discover a connected series of price-lists of commodities of the early part of last century. The accounts of prices of goods at Greenwich Hospital, to be found in several statistical works, are not only incomplete, but probably misleading. Any reader of this article who can point out to me series of prices of metals or other commodities, not merely agricultural, before 1782, will confer a very great obligation upon me by doing so.

Deferring, however, for the present, any minuter inquiry, I permit myself to assume that there were about the years 1742 and 1752 fluctuations of trade which connect the undoubted decennial series of 1711, 1721, and 1732, with that commencing again in the most unquestionable manner in 1763. Thus the whole series of decennial crises may be stated as follows: (1701?), 1711, 1721, 1731-32, (1742? 1752?), 1763, 1772-73, 1783, 1793, (1804-5?), 1815, 1825, 1836-39 (1837 in the United States), 1847, 1857, 1866, 1878. A series of this sort is not, like a chain, as weak as its weakest part; on the contrary, the strong parts add strength to the weak parts. In spite, therefore, of the doubtful existence of some of the crises, as marked in the list, I can entertain no doubt whatever that the principal commercial crises do fall into a series having the average period of about 10.466 years. Moreover, the almost perfect coincidence of this period with Broun's estimate of the sun-spot period (10.46) is by itself strong evidence that the phenomena are causally connected. The exact nature of the connection cannot at present be established. As we have seen, Hyde Clarke, Wilson, and Danson all argued, some thirty or forty years ago, that commercial fluctuations must be governed by physical causes. But here we are embarrassed by the fact that no inquirer has been able to discover a clear periodic variation in the price of corn. This is what Sir William Herschel attempted to do, at the beginning of this century, in his truly prophetic inquiry about the economic effects of the sun-spots; but his facts are evidently too few to justify any sure inference. Carrington also compared the sun-spot curve with that of the price of corn, without detecting any coincidence; and my own repeated inquiries have been equally without result as to this point. The fact is, I believe, that cereal crops, as grown and gathered in Europe, depend for their success upon very complicated conditions, so that the solar influence is disguised. But it does not follow that other crops in other latitudes may not manifest the decennial period. Dr. Sohuster has pointed out a coincidence between good vintages and minima of sun-spots which can hardly be due to accident, and the whole controversy about the connection of Indian famines with the sun-spot period is of course familiar to all readers of *Nature*. Now if we may assume Dr. Hunter's famine theory to be true, there is little difficulty in explaining the remarkable series of periodic crises which I have pointed out.

The trade of Western Europe has always been strongly affected by communication with the Indies. Several of the crises are distinctly traceable to this cause, especially those at the beginning of the eighteenth century. That was a time of wild enterprise in the tropical regions, as the very names of the South Sea Company, the Mississippi scheme, the Darien project, etc. show. The Dutch, English, and French East India Companies were then potent bodies, the constant subject of legislation and controversy. Thus it is my present belief that to trade with India, China, and probably other parts of the tropical and semi-tropical regions, we must attribute the principal fluctuations in European commerce. Surely there is nothing absurd in such a theory when we remember that the present crisis is at least partly due to the involvement of the City of Glasgow Bank in the India trade, through the medium of some of their chief debtors. Thus the crisis of 1878 is clearly connected with the recent famines in India and China, and these famines are confidently attributed to solar disturbance.

To establish this view of the matter in a satisfactory manner; it would be desirable to show that there has been a decennial variation of trade with India during the one hundred and seventy years under review. The complications and disturbances produced in the statistics of such a trade by various events are so considerable that I have not yet attempted to disentangle them properly. Yet the accounts of the merchandise (not including bullion) exported by the English East India Company between the years 1708-9 and 1733-34 display a wonderful tendency to decennial variation.

Probably, however, we ought not to attribute the decennial fluctuation wholly to Indian trade. It is quite possible that tropical Africa, America, the West Indies, and even the Levant are affected by the same meteorological influences which occasion the famines in India. Thus it is the nations which trade most largely to those parts of the world, *and which give long credits to their customers,* which suffer most from these crises. Holland was most easily affected a century ago; England is most deeply affected now; France usually participates, together with some of the German trading towns. But I am not aware that these decennial crises extend in equal severity to such countries as Austria, Hungary, Switzerland, Italy, and Russia, which have comparatively little foreign trade. Even when they are affected, it may be indirectly through sympathy with the great commercial nations.

There is nothing in this theory inconsistent with the fact that crises and panics arise from other than meteorological causes. There was a great political crisis in 1798, a great commercial collapse in 1810-11 (which will not fall into the decennial series); there was a Stock Exchange panic in 1859; and the great American collapse of 1873-75. There have also been several minor disturbances in the money market, such as those of February, 1861, May and September; 1864, August, 1870, November, 1873; but they are probably due to exceptional and disconnected reasons. Moreover, they have seldom, if ever, the intensity, profundity, and wide extension of the true decennial crises.

If it were permitted to draw any immediate conclusion from these speculations, I should point to the necessity of at once undertaking direct observations upon the varying power and character of the sun's rays. There are hundreds of meteorological observatories registering, at every hour of the day and night, the most minute facts about the atmosphere; but that very influence, upon which all atmospheric changes ultimately depend, *the solar radiation*, is not, I believe, measured in any one of them, at least in the proper manner. Pouillet showed long ago (1838) how the absolute heating power of the sun's rays might be accurately determined by his Pyrheliometer. This instrument, and the results which he drew from its use, are fully described, in his *Élements de Physique Expérimentale et de Météorologie*, (livre 8 chap. i. section 285). But I have never heard that his experiments have been repeated, except so far as this may have been done by Sir John Herschel, with his so-called Actinometer, as described by him in the *Admiralty Manual of Scientific Inquiry*. I fancy that physicists still depend upon Pouillet's observations in 1837 and 1838 for one of the most important constants of the solar system, if constant it can be called. While astronomers agitate themselves and spend infinite labour about the two-hundredth planetoid, or some imperceptible satellite, the very fountain of heat and light and life is left unmeasured. Pouillet indeed assumed that the heating power of the sun's rays is a constant quantity, which accounts for his not continuing the solar observations. But, if there is any truth in all the sun-spot speculations, there must be a periodic variation in the sun's rays, of which the sun-spots are a mere sign, and perhaps an unsatisfactory one. It is possible that the real variations are more regular than the sun-spot indications, and thus perhaps may be explained the curious fact that the decennial crises recur more regularly on the whole than the maxima and minima of sun-spots.

PART II

151

I have been repeatedly told by men who have good opportunity of hearing current opinions, that they who theorise about the relations of sun-spots, rainfall, famines, and commercial crises are supposed to be jesting, or at the best romancing. I am, of course, responsible only for a small part of what has been put forth on this subject, but so far as I am concerned in the matter, I beg leave to affirm that I never was more in earnest, and that after some further careful inquiry, I am perfectly convinced that these decennial crises do depend upon meteorological variations of like period, which again depend, in all probability, upon cosmical variations of which we have evidence in the frequency of sun-spots, auroras, and magnetic perturbations. I believe that I have, in fact, found the missing link required to complete the first outline of the evidence.

About ten years ago it was carefully explained by Mr. J. C. Ollerenshaw, in a communication to the Manchester Statistical Society (*Transactions*, 1869-70, p. 109), that the secret of good trade in Lancashire is the low price of rice and other grain in India. Here again some may jest at the folly of those who theorise about such incongruous things as the cotton-mills of Manchester and the paddy-fields of Hindostan. But to those who look a little below the surface the connection is obvious. Cheapness of food leaves the poor Hindoo ryot a small margin of earnings, which he can spend on new clothes; and a small margin multiplied by the vast population of British India, not to mention China, produces a marked change in the demand for Lancashire goods. Now, it has been lately argued by Dr. Hunter, the Government statist of India, that the famines of India do recur at intervals of about ten or eleven years. The idea of the periodicity of Indian famines is fur from being a new one; it is discussed in various previous publications, as, for instance, "The Companion to the British Almanack" for 1857, p. 76. The principal scarcities in the North-Western and Upper Provinces of Bengal are there assigned to the years 1782-83, 1792-93, 1802-3, 1812-13, 1819-20, 1826, 1832-33. Here we notice precise periodicity up to 1812-13, which, after being broken for a time, seems to recur in 1832-33.

Partly through the kind assistance of Mr. Garnett, the Superintendent of the British Museum Reading Room, I have now succeeded in finding the data so much wanted to confirm these views —namely, a long series of prices of grain in Bengal (Delhi). These data are found in a publication so accessible as the *Journal of the London Statistical Society* for 1843, vol. vi. pp. 246-48, where is printed a very brief but important paper by the Rev. Robert Everest, chaplain to the East India Company, "On the Famines that have devastated India, and on the Probability of their being Periodical."

Efforts have, I believe, been made by Dr. Hunter, Mr. J. H. Twigg, and probably others, to obtain facts of this kind, which would confirm or controvert prevailing theories; but this little paper, which seems to contain almost the only available table of prices, has hitherto escaped the notice of all inquirers, except, indeed, Mr. Cornelius Walford. The last number of the *Journal of the London Statistical Society* contains the second portion of Mr. Walford's marvelously complete account of "The Famines of the World, Past and Present," a kind of digest of the facts and literature of the subject. At pp. 260, 261 (vol.

xlii.) we find Everest's paper noticed. In this latter paper we have a list of prices of wheat at Delhi for seventy-three years, ending with 1835, stated in terms of the numbers of seers of wheat a seer is equal to about 2 lb. avoirdupois—to be purchased with one rupee. As this mode of quotation is confusing, I have calculated the prices in rupees per 1000 seers of wheat, and have thus obtained the following remarkable table:

### Price of Wheat at Delhi.

| Year | Price | Year | Price |
|---|---|---|---|
| 1763 | 50 M.C. | 1800 | 22 |
| 1764 | 35 | 1801 | 23 |
| 1765 | 27 | 1802 | 25 |
| 1766 | 24 | 1803 | 65 C. |
| 1767 | 23 | 1804 | 48 C. |
| 1768 | 21 | 1805 | 33 |
| 1769 | 24 | 1806 | 31 |
| 1770 | 28 | 1807 | 28 |
| 1771 | 33 | 1808 | 36 |
| 1772 | 38 C. | 1809 | 40 |
| 1773 | 100 M.C. | 1810 | 25 C. |
| 1774 | 53 | 1811 | 28 |
| 1775 | 40 | 1812 | 44 |
| 1776 | 25 | 1813 | 43 |
| 1777 | 17 | 1814 | 30 |
| 1778 | 25 | 1815 | 23 C. |
| 1779 | 33 | 1816 | 28 |
| 1780 | 45 | 1817 | 41 |
| 1781 | 55 | 1818 | 39 |
| 1782 | 91 | 1819 | 42 |
| 1783 | 167 M.C. | 1820 | 46 |
| 1784 | 40 | 1821 | 38 |
| 1785 | 25 | 1822 | 35 |
| 1786 | 23 | 1823 | 33 |
| 1787 | 22 | 1824 | 39 |
| 1788 | 23 | 1825 | 39 C. |
| 1789 | 24 | 1826 | 48 M.C. |
| 1790 | 26 | 1827 | 30 |
| 1791 | 33 | 1828 | 22 |
| 1792 | 81 M. | 1829 | 21 |
| 1793 | 54 C. | 1830 | 21 |
| 1794 | 32 | 1831 | 26 |
| 1795 | 14 | 1832 | 22 |
| 1796 | 14 | 1833 | 33 |
| 1797 | 15 | 1834 | 40 M.. |
| 1798 | 8 | 1835 | 25 |
| 1799 | 17 | 1836 | - C. |

The letter M indicates the maxima attained by the price, and we see that up to 1803, at least, the maxima occur with great regularity at intervals of ten years. Referring to Mr. Macleod's *Dictionary of Political Economy*, pp. 627, 628, we learn that commercial crises occurred in the years 1763,1772-73, 1783, and 1793, in almost perfect coincidence with scarcity at Delhi. M. Clément Juglar, in his work, *Des Crises commercials, et de leur Retour périodique*, also assigns one to the year 1804. After this date the variation of prices becomes for a time much less marked and regular, and there also occurs a serious crisis about the year 1810, which appears to be exceptional; but in 1825 and 1836 the decennial periodicity again manifests itself, both in the prices of wheat at Delhi and in the state of English trade. The years of crisis are marked with the letter C.

When the above numbers are plotted out in the form of a curve, the earlier part of the series presents the appearance of a saw, with four or five high sharp pointed teeth at almost exactly equal distances of ten years. The first maximum, that of 1763, is perhaps imperfectly represented, and were the table extended backwards, the true maximum might fall in 1762. It is remarkable that after about the year 1807 the character of the curve suddenly and entirely changes, the oscillations becoming comparatively small, irregular, and rounded, although the periodicity, as already remarked, seems to recur in a less intense degree after 1823. This change in the curve may be due to some local causes, such as the opening of new roads and markets, and it is obviously important that we should learn whether this is the case, or whether some important meteorological variation is here manifested. This is not the only instance in which a well-marked decennial oscillation appears to be for a time suddenly arrested or thrown into confusion.

One difficulty which presents itself in connection with the above table is that the commercial crises in England occur *simultaneously* with the high prices in Delhi, or even in anticipation of the latter; now the effect cannot precede its cause, and in commercial matters we should expect an interval of a year or two to elapse before bad seasons in India make their effects felt here. The fact, however, is, that the famines in Bengal appear to follow similar events in Madras. Thus it is well known that the great famine occurred in the year 1770, or even began in 1769, though it seems not to have made its mark at Delhi until 1773. This quite explains the fact that the English crisis was in 1772-73. Mr. F. C. Danvers of the India Office (*Journal of Science*, N.S., vol. viii. p. 4) assigns famines in the Madras Presidency to the years 1781-83 and 1790-92. In fact Mr. Danvers explicitly points out this tendency of famines to travel northward, saying (p. 441): "It is a point worthy of remark that severe droughts in Northern India have, on several occasions, followed closely upon distress similarly caused in the Peninsula of India: thus, the Madras famine of 1781 to 1783 was followed by one which affected Bengal, the North-Western Provinces, and the Punjab in 1783-84; the failure of rains which resulted in scarcity in many of the provinces of the Madras Presidency in 1824-25 was followed by a similar calamity in the North-Western Provinces in the succeeding years. The 'Guntoor' famine of

1833 preceded, only by a few years, one which affected the North-West and Lower Provinces of Bengal in 1837-38, and the Madras famine of 1866 was very closely followed by one in the North-West Provinces and the Punjab in 1868 to 1870." We see, then, that in looking for periodicity, we must confine each comparison to events of the same locality. It must also be allowed that the *commencement* of famine in India precedes by about two years the occurrence of commercial collapse in England.

It ought to be added that Everest refers to a journal published at Calcutta, called *Gleanings in Science*, which contains (vol. i. p. 368) a table of the prices of various kinds of grain at Chinsurah, in Bengal, from 1700 to 1813. The volume is to be found in the British Museum; but on referring to it and plotting out the curve for the price of rice, it was very disappointing to find the series broken by gaps of several years every here and there, which renders it impossible to draw any safe inference, affirmative or negative. The table is said to have been drawn up by G. Herklots, the fiscal of Chinsurah, from authentic documents. Now, if such documents existed half a century ago, it is indispensable that minute inquiry should be made for any local records of the kind which may still exist.

Returning to the prices at Delhi, and taking the above table in connection with a mass of considerations of which I have given a mere outline at the last meeting of the British Association, I hold it to be established with a high degree of probability that the recurrence of manias and crises among the principal trading nations depends upon commerce with the East. This conclusion is confirmed by the fact that these fluctuations are but slightly felt by the non-trading nations, and that what these nations do feel is easily accounted for as an indirect effect.

It has been objected by The *Economist* that this explanation cannot be applied to the earlier crises in the years 1711, 1721, and 1732, because trade with India was then of insignificant dimensions. But the reading of many old books and tracts of the seventeenth and eighteenth centuries has convinced me that trade with India was always looked upon as of the highest importance. A large part of the political literature of the time was devoted to the subject, and under the Mercantile Theory the financial system of the country was framed mainly with an eye to Indian trade. The published returns of exports and imports probably give us little idea of the real amount of trade, as smuggling was very common in those days, and much of the Indian trade went on secretly in private ships or indirectly through Holland.

Dr. George Birdwood has lately been studying the records of the India Office, and he gives as the result of his extensive reading "that the history of modern Europe, and emphatically of England, has been the quest of the aromatic gum-resins, and balsams and condiments, and spices of India and the Indian Archipelago" (*Journal of the Society of Arts*, February 7th, 1879, vol. xxvii. p. 192). This closely corresponds with the view which I have been gradually led to adopt of the cause of decennial crises.

While India is, no doubt, together with China, the principal source of disturbance, there is no reason to suppose that it is the only source. A nearly exhaustive analysis which I have made of the trade of England with various parts of the world during the last century, as given in Whitworth's valuable tables, fails to disclose any clear periodicity as regards European trade. The investigation of various long series of prices of agricultural produce in Europe also lends me to believe that the decennial periodicity, if felt in Europe at all, is overborne by disturbing causes, or involved in too great complication to admit of discovery. On the other hand, I have fallen upon the very interesting and significant fact that the export trade from Maryland and Virginia exhibits what seems to me unquestionable periodicity, with maxima in the years 1701, 1711-13, 1720, 1742, 1753, 1764, and 1774. The same tendency is not apparent in the trade of New England. Thus it is likely that crises may have an independent meteorological origin in the semi-tropical States of the Union; and, if so, it is probable that there are other tropical parts of the world where the meteorological conditions allow the cycle to manifest itself. This subject, so far as it has yet been studied, is full of important and mysterious facts, which stimulate the interest of the inquirer in a high degree. At the same time it is plain that sound conclusions can be reached only by most extensive analyses and comparisons of large series of facts. The search for the facts, too, among the records of the last two centuries, the suitable part of which has in too many cases probably perished, is so tedious and disappointing that it taxes the patience of the inquirer very severely. It is no jest at all.

But whatever be the area of the tropical and semi-tropical regions from which the decennial impulse comes, mainly India and China, no doubt, it does not follow that the extent of the commercial mania or crisis here is bounded by the variation of the foreign trade. The impulse from abroad is like the match which fires the inflammable spirits of the speculative classes. The history of many bubbles shows that there is no proportion between the stimulating cause and the height of folly to which the inflation of credit and prices may be carried. A mania is, in short, a kind of explosion of commercial folly followed by the natural collapse. The difficulty is to explain why this collapse so often comes at intervals of ten or eleven years, and I feel sure the explanation will be found in the cessation of demand from India and China occasioned by the failure of harvests there, ultimately due to changes of solar activity. Certainly the events of the last few years, as too well known to many sufferers, entirely coincide with this view.

# Chapter 14

# Marshall on Elasticity

In a paper read before the International Statistical Congress in 1885, Alfred Marshall said: "We may want to find a measure of what may be called *the elasticity of demand*: that is, when a fall of price leads to an increase in the amount demanded, we may want to know the ratio in which the percentage by which the amount demanded has increased stands to the percentage by which the price has fallen." He then proceeded to outline a mathematical formula for the derivation of this measure. Five years later, he showcased the concept in his *Principles of Economics*, a book that established Marshall's enduring reputation as a master economist. Legend has it that the notion of elasticity struck Marshall in 1881 as he was sunning himself on the rooftop of a Palermo hotel (while on recuperative leave from teaching), and that he was highly delighted with the idea. Commenting on Marshall's contribution of this important tool, John Maynard Keynes, who was not always sparing in his criticism of his former professor, declared: "In the provision of terminology and apparatus to aid thought I do not think that Marshall did economists any greater service than by the explicit introduction of the idea of 'elasticity'." Keynes added that the advanced theory of value and distribution could scarcely have made progress without the concept.

The excerpt below on elasticity, taken from Marshall's *Principles,* is noteworthy for several reasons. For one, it contains a workable, if not precise definition of "perfect" competition; for another it emphasizes the significance of the element of time in Marshall's economics, and finally, it underscores the shortcomings of statistical data. See if you can extract from Marshall's discussion the four "determinants" of elasticity embodied therein.

Source: Marshall, Alfred. *Principles of Economics*, 8th ed. London: Macmillan, 1920. Pages 102-113.

## Chapter IV

### THE ELASTICITY OF WANTS

§ 1. We have seen that the only universal law as to a person's desire for a commodity is that it diminishes, other things being equal, with every increase in his supply of that commodity. But this diminution may be slow or rapid. If it is slow the price that he will give for the commodity will not fall much in consequence of a considerable increase in his supply of it; and a small fall in price will cause a comparatively large increase in his purchases. But if it is rapid, a small fall in price will cause only a very small increase in his purchases. In the former case his willingness to purchase the thing stretches itself out a great deal under the action of a small inducement: the elasticity of his wants, we may say, is great. In the latter case the extra inducement given by the fall in price causes hardly any extension of his desire to purchase: the elasticity of his demand is small. If a fall in price from say 16d. to 15d. per lb. of tea would much increase his purchases, then a rise in price from 15d. to 16d. would much diminish them. That is, when the demand is elastic for a fall in price, it is elastic also for a rise.

And as with the demand of one person so with that of a whole market. And we may say generally: The *elasticity* (or *responsiveness) of demand* in a market is great or small according as the amount demanded increases much or little for a given fall in price, and diminishes much or little for a given rise in price.

§ 2. The price which is so high relatively to the poor man as to be almost prohibitive, may be scarcely felt by the rich; the poor man, for instance, never tastes wine, but the very rich man may drink as much of it as he has a fancy for, without giving himself a thought of its cost. We shall therefore get the clearest notion of the law of the elasticity of demand by considering one class of society at a time. Of course there are many degrees of richness among the rich, and of poverty among the poor; but for the present we may neglect these minor subdivisions.

When the price of a thing is very high relatively to any class, they will buy but little of it; and in some cases custom and habit may prevent them from using it freely even after its price has fallen a good deal. It may still remain set apart for a limited number of special occasions, or for use in extreme illness, etc. But such cases, though not infrequent, do not form the general rule; and anyhow as soon as it has been taken into common use, any considerable fall in its price causes a great increase in the demand for it. The elasticity of demand is great for high prices, and great, or at least considerable, for medium prices; but it declines as the price falls; and gradually fades away if the fall goes so far that satiety level is reached.

This rule appears to hold with regard to nearly all commodities and with regard to the demand of every class; save only that the level at which high prices end and low prices begin, is different for different classes; and so again is the level at which low prices end and very low prices begin. There are however many varieties in detail; arising chiefly from the fact that there are some commodities with which people are easily satiated, and others chiefly things used for display for which their desire is almost unlimited. For the latter the elasticity of demand remains considerable, however low the price may fall, while for the former the demand loses nearly all its elasticity as soon as a low price has once been reached.

§ 3. There are some things the current prices of which in this country are very low relatively even to the poorer classes; such are for instance salt, and many kinds of savours and flavours, and also cheap medicines. It is doubtful whether any fall in price would induce a considerable increase in the consumption of these.

The current prices of meat, milk and butter, wool, tobacco, imported fruits, and of ordinary medical attendance, are such that every variation in price makes a great change in the consumption of them by the working classes, and the lower half of the middle classes; but the rich would not much increase their own personal consumption of them however cheaply they were to be had. In other words, the direct demand for these commodities is very elastic on the part of the working and lower middle classes, though not on the part of the rich. But the working class is so numerous that their consumption of such things as are well within their reach is much greater than that of the rich; and therefore the aggregate demand for all things of the kind is very elastic. A little while ago sugar belonged to this group of commodities: but its price in England has now fallen so far as to be low relatively even to the working classes, and the demand for it is therefore not elastic.

The current prices of wall-fruit, of the better kinds of fish, and other moderately expensive luxuries are such as to make the consumption of them by the middle class increase much with every fall in price; in other words, the middle class demand for them is very elastic: while the demand on the part of the rich and on the part of the working class is much less elastic, the former because it is already nearly satiated, the latter because the price is still too high.

The current prices of such things as rare wines, fruit out of season, highly skilled medical and legal assistance, are so high that there is but little demand for them except from the rich: but what demand there is, often has considerable elasticity. Part of the demand for the more expensive kinds of food is really a demand for the means of obtaining social distinction, and is almost insatiable.

§ 4. The case of necessaries is exceptional. When the price of wheat is very high, and again when it is very low, the demand has very little elasticity: at all events if we assume that wheat, even when scarce, is the cheapest food for man; and that, even when most plentiful, it is not consumed in any other way. We know that a fall in the price of the quartern loaf from 6d. to 4d. has scarcely any effect in increasing the consumption of bread. With regard to the other end of the scale it is more difficult to speak with certainty, because there has been no approach to a scarcity in England since the repeal of the corn laws. But, availing ourselves of the experience of a less happy time, we may suppose that deficits in the supply of 1, 2, 3, 4, or 5 tenths would cause a rise in price of 3, 8, 16, 28, or 45 tenths respectively. Much greater variations in prices indeed than this have not been uncommon. Thus wheat sold in London for ten shillings a bushel in 1335, but in the following year it sold for ten-pence.

There may be even more violent changes than this in the price of a thing which is not necessary, if it is perishable and the demand for it is inelastic: thus fish may be very dear one day, and sold for manure two or three days later.

Water is one of the few things the consumption of which we are able to observe at all prices, from the very highest down to nothing at all. At moderate prices the demand for it is very elastic. But the uses to which it can be put are capable of being completely filled: and as its price sinks towards zero the demand for it loses its elasticity. Nearly the same may be said of salt. Its price in England is so low that the demand for it as an article of food is very inelastic: but in India the price is comparatively high and the demand is comparatively elastic.

The price of house room, on the other hand, has never fallen very low except when a locality is being deserted by its inhabitants. Where the condition of society is healthy, and there is no check to general prosperity, there seems always to be an elastic demand for house room, on account both of the real conveniences and the social distinction which it affords. The desire for those kinds of clothing which are not used for the purpose of display, is satiable: when their price is low the demand for them has scarcely any elasticity.

The demand for things of a higher quality depends much on sensibility: some people care little for a refined flavour in their wine provided they can get plenty of it: others crave a high quality, but are easily satiated. In the ordinary working class districts the inferior and the better joints are sold at nearly the same price: but some well-paid artisans in the north of England have developed a liking for the best meat, and will pay for it nearly as high a price as can be got in the west end of London, where the price is kept artificially high by the necessity of sending the inferior joints away for sale elsewhere. Use also gives rise to acquired distastes as well as to acquired tastes. Illustrations which make a book attractive to many readers, will repel those whose familiarity with better work has rendered them fastidious. A person of high musical sensibility in a large town will avoid bad concerts: though he might go to them gladly if he lived in a small town, where no good concerts are to be heard, because there are not enough persons willing to pay the high price required to cover their expenses. The effective demand for first-rate music is elastic only in large towns; for second-rate music it is elastic both in large and small towns.

Generally speaking those things have the most elastic demand, which are capable of being applied to many different uses. Water for instance is needed first as food, then for cooking, then for washing of various kinds and so on. When there is no special drought, but water is sold by the pailful, the price may be low enough to enable even the poorer classes to drink as much of it as they are inclined, while for cooking they sometimes use the same water twice over, and they apply it very scantily in washing. The middle classes will perhaps not use any of it twice for cooking; but they will make a pail of water go a good deal further for washing purposes than if they had an unlimited supply at command. When water is supplied by pipes, and charged at a very low rate by meter, many people use as much of it even for washing as they feel at all inclined to do; and when the water is supplied not by meter but at a fixed annual charge, and is laid on in every place where it is wanted, the use of it for every purpose is carried to the full satiety limit.

On the other hand, demand is, generally speaking, very inelastic, firstly, for absolute necessaries (as distinguished from conventional necessaries and necessaries for efficiency); and secondly, for some of those luxuries of the rich which do not absorb much of their income.

§ 5. So far we have taken no account of the difficulties of getting exact lists of demand prices, and interpreting them correctly. The first which we have to consider arises from the element of *time,* the source of many of the greatest difficulties in economics.

Thus while a list of demand prices represents the changes in the price at which a commodity can be sold consequent on changes in the amount offered for sale, *other things being equal;* yet other things seldom are equal in fact over periods of time sufficiently long for the collection of full and trustworthy statistics. There are always occurring disturbing causes whose effects are commingled with, and cannot easily be separated from, the effects of that particular cause which we desire to isolate. This difficulty is aggravated by the fact that in economics the full effects of a cause seldom come at once, but often spread themselves out after it has ceased to exist.

To begin with, the purchasing power of money is continually changing, and rendering necessary a correction of the results obtained on our assumption that money retains a uniform value. This difficulty can however be overcome fairly well, since we can ascertain with tolerable accuracy the broader changes in the purchasing power of money.

Next come the changes in the general prosperity and in the total purchasing power at the disposal of the community at large. The influence of these changes is important, but perhaps less so than is generally supposed. For when the wave of prosperity is descending, prices fall, and this increases the resources of those with fixed incomes at the expense of those whose incomes depend on the profits of business. The downward fluctuation of prosperity is popularly measured almost entirely by the conspicuous losses of this last class; but the statistics of the total consumption of such commodities as tea, sugar, butter, wool, etc. prove that the total purchasing power of the people does not meanwhile fall very fast. Still there is a fall, and the allowance to be made for it must be ascertained by comparing the prices and the consumption of as many things as possible.

Next come the changes due to the gradual growth of population and wealth. For these an easy numerical correction can be made when the facts are known.

§ 6. Next, allowance must be made for changes in fashion, and taste and habit for the opening out of new uses of a commodity, for the discovery or improvement or cheapening of other things that can be applied to the same uses with it. In all these cases there is great difficulty in allowing for the time that elapses between the economic cause and its effect. For time is required to enable a rise in the price of a commodity to exert its full influence on consumption. Time is required for consumers to become familiar with substitutes that can be used instead of it, and perhaps for producers to get into the habit of producing

161

them in sufficient quantities. Time may be also wanted for the growth of habits of familiarity with the new commodities and the discovery of methods of economizing them.

For instance when wood and charcoal became dear in England, familiarity with coal as a fuel grew slowly, fireplaces were but slowly adapted to its use, and an organized traffic in it did not spring up quickly even to places to which it could be easily carried by water: the invention of processes by which it could be used as a substitute for charcoal in manufacture went even more slowly, and is indeed hardly yet complete. Again, when in recent years the price of coal became very high, a great stimulus was given to the invention of economies in its use, especially in the production of iron and steam; but few of these inventions bore much practical fruit till after the high price had passed away. Again, when a new tramway or suburban railway is opened, even those who live near the line do not get into the habit of making the most of its assistance at once; and a good deal more time elapses before many of those whose places of business are near one end of the line change their homes so as to live near the other end. Again, when petroleum first became plentiful few people were ready to use it freely; gradually petroleum and petroleum lamps have become familiar to all classes of society: too much influence would therefore be attributed to the fall in price which has occurred since then, if it were credited with all the increase of consumption.

Another difficulty of the same kind arises from the fact that there are many purchases which can easily be put off for a short time, but not for a long time. This is often the case with regard to clothes and other things which are worn out gradually, and which can be made to serve a little longer than usual under the pressure of high prices. For instance, at the beginning of the cotton famine the recorded consumption of cotton in England was very small. This was partly because retail dealers reduced their stock, but chiefly because people generally made shift to do as long as they could without buying new cotton goods. In 1864 however many found themselves unable to wait longer; and a good deal more cotton was entered for home consumption in that year, though the price was then much higher than in either of the preceding years. For commodities of this kind then a sudden scarcity does not immediately raise the price fully up to the level, which properly corresponds to the reduced supply. Similarly after the great commercial depression in the United States in 1873 it was noticed that the boot trade revived before the general clothing trade; because there is a great deal of reserve wear in the coats and hats that are thrown aside in prosperous times as worn out, but not so much in the boots.

§ 7. The above difficulties are fundamental: but there are others which do not lie deeper than the more or less inevitable faults of our statistical returns.

We desire to obtain, if possible, a series of prices at which different amounts of a commodity can find purchasers during a given time in a market. A perfect market is a district, small or large, in which there are many buyers and many sellers all so keenly on the alert and so well acquainted with one another's affairs that the price of a commodity is always practically the same for the whole of the district. But independently of the fact that those who buy for their own consumption, and not for the purposes of trade, are not always on the look out for every change in the market, there is no means of ascertaining exactly what prices are paid in many transactions. Again, the geographical limits of a market are seldom clearly drawn, except when they are marked out by the sea or by custom-house barriers; and no country has accurate statistics of commodities produced in it for home consumption.

Again, there is generally some ambiguity even in such statistics as are to be had. They commonly show goods as entered for consumption as soon as they pass into the hands of dealers; and consequently an increase of dealers' stocks cannot easily be distinguished from an increase of consumption. But the two are governed by different causes. A rise of prices tends to check consumption; but if the rise is expected to continue, it will probably, as has already been noticed, lead dealers to increase their stocks.

Next it is difficult to insure that the commodities referred to are always of the same quality. After a dry summer what wheat there is, is exceptionally good; and the prices for the next harvest year appear to be higher than they really are. It is possible to make allowance for this, particularly now that dry Californian wheat affords a standard. But it is almost impossible to allow properly for the changes in quality of many kinds of manufactured goods. This difficulty occurs even in the case of such a thing as tea: the substitution in recent years of the stronger Indian tea for the weaker Chinese tea has made the real increase of consumption greater than that which is shown by the statistics.

# Chapter 15

## Hicks on the Walrasian System

Léon Walras (1834-1910), co-discoverer of the marginal utility theory of value along with Jevons and Menger, made contributions to economics that are peculiarly his own. In the selection that follows, John R. Hicks, 1972 Nobel laureate in Economics, explores those special contributions which distinguish Walras from his fellow-pioneers. Hicks himself was steeped in the economics of Marshall and the Austrians; and although his admiration for Walras is obvious, he nevertheless offers a balanced appraisal of Walras's strengths and weaknesses.

Most contrasts of Walras and Marshall emphasize their differences. Hicks bucks this trend by emphasizing their similarities. The common ground between these two giants of neoclassical economics at the turn of the twentieth century persists up to a point, and therefore provide a heightened basis for understanding their ultimate differences, which Hicks claims are due more to divergence "of interest, rather than of technique." Hicks claims two main achievements for Walras. One is his discovery of the conditions of static equilibrium under perfect competition. The other is his realization of the unity of economic life. This unity is strongly emphasized in Walras's formulation of 'general equilibrium'. The abstract, formalized, mathematical specification that Walras gave to his general equilibrium system should not be allowed to obscure its basic truth, namely that diverse individual ends are reconciled through the mechanism of the market. Underlying everything else was Walras's conviction "that the only economic explanation of a phenomenon is its reference back to individual choice." More than anything else, this conviction lies at the heart of the neoclassical developments in economic theory.

Source: Hicks, J. R. "Léon Walras," *Econometrica*, vol. 2 (October 1934), pp. 338-348.

I

Like John Stuart Mill and John Maynard Keynes, Léon Walras was the son of an economist. His father, Auguste Walras, was one of those excellent people (they seem to have existed since very near the dawn of history) who taught the true but unhelpful doctrine that value depends on scarcity (*rareté*); the son followed the father's teaching, but added to it something which lifts it on to another plane of precision. He defined *rareté* as

165

*l'intensité du dernier besoin satisfait par une quantité consommée de marchandise;* scarcity equals marginal utility.

His position with Jevons and Menger as one of the independent discoverers of the Marginal Utility principle is generally regarded as Leon Walras' chief title to fame; and this no doubt justly enough. But anyone who comes a little closer to these writers cannot help feeling a little resentment at the habit of classifying them together, even for the joint receipt of such an honorable title. For each of them made contributions to economics which are peculiarly his own, and it is for these special contributions that they are still worth reading today.

Indeed, the modern reader of Walras' *Éléments d'Économie Politique Pure is* struck by its affinity, not with the work of Jevons or Menger, but with that of Marshall. For a quite considerable part of the way Walras and Marshall go together; and when they separate, it is a difference of interests, rather than of technique, that divides them. While Walras was seeking for the general principles which underlie the working of an exchange economy, Marshall forged an analytical instrument capable of easier application to particular problems of history or experience. Yet, since the followers of Walras cannot always afford to be pure philosophers, and Marshallians have their moments of reflection, the two systems have inevitably tended to grow back into one another as the years pass by.

This affinity between two writers of different upbringing and obviously very different mental outlook—their simultaneous development of what was then a very new line of thought—looks at first sight surprising, and one feels almost obliged to explain it by the intrinsic excellence of the path they followed: "it seems no honest heart can stray." Yet in fact there is a clear historical reason for it, one decisive influence we know to have been felt by both. Each of them had read Cournot.

Now although each makes a specific acknowledgment to Cournot, it is in each case couched in very general terms. They each tell us that Cournot showed them how to use the differential calculus in economics, and this may mean much or little. But it is at least striking that certain very significant elements of Cournot's mathematical economics, going far beyond the mere idea of using mathematical methods, appear in Walras and appear in Marshall.

One of these is of course the demand curve itself (which already implies a resolution to treat economic quantities as if they are continuous variables). But more important, and less obvious, is the conception of perfect competition. Cournot's analysis, it will be remembered, passed from Monopoly to Duopoly (or Limited Competition), and from Duopoly to Unlimited Competition, which he defined as a state of affairs in which no single producer is able to influence appreciably the prices of the market. It was this last conception (applied to the theory of exchange value generally) which enabled Walras and Marshall to overcome the difficulties which had baffled Jevons, those difficulties which arise from the differences in the wants of different buyers of a particular commodity. In the hands of Walras, this conception of perfect competition was converted into a special technique of using prices as economic parameters. Although of course this technique was used by Marshall as well, its very consistent employment is highly characteristic of Walras' work.

With this equipment, it was fairly easy to give an adequate analysis of the simple exchange of two commodities under competitive conditions. (Cournot had confined himself to the selling of products by producers, and did not examine the logically prior problem.) Accordingly, we find Walras beginning his *Éléments* in this way (1874), and Marshall following with a substantially equivalent analysis, hidden under the guise of a theory of International Values (1879).

Walras' treatment fails of complete generality in only one respect; the downward slope of the demand curve is not quite so inevitable an assumption as he thought it. But he was well aware that the downward slope of the demand curve does not necessarily imply that the supply curve derived from it is upward sloping. If a person is buying X, and giving Y in exchange, then, if his demand for X becomes inelastic, his supply curve of Y will turn back towards the price-axis. In this case it becomes possible that the demand and supply curves for may cut several times; but some of these intersections will be points of unstable equilibrium.

Faced with this difficulty of multiple intersections, Marshall cut the knot by his distinction between the "theory of International Values" and the "theory of Domestic Values." In "International Values," the possibility of negatively inclined supply curves is serious; but they are unlikely to be particularly important in practice, because the competition of domestic industry generally suffices to keep a country's demand for imports in terms of exports fairly elastic. In the theory of "Domestic Values," we may take commodities to be usually sold by producers or dealers who have themselves no direct demand for Y what they sell. Negatively-inclined supply curves can then only arise from increasing returns.

Apart from the reference to increasing returns (a problem he never seriously examined), this reliance on sale by producers, whose reservation demand is negligible, was Walras' way out also. But before coming to that point, he widened the problem by a consideration of multiple exchange, where more than two commodities enter into the picture. In order to treat this question, he supposed one of the $n$ commodities to be chosen as a standard of value *(numéraire),* in which prices are reckoned, but which is itself subject to no demand other than that which arises from its ordinary properties as a commodity. There thus remained $n-1$ prices to determine. From the conditions of given stocks at the commencement of trading, and equalization of the marginal utilities of expenditure in all directions, he derived each individual's demand (or supply) for each commodity. Then the ordinary equations of supply and demand in each market give the conditions of equilibrium. They are $n$ in number, but that in the market for the *numéraire* is superfluous, as it follows from the rest. There are thus $n-1$ equations and $n-1$ unknowns; a set of prices must therefore exist which satisfies the conditions of equilibrium.

Here, for the first time, we have a characteristically Walrasian doctrine. What is it worth? On our estimation of it our view of Walras' individual contribution to economics must largely depend.

Now it is, of course, quite clear that, even when they are applied to this pure problem of exchange, the equations are far too complicated to be of much use in analysing any actual situation. But that is surely not their function. Where they are supremely useful is in elucidating the general way the price-system works, and in giving us a classification of those factors which may be relevant to any particular case. In practice we have to select out of that over-long list those which are most important for each special problem. When that selection is performed, we may get a result which conforms to the simpler scheme employed by Marshall; but on the other hand we may not.

The types of equations used by Walras in determining exchange equilibrium are two; those which express the dependence of the amounts demanded and supplied by particular individuals on the system of market prices, and those which express the equality of demand and supply in particular markets. These two classes stand on very different footings. So far as the first class is concerned, they have become the essential foundation for the whole branch of economics to which they refer. On them is based, and had to be based, all the work in the field of demand and of related goods, which has been carried out by Edgeworth, Pareto, and others. In the process of development Walras' conception of utility has been much refined; but we still work with Walras' equations, however differently we write them.

The second class, which expresses the equation of supply and demand in the different markets, seems much more simple and obvious; yet it has proved much more open to criticism, for it is on this class that the meaning of Walras' system of general equilibrium depends, and by far the most important divergence between Walras and Marshall turns on this point.

Walras' own account of the nature of equilibrium is this. Persons come on to the market with certain stocks of commodities, and certain dispositions to trade ("dispositions à l'enchère") and a particular set of prices is proposed. If at these prices supplies and demands are equal, then there is equilibrium straight away. But if demands and supplies are not equal, prices will be changed until equilibrium is reached.

What, however, Walras does not make really clear is whether any exchanges do or do not actually take place at the prices originally proposed, when those prices are not equilibrium prices. If there is no actual exchange until the equilibrium prices are reached by bidding, then Walras' argument is beyond reproach on the score of logical consistency, though it may be called unrealistic. (The market then proceeds under Edgeworth's principle of "recontract," or provisional contract.) But if such exchanges do take place, then, in general, the final equilibrium prices will be affected by them.

Marshall's way out of this dilemma was to concentrate on a particular market, where he could show that if the marginal utility of one of the commodities exchanged could be treated as constant, then the final rate of interchange would be independent of the path followed to reach it. But this solution which is, after all, only a very particular solution is usually not available in the case of General Equilibrium.

Neither Walras nor Pareto faced up to this difficulty; when we do so, it is impossible to avoid the conclusion that the "Lausanne equations" are of rather less significance than they imagined. The equations of Walras' are not by any means a complete solution of the problem of exchange; but they remain a very significant step towards such a solution. For Walras' system of prices will be reached, either if contracts are made provisionally or (a more important case) if people come on to the market on successive "days" with the same dispositions to trade, and there is no carry-over of stocks (or a constant carry-over) from one day to the next. When it is understood in the last sense, the theory of static equilibrium of exchange takes its place as a step towards the development of a complete theory with which future exposition is unlikely to dispense.

## II

From the General Equilibrium of Exchange, Walras passed to the General Equilibrium of Production. For him, as for the Austrians, the problem of production fell into two parts: one relating to the pricing of factors of production, which are only used in combination with one another; the other relating to the role of time in production—the theory of capital.

The first of these problems (which corresponds to the Austrian theory of imputation) is really no more than an extension of the theory of value: it studies one particular kind of interrelation of prices. In this field Walras' original work was chiefly confined to a consideration of that problem which from his point of view is the simplest (though the Austrians naturally found it the hardest from their standpoint); the case where the "coefficients of production" are fixed, so that the quantities of all factors needed to produce a unit of each kind of finished product are technically given.

With fixed coefficients, and with perfect competition, the equilibrium prices of the products must depend on the prices of the factors; thus, given the prices of the factors, the whole price-system (of products and factors) can be derived by simple process of addition. But, given this whole price-system, the demands for products and the supply of factors can be determined from the tastes and abilities of the individuals composing the economy. Again, once the demands for the products are determined, the demands for the factors can be technically deduced. We can thus write both the demands for the factors and the supplies of the factors as functions of the set of factor-prices; and determine equilibrium in the factor markets as before. The equilibrium prices in the factor markets now determine the equilibrium prices of the products.

This solution is of course valid only under the assumption of fixed coefficients; but Walras was quite aware that it could easily be extended to the more realistic case of variable coefficients. One cannot help thinking it to be a great pity that he did not trouble to work out this hint, for it would have led directly to the general law of marginal productivity.

Nevertheless, even as it is, this part of Walras' work has great merits. The particular relation which it exhibits has quite general significance, and could hardly have been discovered in any other way than this. Even when the coefficients of production are variable, so that a rise in the price of one particular factor influences the demand for it mainly by encouraging a substitution of other factors within industries, there will still be present this further tendency: that the factors which cooperate with this first factor will find it more profitable to devote themselves to the production of products for which relatively little (or none at all) of the first factor is required.

Again, we have here an excellent illustration of the value of Walras' work for the clearing up of questions of principle—the sort of question which Marshall so frequently left rather confused. Walras' equations give the most exact  version that has ever been given of the "opportunity cost" element in value; and at the same time they preserve the essence of the "real cost" principle for which Edgeworth and Marshall contended. They exhibit the supplies of the factors as variable, but as determined by the system of prices in fundamentally the same way as the demands for commodities, with which they are interdependent.

It is hardly necessary, at this date, to discuss at any length that one of Walras' conditions which was so vehemently attacked by Edgeworth—the condition that prices equal costs of production, so that the entrepreneur makes "neither profit nor loss." For this device, in spite of its paradoxical appearance, is nothing else than the reckoning of "normal profits" (the profits which the entrepreneur could earn in other activities) into costs; and similar forms of definition are now adopted for their extreme convenience by many economists who would acknowledge no direct debt to Walras. It may indeed be questioned whether the full implications of this method of statement have been explored particularly with respect to its application to dynamic conditions. But the device itself needs no defence nowadays.

### III

Those parts of Walras' doctrine which we have hitherto considered are on the whole uncontroversial; it is true that they raise difficult problems of interpretation, but no one seems to doubt that in some sense they are valid enough. It is these parts  which have passed into the body of economic teaching; and when we want to study them we are inclined to go, not to Walras' own works, but to the rather more elegantly stated versions of his successors, such as Pareto or  Wicksell.

Walras' theory of capital, however, has not reached this happy position. By Pareto it was simply ignored; by Wicksell it was attacked. It has therefore not passed into any recognized "Lausanne" tradition, and is liable to be dismissed as something of an aberration. In spite of this, it has its merits; though there can be no question that it needs a good deal of repair in details before it can become a usable theory.

If a reader who is acquainted with the work of Böhm-Bawerk and Wicksell approaches Walras' theory of capital, the first thing which will strike him is that it is purely a theory of fixed capital. Walras begins from a discussion of the capital value of income-yielding goods. He shows that the ratio of capital value to net income-yielded (after allowance for depreciated insurance) must tend to equality for all such goods; otherwise people would sell the more expensive (relatively to yield) and buy the cheaper. Thus there emerges a "rate of net yield" (*taux du revenu net*), which, in equilibrium, must be equal for all capital goods.

How is the "rate of net yield" determined? By the condition that the prices of new capital goods must equal their costs of production. Granted that a certain amount of new saving is coming forward, this saving will give the demand for new capital goods. The saving has then to be divided among the various capital goods that can be produced in such a way as to maximize the rate of net yield.

Substantially, that is Walras' theory; it is a theory, which, if taken literally, is open to very serious objections.

For one thing, as Wicksell pointed out, it determines the rate of interest on the market for new capital; and is therefore apparently inapplicable to stationary conditions, when no net addition to the capital equipment of the community is being made. Further, as Walras would have realized if it had not been for his confusion about the exact meaning of equilibrium, it is only in a stationary state that we can get any sensible sort of equilibrium, so long as people expect the prices of products to remain unchanged in the future (as Walras tacitly assumes they do). This dilemma is fatal to the theory as Walras presents it.

But it is not necessarily fatal to the whole method of approach. For once we assume that the reinvestment of depreciation allowances is not technically given (in the way Walras supposed), but that these funds are reinvested according to the best prospects open for them at the moment of reinvestment; then the "new capital goods" become not only net additions to the capital stock, but also replacements, and the demand for these goods is no longer confined to new savings, but consists of depreciation allowances as well. With this slight extension, Walras' system becomes immune from Wicksell's criticisms; the capital market does not disappear in the stationary state.

Walras did not make this amendment, but its possibility deserves attention; for it shows the essential rightness of his method, which survives the imperfect way in which he used it. Once the amendment is made, Walras' theory of capital becomes as good as Wicksell's, and better than Böhm-Bawerk's. It is still subject to the static limitations within which their theories are also confined, but it is as good a basis for extension in a dynamic direction as theirs and in some ways it is perhaps better.

# IV

Walras' work on the theory of money, and his relatively uninteresting writings on applied Economics, cannot detain us here. It was in pure economics that his real interest lay, and the discovery of the conditions of static equilibrium under perfect competition was his central achievement. Like many pioneers, he was a little vague about the exact meaning of some of his results, and was perhaps inclined to claim for them more than they are actually worth. Yet our consciousness of its limitations should not blind us to the greatness of his achievement. Static equilibrium is far from being the whole of economics, but it is an indispensable foundation; and the greater part of that foundation was laid by Cournot and Walras. There are very few economists who have contributed so much to the permanent body of established truth as Walras did.

Comment may be made in conclusion on two qualities of his work taken as a whole. One is the realization of the unity of economic life which emerges so forcefully from his pages. Other economists had had a sense of this unity, but none before had shown it so well. For the unity which Walras demonstrated is not a unity of resources being allotted among a single system of ends—the only unity which really appears in Menger—it is a unity of diverse individual ends reconciled through the mechanism of the market. Yet this unity is as real as the other. In a free economic system, under perfect competition,

> thou canst not stir a flower
> Without troubling of a star.

The other great quality of Walras' work to which we may here allude is its rigorous "methodological individualism." Far better than any earlier economist better even than Marshall he realized that the only economic explanation of a phenomena is its reference back to individual acts of choice. Even he did not emancipate himself entirely from that sham utilitarianism which was the bane of his contemporaries, and which led them to suppose that the working of the market "maximized utility" for the community as a whole. But this in his work is a mere excrescence, and is easily disregarded. In his central doctrines he held firmly to the true significance of economic subjectivism, and therefore broke with the Labour Theory of Value more drastically than Marshall, and quite as drastically as the Austrians. For him individual choice was all-important in its function as explanation; and it is our realization of this which has led us to understand that it is not, for the economist, necessarily anything more.

# Chapter 16

## Veblen on Conspicuous Consumption

The kind of inquiry which Thorstein Veblen (1857-1929) wished economics to become was unlike any which had preceded him and unlike any which followed him. He wanted to analyze the wider social and cultural causes and consequences of evolutionary changes in economic patterns, such as the change from a hunter-gatherer society to that of settled farming; or from handicrafts to industrial production. Neither classical economics nor neoclassical economics attempted anything of the sort, and Veblen criticized them, not for giving wrong answers but for asking the wrong questions. In his own investigations, Veblen blurred the lines between economics and sociology, history, and anthropology. On occasion, he even confounded empirical investigation with self-indulgent speculation.

Although Veblen founded institutionalist economics, his practice of the subject was quite different from later variants, in part because of his definition of institutions. He did not think of institutions as organizations but rather as 'settled habits of thought, common to the generality of men.' Thus, customs, habits, canons of conduct, and principles of propriety were viewed by Veblen as institutions, and he directed his inquiry to the underlying social and cultural visions that gave them meaning. He strove for *analysis* rather than *ad hoc* description, but many of his followers lapsed into mere description. As a consequence, technical economics quickly outpaced institutional economics, leaving the latter as an outlier of contemporary theory.

In the excerpt below from Veblen's first book, *The Theory of the Leisure Class*, note how Veblen weaves culture, habit, and status into an evolutionary analysis of 'conspicuous' consumption. Also, in contrast to contemporary orthodox economics, note the anthropological and sociological strains of Veblen's argument.

Source: Veblen, Thorstein. *The Theory of the Leisure Class*. New York: Viking Press, 1931. Pages 68-78; 85-86.

# Chapter IV

## CONSPICUOUS CONSUMPTION

In what has been said of the evolution of the vicarious leisure class and its differentiation from the general body of the working classes, reference has been made to a further division of labor,—that between different servant classes. One portion of the servant class, chiefly those persons whose occupation is vicarious leisure, come to undertake a new, subsidiary range of duties—the vicarious consumption of goods. The most obvious form in which this consumption occurs is seen in the wearing of liveries and the occupation of spacious servants' quarters. Another, scarcely less obtrusive or less effective form of vicarious consumption, and a much more widely prevalent one, is the consumption of food, clothing, dwelling, and furniture by the lady and the rest of the domestic establishment.

But already at a point in economic evolution far antedating the emergence of the lady, specialized consumption of goods as an evidence of pecuniary strength had begun to work out in a more or less elaborate system. The beginning of a differentiation in consumption even antedates the appearance of anything that can fairly be called pecuniary strength. It is traceable back to the initial phase of predatory culture, and there is even a suggestion that an incipient differentiation in this respect lies back of the beginnings of the predatory life. This most primitive differentiation in the consumption of goods is like the later differentiation with which we are all so intimately familiar, in that it is largely of a ceremonial character, but unlike the latter it does not rest on a difference in accumulated wealth. The utility of consumption as an evidence of wealth is to be classed as a derivative growth. It is an adaptation to a new end, by a selective process, of a distinction previously existing and well established in men's habits of thought.

In the earlier phases of the predatory culture the only economic differentiation is a broad distinction between an honorable superior class made up of the able-bodied men on the one side, and a base inferior class of laboring women on the other. According to the ideal scheme of life in force at that time it is the office of the men to consume what the women produce. Such consumption as falls to the women is merely incidental to their work; it is a means to their continued labor, and not a consumption directed to their own comfort and fullness of life. Unproductive consumption of goods is honorable, primarily as a mark of prowess and a perquisite of human dignity; secondarily it becomes substantially honorable in itself, especially the consumption of the more desirable things. The consumption of choice articles of food, and frequently also of rare articles of adornment, becomes taboo to the women and children; and if there is a base (servile) class of men, the taboo holds also for them. With a further advance in culture this taboo may change into simple custom of a more or less rigorous character; but whatever be the theoretical basis of the distinction which is maintained, whether it be a taboo or a larger conventionality, the features of the conventional scheme of consumption do not change easily. When the quasi-peaceable stage of industry is reached, with its fundamental institution of chattel slavery, the general principle, more or less rigorously applied, is that the base, industrious class should consume only what may be necessary to their subsistence. In the nature of things, luxuries and the comforts of life belong to the leisure class. Under the taboo certain victuals, and more particularly certain beverages, are strictly reserved for the use of the superior class.

The ceremonial differentiation of the dietary is best seen in the use of intoxicating beverages and narcotics. If these articles of consumption are costly, they are felt to be noble and honorific. Therefore the base classes, primarily the women, practice an enforced continence with respect to these stimulants, except in countries where they are obtainable at a very low cost. From archaic times down through all the length of the patriarchal regime it has been the office of the women to prepare and administer these luxuries, and it has been the perquisite of the men of gentle birth and breeding to consume them. Drunkenness and the other pathological consequences of the free use of stimulants therefore tend in their turn to become honorific, as being a mark, at the second remove, of the superior status of those who are able to afford the indulgence. Infirmities induced by over-indulgence are among some peoples freely recognized as manly attributes. It has even happened that the name for certain diseased conditions of the body arising from such an origin has passed into everyday speech as a synonym for "noble" or "gentle." It is only at a relatively early stage of culture that the symptoms of expensive vice are conventionally accepted as marks of a superior status, and so tend to become virtues and command the deference of the community; but the reputability that attaches to certain expensive vices long retains so much of its force as to appreciably lessen the disapprobation visited upon the men of the wealthy or noble class for any excessive indulgence. The same invidious distinction adds force to the current disapproval of any indulgence of this kind on the part of women, minors, and inferiors. This invidious traditional distinction has not lost its force even among the more advanced peoples of to-day. Where the example set by the leisure class retains its imperative force in the regulation of the conventionalities, it is observable that the women still in great measure practice the same traditional continence with regard to stimulants.

This characterization of the greater continence in the use of stimulants practiced by the women of the reputable classes may seem an excessive refinement of logic at the expense of common sense. But facts within easy reach of any one who cares to know them go to say that the greater abstinence of women is in some part due to an imperative conventionality; and this conventionality is, in a general way, strongest where the patriarchal tradition—the tradition that the woman is a chattel—has retained its hold in greatest vigor. In a sense which has been greatly qualified in scope and rigor, but which has by no means lost its meaning even yet, this tradition says that the woman, being a chattel, should consume only what is necessary to her sustenance,—except so far as her further consumption contributes to the comfort or the good repute of her master. The consumption of luxuries, in the true sense, is a consumption directed to the comfort of the consumer himself, and is, therefore, a mark of the master. Any such consumption by others can take place only on a basis of sufferance. In communities where the popular habits of thought have been profoundly shaped by the patriarchal tradition we may accordingly look for survivals of the taboo on luxuries at least to the extent of a conventional deprecation of their use by the unfree and dependent class. This is more particularly true as regards certain luxuries, the use of which by the dependent class would detract sensibly from the comfort or pleasure of their masters, or which are held to be of doubtful legitimacy on other grounds. In the apprehension of the great conservative middle class of Western civilization the use of these various stimulants is obnoxious to at least one, if not both, of these objections; and it is a fact too significant to be passed over that it is precisely among these middle classes of the Germanic culture, with their strong surviving sense of the patriarchal proprieties, that the women are to the greatest extent subject to a qualified taboo on narcotics and alcoholic beverages. With many qualifications—with more qualifications as the patriarchal tradition has gradually weakened—the general rule is felt to be right and binding that women should consume only for the benefit of their masters. The objection of course presents itself that expenditure on women's dress and household paraphernalia is an obvious exception to this rule; but it will appear in the sequel that this exception is much more obvious than substantial.

During the earlier stages of economic development, consumption of goods without stint, especially consumption of the better grades of goods,—ideally all consumption in excess of the subsistence minimum,—pertains normally to the leisure class. This restriction tends to disappear, at least formally, after the later peaceable stage Has been reached, with private ownership of goods and an industrial system based on wage labor or on the petty household economy. But during the earlier quasi-peaceable stage, when so many of the traditions through which the institution of a leisure class has affected the economic life of later times were taking form and consistency, this principle has had the force of a conventional law. It has served as the norm to which consumption has tended to conform, and any appreciable departure from it is to be regarded as an aberrant form, sure to be eliminated sooner or later in the further course of development.

The quasi-peaceable gentleman of leisure, then, not only consumes of the staff of life beyond the minimum required for subsistence and physical efficiency, but his consumption also undergoes a specialization as regards the quality of the goods consumed. He consumes freely and of the best, in food, drink, narcotics, shelter, services, ornaments, apparel, weapons and accouterments, amusements, amulets and idols or divinities. In the process of gradual amelioration which takes place in the articles of his consumption, the motive principle and the proximate aim of innovation is no doubt the higher efficiency of the improved and more elaborate products for personal comfort and well-being. But that does not remain the sole purpose of their consumption. The canon of reputability is at hand and seizes upon such innovations as are, according to its standard, fit to survive. Since the consumption of these more excellent goods is an evidence of wealth, it becomes honorific; and conversely, the failure to consume in due quantity and quality becomes a mark of inferiority and demerit.

This growth of punctilious discrimination as to qualitative excellence in eating, drinking, etc., presently affects not only the manner of life, but also the training and intellectual activity of the gentleman of leisure. He is no longer simply the successful, aggressive male,—the man of strength, resource, and intrepidity. In order to avoid stultification he must also cultivate his tastes, for it now becomes incumbent on him to discriminate with some nicety between the noble and the ignoble in consumable goods. He becomes a connoisseur in creditable viands of various degrees of merit, in manly beverages and trinkets, in seemly apparel and architecture, in weapons, games, dancers, and the narcotics. This cultivation of the aesthetic faculty requires time and application, and the demands made upon the gentleman in this direction therefore tend to change his life of leisure into a more or less arduous application to the business of learning how to live a life of ostensible leisure in a becoming way. Closely related to the requirement that the gentleman must consume freely and of the right kind of goods, there is the requirement that he must know how to consume them in a seemly manner. His life of leisure must be conducted in due form. Hence arise good manners in the way pointed out in an earlier chapter. High-bred manners and ways of living are items of conformity to the norm of conspicuous leisure and conspicuous consumption.

Conspicuous consumption of valuable goods is a means of reputability to the gentleman of leisure. As wealth accumulates on his hands, his own unaided effort will not avail to sufficiently put his opulence in evidence by this method. The aid of friends and competitors is therefore brought in by resorting to the giving of valuable presents and expensive feasts and entertainments. Presents and feasts had probably another origin than that of naive ostentation, but they acquired their utility for this purpose very early, and they have retained that character to the present; so that their utility in this respect has now long been the substantial ground on which these usages rest. Costly entertainments, such as the potlatch or the ball, are peculiarly adapted to serve this end. The competitor with whom the entertainer wishes to institute a comparison is, by this method, made to serve as a means to the end. He consumes vicariously for his host at the same time that he is a witness to the consumption of that excess of good things which his host is unable to dispose of single-handed, and he is also made to witness his host's facility in etiquette.

In the giving of costly entertainments other motives, of a more genial kind, are of course also present. The custom of festive gatherings probably originated in motives of conviviality and religion; these motives are also present in the later development, but they do not continue to be the sole motives. The latter-day leisure class festivities and entertainments may continue in some slight degree to serve the religious need and in a higher degree the needs of recreation and conviviality, but they also serve an invidious purpose; and they serve it none the less effectually for having a colorable non-invidious ground in these more avowable motives. But the economic effect of these social amenities is not therefore lessened, either in the vicarious consumption of goods or in the exhibition of difficult and costly achievements in etiquette.

As wealth accumulates, the leisure class develops further in function and structure, and there arises a differentiation within the class. There is a more or less elaborate system of rank and grades. This differentiation is furthered by the inheritance of wealth and the consequent inheritance of gentility. With the inheritance of gentility goes the inheritance of obligatory leisure; and gentility of a sufficient potency to entail a life of leisure may be inherited without the complement of wealth required to maintain a dignified leisure. Gentle blood may be transmitted without goods enough to afford a reputably free consumption at one's ease. Hence results a class of impecunious gentlemen of leisure, incidentally referred to already. These half-caste gentlemen of leisure fall into a system of hierarchical gradations. Those who stand near the higher and the highest grades of the wealthy leisure class, in point of birth, or in point of wealth, or both, outrank the remoter-born and the pecuniarily weaker. These lower grades, especially the impecunious, or marginal, gentlemen of leisure, affiliate themselves by a system of dependence or fealty to the great ones; by so doing they gain an increment of repute, or of the means with which to lead a life of leisure, from their patron. They become his courtiers or retainers, servants; and being fed and countenanced by their patron they are indices of his rank and vicarious consumers of his superfluous wealth. Many of these affiliated gentlemen of leisure are at the same time lesser men of substance in their own right; so that some of them are scarcely at all, others only partially, to be rated as vicarious consumers. So many of them, however, as make up the retainers and hangers-on of the patron may be classed as vicarious consumers without qualification. Many of these again, and also many of the other aristocracy of less degree, have in turn attached to their persons a more or less comprehensive group of vicarious consumers in the persons of their wives and children, their servants, retainers, etc.

Throughout this graduated scheme of vicarious leisure and vicarious consumption the rule holds that these offices must be performed in some such manner, or under some such circumstance or insignia, as shall point plainly to the master to whom this leisure or consumption pertains, and to whom therefore the resulting increment of good repute of right inures. The consumption and leisure executed by these persons for their master or patron represents an investment on his part with a view to an increase of good fame. As regards feasts and largesses this is obvious enough, and the imputation of repute to the host or patron here takes place immediately, on the ground of common notoriety. Where leisure and consumption is performed vicariously by henchmen and retainers, imputation of the resulting repute to the patron is effected by their residing near his person so that it may be plain to all men from what source they draw. As the group whose good esteem is to be secured in this way grows larger, more patent means are required to indicate the imputation of merit for the leisure performed, and to this end uniforms, badges, and liveries come into vogue.

. . . . . . . . . . . . . . . . . . . . . . . . . . . . . . . . . . . . . . . . . . . . . . . . . . . . . . . .

From the foregoing survey of the growth of conspicuous leisure and consumption, it appears that the utility of both alike for the purposes of reputability lies in the element of waste that is common to both. In the one case it is a waste of time and effort, in the other it is a waste of goods. Both are methods of demonstrating the possession of wealth, and the two are conventionally accepted as equivalents. The choice between them is a question of advertising expediency simply, except so far as it may be affected by other standards of propriety, springing from a different source. On grounds of expediency the preference may be given to the one or the other at different stages of the economic development. The question is, which of the two methods will most effectively reach the persons whose convictions it is desired to affect. Usage has answered this question in different ways under different circumstances.

So long as the community or social group is small enough and compact enough to be effectually reached by common notoriety alone,—that is to say, so long as the human environment to which the individual is required to adapt himself in respect of reputability is comprised within his sphere of personal acquaintance and neighborhood gossip so long the one method is about as effective as the other. Each will therefore serve about equally well during the earlier stages of social growth. But when the differentiation has gone farther and it becomes necessary to reach a wider human environment, consumption begins to hold over leisure as an ordinary means of decency. This is especially true during the later peaceable economic stage. The means of communication and the mobility of the population now expose the individual to the observation of many persons who have no other means of judging of his reputability than the display of goods (and perhaps of breeding) which he is able to make while he is under their direct observation.

# Chapter 17

## Chamberlin on Product Differentiation

Along with Joan Robinson of Cambridge University, Harvard Professor Edward Hastings Chamberlin (1899-1967) pioneered the development of the theory of imperfect competition. From the start of his dissertation research in 1925 to the end of his life four decades later, Chamberlin opposed the popular microeconomic theory of the 1920s, with its alternative polar frameworks of competition and monopoly. Instead, he advanced the notion of market structure as a *continuum* that connected these polar opposites, but offered gradations in between. In Chamberlin's theory, which he called "monopolistic competition," location on the continuum is determined by numbers of firms and degree of product differentiation. His work gave birth to modern industrial organization theory by giving a theoretical core to what had formerly been institutional and anecdotal. In the process, Chamberlin reoriented microeconomics from the industry to the firm.

Central to Chamberlin's theoretical merger was the concept of *product differentiation*, by which he meant the ability of a firm to distinguish its product in the preferences of consumers. The meaning of 'product' itself underwent a subtle transformation in this new theory, emerging in its new definition as an amalgam of characteristics besides those inherent in the physical good. According to Chamberlin, such features as location, convenience, reliability, reputation, etc., enter into the notion of 'product'. Robinson, who was more steeped in the Marshallian tradition than Chamberlin, saw the threat to the Marshallian construct of 'industry' posed by non-homogeneous products, and consequently de-emphasized this aspect of "imperfect" competition in her formulation. In the long run, therefore, Chamberlin's theoretical innovations were more seminal, even though he personally was unsuccessful in breaking away entirely from the Marshallian mold.

Source: Chamberlin, E. H. *The Theory of Monopolistic Competition*, 7th ed. Cambridge, MA: Harvard University Press, 1956. Pages 56-70.

## Chapter IV

## THE DIFFERENTIATION OF THE PRODUCT

### I. The Meaning Of Differentiation

The interplay of monopolistic and competitive forces…arises from what we shall call the differentiation of the product. This chapter introduces the subject by explaining what differentiation means, and how and in what relationship it involves both monopoly and competition.

A general class of product is differentiated if any significant basis exists for distinguishing the goods (or services) of one seller from those of another. Such a basis may be real or fancied, so long as it is of any importance whatever to buyers, and leads to a preference for one variety of the product over another. Where such differentiation exists, even though it be slight, buyers will be paired with sellers, not by chance and at random (as under pure competition), but according to their preferences.

Differentiation may be based upon certain characteristics of the product itself, such as exclusive patented features; trademarks; trade names; peculiarities of the package or container, if any; or singularity in quality, design, color, or style. It may also exist with respect to the conditions surrounding its sale. In retail trade, to take only one instance, these conditions include such factors as the convenience of the seller's location, the general tone or character of his establishment, his way of doing business, his reputation for fair dealing, courtesy, efficiency, and all the personal links which attach his customers either to himself or to those employed by him. In so far as these and other intangible factors vary from seller to seller, the "product" in each case is different, for buyers take them into account, more or less, and may be regarded as purchasing them along with the commodity itself. When these two aspects of differentiation are held in mind, it is evident that virtually all products are differentiated, at least slightly, and that over a wide range of economic activity differentiation is of considerable importance.

In explanation of the adjustment of economic forces over this field, economic theory has offered (a) a theory of competition, and (b) a theory of monopoly. If the product is fairly individual, as the services of an electric street railway, or if it has the legal stamp of patent or a copyright, it is usually regarded as a monopoly. On the other hand, if it stands out less clearly from other "products " in a general class, it is grouped with them and regarded as part of an industry or field of economic activity which is essentially competitive. Thus, although patents are usually classed as monopolies, trademarks are more often looked upon as conferring a lesser degree of individuality to a product, and hence as quite compatible with competition (sometimes even as requisite to it). By this dispensation, the value of patented goods is explained in terms of the monopolist's maximizing his total profit within the market which he controls, whereas that of trade-marked goods is described in terms of an equilibrium between demand and supply over a much wider field. All value problems are relegated to one category or the other according to their predominant element; the partial check exerted by the other is ignored.

This procedure has led to a manner of thinking which goes even further and denies the very existence of the supposedly minor element. Monopoly and competition are very generally regarded, not simply as antithetical, but as mutually exclusive. To demonstrate competition is to prove the absence of monopoly, and vice versa. Indeed, to many the very phrase "monopolistic competition" will seem self-contradictory—a juggling of words. This conception is most unfortunate. Neither force excludes the other, and more often than not both are requisite to an intelligible account of prices.

## 2. Patents And Trade-marks

The general case for a theory which recognizes both elements concurrently may be presented by inquiring into a particular problem: does any basis really exist for distinguishing between patents and trade-marks? Patents (and copyrights) are ordinarily considered as monopolies. They are granted under the authority vested in Congress by the United States Constitution to secure "for limited times, to authors and inventors, exclusive rights to their respective writings and discoveries." The privilege granted is *exclusive*—the inventor has the sole right to manufacture and sell his invention for seventeen years. The monopoly nature of this privilege is generally recognized both in the literature of patents and in that of general economics. To be sure, the issue is usually not sharply drawn, but one gains the impression that here are instances where the principles of monopoly value are true without qualification.

On the other hand, the competitive element has been pointed out, and it has even been claimed that patents are, in their essence, competitive rather than monopolistic. Vaughn argues that "Patented products may be in competition both with patented and unpatented goods. In fact, the patent law is conducive to competition in that it stimulates individual initiative and private enterprise." Seager points out that "a large number of them [patents] are for the protection of rival processes and serve to stimulate rather than to diminish competition among those employing the different methods." The Committee on Patents in the House of Representatives reported in 1912 that before the era of trusts and combinations in restraint of trade "the monopoly granted by the patent law, limited as it was, in time tended to stimulate competition. It incited inventors to new effort, and capitalists and business men were encouraged to develop inventions. Under these conditions a patent, while granting a monopoly in a specific article, had rarely a tendency to monopolize any branch of the trade, because few inventions were so fundamental in character as to give the owner of patent a monopoly in any branch of the trade, and every great financial success arising from an individual patent was sure to result in rival inventions." The report goes on to demonstrate the competition normally present if patents are separately held, in the following words: "Capital seeking to control industry through the medium of patents proceeds to buy up all important patents pertaining to the particular field. The effect of this is to shut out competition that would be inevitable if the various patents were separately and adversely held." Evidently, when they are so held, the fact that they are monopolies does not preclude their being in competition with each other. Every patented article is subject to the competition of more or less imperfect substitutes.

It is the same with copyrights. Copyrighted books, periodicals, pictures, dramatic compositions, are monopolies; yet they must meet the competition of similar productions, both copyrighted and not. The individual's control over the price of his own production is held within fairly narrow limits by the abundance and variety of substitutes. Each copyrighted production is monopolized by the holder of the copyright; yet it is also subject to the competition which is present over a wider field.

Let us turn to trade-marks. Their monopolistic nature has not been entirely ignored. Says Johnson, "Somewhat analogous to the profits arising from a patent are the profits arising from the use of a trade-mark or from the 'good-will' of a concern." These returns "fall under the general head of monopoly profits." The tone of hesitancy should, however, be noted, for it is characteristic. These profits are not *the same* as those arising from a patent; they are only "somewhat analogous." Ely classifies trade-marks as "general welfare monopolies," and, although "it may be questioned whether they ought to be placed here," he argues that they should be. "They give the use or monopoly of a certain sign or mark to distinguish one's own productions. . . . Of course, another person may build up another class of goods, and may establish value for another trade-mark." He therefore concludes that "it is a monopoly only in a certain line, marking off the goods of one manufacturer." Veblen speaks of monopolies "resting on custom and prestige" as "frequently sold under the name of good-will, trade-marks, brands, etc." Knight puts "in the same category of monopoly. . . the use of trade-marks, trade names, advertising slogans, etc., and we may include the services of professional men with established reputations (whatever their real foundation)." The list might be extended further.

On the other hand, trade-marks and brands are commonly regarded in the business world as a means of enabling one seller to compete more effectively with another as congruous with and even necessary to competition. The view is implicitly sanctioned in economic literature by a common failure to take any cognizance of trade-marks whatever. They are simply taken for granted as a part of the essentially competitive regime. Frequently patents and copyrights alone are mentioned as monopolies; the implication is that trade-marks are not. A positive stand is taken by the late Professor Young in Ely, *Outlines of Economics,* where the elaborate classification found in Ely, *Monopolies and Trusts,* is reproduced with the significant change that trade-marks are omitted. "Trade-marks, like patents, are monopolies in the strictly legal sense that no one else may use them. But, unlike patents, they do not lead to a monopoly in the economic sense of giving exclusive control of one sort of business." By means of a trade-mark a successful business man " may be able to lift himself a little above the 'dead level' of competition . . . he is able to obtain what might be called a quasi-monopoly. But because his power to control the price of his product is in general much more limited than that of the true monopolist, and because competition limits and conditions his activities in other ways, his business is more properly called competitive than monopolistic."   Against this position it may be urged, first, that single patents, as has been shown, do not ordinarily give exclusive control of one sort of business and do not confer a monopoly in this sense of the term; and secondly, that, even granting that patents do give *more* control, this is simply a matter of degree, reducible to relative elasticity of demand. Both patents and trade-marks may be conceived of as monopoly elements of the goods to which they are attached; the competitive elements in both cases are the similarities between these goods and others. To neglect either the monopoly element in trade-marks or the competitive element in patents by calling the first competitive and the second monopolistic is to push to opposite extremes and to represent as *wholly* different two things which are, in fact, essentially alike.

An uncompromising position as to the competitive nature of trade-marks is found in Rogers, *Goodwill, Trade-Marks and Unfair Trading.* "These things [patents and copyrights] are monopolies created by law. . . A trade-mark is quite a different thing. There is no element of monopoly involved at all. . . A trade-mark precludes the idea of monopoly. It is a means of distinguishing one product from another; it follows therefore that there must be others to distinguish from. If there are others there is no monopoly, and if there is a monopoly there is no need for any distinguishing."   Here explicitly is the dialectic behind the attitude widely prevalent in economic and legal thinking, to which reference has already been made, that monopoly and competition must be regarded as alternatives. Evidently, it applies equally well to patents, for, to paraphrase the argument, no matter how completely the patented article may be different from others, there are always others, and therefore no monopoly. Monopoly becomes, by this reasoning, a possibility only if there is but one good in existence. What is the difficulty? Assuredly, two things may be alike in some respects and different in others. To center attention upon either their likeness or their unlikeness is, in either case, to give only half of the picture. Thus, if a trade-mark distinguishes, that is, marks off one product as different from another, it gives the seller of that product a monopoly, from which we might argue, following Rogers, that there is no competition. Indeed, Rogers himself falls into the trap and refutes his own argument a few pages further on, where, speaking of a buyer's assumed preference for "Quaker Oats," he says, "It is a habit pure and simple, and it is a *brand* habit, a *trade-mark* habit that we and others like us have, and that habit is worth something to the producer of the goods to whose use we have become habituated. It *eliminates competition,* for to us there is nothing 'just as good'." If trade-marks "preclude monopoly" and "eliminate competition," one may well ask the nature of the remainder.

Are there any bases, after all, for distinguishing between patents and trade-marks? Each makes a product unique in certain respects; this is its monopolistic aspect. Each leaves room for other commodities almost but not quite like it; this is its competitive aspect. The differences between them are only in degree, and it is doubtful if a significant distinction may be made even on this score. It would ordinarily be supposed that the degree of monopoly was greater in the case of patents. Yet the huge prestige of value of such names as "Ivory," "Kodak," "Uneeda," "Coca-Cola," and "Old Dutch Cleanser," to cite only a few, is sufficient at least to make one skeptical. It would be impossible to compute satisfactorily for comparison the value of the monopoly rights granted by the United States Government in the form of patents and copyrights, and the value of those existing in the form of trade-marks, trade names, and good-will. The insuperable difficulty would be the definition (for purposes of deduction from total profits) of "competitive" returns, and of profits attributable to other monopoly elements. Allowance would also have to be made for the difference in duration of patents and trade-marks, for the enhanced value of patents in many cases by combination, and for other factors. But merely to suggest such a comparison is to raise serious doubts as to whether the monopoly element in patents is even quantitatively as important as that in trade-marks.

Let us apply the reasoning to the second phase of differentiation mentioned above, that with respect to the conditions surrounding a product's sale. An example is the element of location in retail trade. The availability of a commodity at one location rather than at another being of consequence to purchasers, we may regard these goods as differentiated spatially and may apply the term "spatial monopoly" to that control over supply which is a seller's by virtue of his location. A retail trader has complete and absolute control over the supply of his "product" when this is taken to include the advantages, to buyers, of his particular location. Other things being equal, those who find his place of business most convenient to their homes, their habitual shopping tours their goings and comings from business or from any other pursuit, will trade with him in preference to accepting more or less imperfect substitutes in the form of identical goods at more distant places; just as, in the case of trade-marked articles and of goods qualitatively differentiated, buyers are led to prefer one variety over another by differences in their personal tastes, needs, or incomes.

In this field of "products" differentiated by the circumstances surrounding their sale, we may say, as in the case of patents and trade-marks, that both monopolistic and competitive elements are present. The field is commonly regarded as competitive, yet it differs only in degree from others which would at once be classed as monopolistic. In retail trade, each "product" is rendered unique by the individuality of the establishment in which it is sold, including its location (as well as by trade-marks, qualitative differences, etc.); this is its monopolistic aspect. Each is subject to the competition of other "products" sold under different circumstances and at other locations; this is its competitive aspect. Here, as elsewhere in the field of differentiated products, both monopoly and competition are always present.

Speaking more generally, if we regard monopoly as the antithesis of competition, its extreme limit is reached only in the case of control of the supply of all economic goods, which might be called a case of pure monopoly in the sense that all competition of substitutes is excluded by definition. At the other extreme is pure competition, where, large classes of goods being perfectly standardized, every seller faces a competition of substitutes for his own product which is perfect. Between the two extremes there are all gradations, but both elements are always present, and must always be recognized. To discard either competition or monopoly is to falsify the result, and in a measure which may be far out of proportion to the apparent importance of the neglected factor.

Hence the theory of pure competition falls short as an explanation of prices when the product is (even slightly) differentiated. By eliminating monopoly elements (i.e., by regarding the product as homogeneous) it ignores the upward force which they exert, and indicates an equilibrium price which is below the true norm. The analogy of component forces although not exact, is helpful. Actual prices are no more approximate to purely competitive prices than the actual course of a twin-screw steamship approximates the course which would be followed if only one propeller were in operation. Pure competition and pure monopoly are extremes, just as the two courses of the ship, when propelled by either screw separately, are extremes. Actual prices tend towards neither, but towards a middle position determined with reference to the relative strength of the two forces in the individual case. A purely competitive price is not a normal price; and except for those few cases in the price system where competition is actually pure, there is no tendency for it to be established.

It might seem that the theory of monopoly would offend equally in the opposite sense by excluding the competitive elements. This would be true, however, only in the case of *pure* monopoly, as defined above—control of the supply of all economic goods by the same person or agency. The theory of monopoly has never been interpreted in this way. It applies to particular goods, and as such always admits competition between the product concerned and others. Indeed, we may go so far as to say that the theory *seems* fully to meet the essential requirement of giving due recognition to both elements, and the interesting possibility is at once suggested of turning the tables and describing economic society as perfectly monopolistic instead of as (almost) perfectly competitive. Subsequent chapters will carry the refutation of this view. Meanwhile the issues are clarified by displaying the large element of truth it contains. Let us see upon what grounds it may not be refuted.

### 3. The Economic Order As Perfectly Monopolistic

The essence of monopoly is control over supply. May not the entire field of differentiated product therefore be described in terms of perfect monopolies, one for each seller?

The first objection which may be made is that substitutes exist for many products which are, in fact, virtually the same product; whence it would appear that the element of monopoly, instead of being absolute and perfect, is almost non-existent.

Now, of course, the owner of a trade-mark does not possess a monopoly or any degree of monopoly over the broader field in which this mark is in competition with others. A monopoly of " Lucky Strikes " does not constitute a monopoly of cigarettes, for there is no degree of control whatever over the supply of other substitute brands. But if, in order to possess a perfect monopoly, control must extend to substitutes, the only perfect monopoly conceivable would be one embracing the supply of everything, since all things are more or less imperfect substitutes for each other. There is no reason to stop with the supply of cigarettes any more than with the supply of cigarettes within a certain quality or price range (which would be narrower) or with that of tobacco in all forms (which would be broader). The term "monopoly" is meaningless without reference to the thing monopolized. A monopoly of diamonds is not a monopoly of precious stones, nor, to go still further, of jewelry. Differentiation implies gradations, and it is compatible with *perfect* monopoly of one product that control stop short of some more general class of which this product is a part, and within which there is competition.

Although the idea has never been developed into a hybrid theory of value, it represents, so far, no departure from currently accepted doctrine. Two writers only need be cited. According to Taussig, "Copyrights and patents supply the simplest cases of absolute monopoly by law." Yet he is explicit that "the holder of such a monopoly must reckon with the competition of more or less available substitutes, and thus is compelled to abate his prices and enlarge his supplies more than he would otherwise do." Ely points out that "the use of substitutes is consistent with monopoly, and we nearly always have them. For almost anything we can think of, there is some sort of a substitute more or less perfect, and the use of substitutes furnishes one of the limits to the power of the monopolist. In the consideration of monopoly we have to ask, what are the substitutes, and how effective are they? "

To the conception of economic society as perfectly monopolistic it may be objected, secondly, that, if differentiation is slight, even perfect control over *supply* may give a control over *price* which is negligible or non-existent. This is the ground upon which Professor Young, choosing between alternatives, preferred to call trade-marks competitive rather than monopolistic. Seager also makes control over price an important element in his definition of monopoly. Now a monopolist's control over price may be limited for either of two reasons: first, because his control over the supply is only partial, or secondly, because the demand for his product is highly elastic. If control over the supply is not complete, clearly the monopoly is not perfect, and control over price is only partial. But a highly elastic demand is a limitation of another sort. A monopolist's control over price is never complete in the sense that he can set it without regard for the conditions of demand for his product. It is to his advantage that the demand be inelastic, to be sure, but it is not in accord with general usage to measure the perfection of his monopoly by the degree of its elasticity.

The demand for a good may be so elastic that the seller's best price is little different from that of others selling products almost identical. It may be lower instead of higher, or it may conform to a commonly accepted price for the general class of goods. But the fact that all the producers set the same price does not indicate absence of monopoly, for, as will be shown later, this price will be higher than it would be if the commodity were perfectly homogeneous and sold under conditions of pure competition. Of course, prices might be higher yet if, instead of a monopoly of each different brand, there existed a monopoly of the entire class of product. The more substitutes controlled by any one seller, the higher he can put his price. But that is another matter. As long as the substitutes are to any degree imperfect, he still has a monopoly of his own product and control over its price within the limits imposed upon any monopolist—those of the demand.

Thirdly, it may be objected that distinctive features often give profits which are not excessive 'unreasonable' or above the "competitive level." This is, of course, true, but it has no bearing on the question. Most patents come to nothing; but they are not for this reason competitive. They are worthless monopolies—things nobody wants. Many copyrighted books are unsuccessful, and others, although sold at prices higher than they would be under pure competition, are sold in such small volume that the profits are nominal or wholly absent. It is quite possible for the preferences of buyers to be distributed with rough uniformity among the products of a number of competing sellers, so that all have about the same profits. Monopoly necessarily involves neither a price higher than that of similar articles nor profits higher than the ordinary rate.

In summary, wherever products are differentiated, the theory of monopoly *seems* adequately to describe their prices. Competition is not eliminated from the explanation; it is fully taken into account by the recognition that substitutes affect the elasticity of demand for each monopolist's product.

## 4. Monopolistic Competition

It may now be asked in what respect monopolistic competition differs from this. Is it anything more than a new name, designed to soften a much wider application of the theory of monopoly than has heretofore been made? And if it is more, wherein lies the deficiency of the theory of monopoly, which has just been defended as adequate?

The answers to these questions are fully developed in the chapters to follow. Monopolistic competition is evidently a different thing from either *pure* monopoly or *pure* competition. As for monopoly, *as ordinarily conceived and defined,* monopolistic competition embraces it and takes it as a starting point. It is possible to do this where it would not be possible to take competition as a starting point, for the reason which has just been set forth at such length: that the theory of monopoly at least recognizes both elements in the problem, whereas the theory of competition, by regarding monopoly elements as "imperfections," eliminates them.

The theory of monopoly, although the opening wedge, is very soon discovered to be inadequate. The reason is that it deals with the isolated monopolist, the demand curve for whose product is given. Although such a theory may be useful in cases where substitutes are fairly remote, in general the competitive interrelationships of groups of sellers preclude taking the demand schedule for the product of any one of them as given. It depends upon the nature and prices of the substitutes with which it is in close competition. Within any group of closely related products (such as that ordinarily included in one imperfectly competitive market) the demand and cost conditions (and hence the price) of any one are defined only if the demand and cost conditions with respect to the others are taken as given. Partial solutions of this sort, yielded by the theory of monopoly, contribute nothing towards a solution of the whole problem, for each rests upon assumptions with respect to the others. Monopolistic competition, then, concerns itself not only with the problem of an *individual* equilibrium (the ordinary theory of monopoly), but also with that of a *group* equilibrium (the adjustment of economic forces within a group of competing monopolists ordinarily regarded merely as a group of competitors). In this it differs both from the theory of competition and from the theory of monopoly.

The matter may be put in another way. It has already been observed that, when products are differentiated, buyers are given a basis for preference, and will therefore be paired with sellers, not in random fashion (as under pure competition). but according to these preferences. Under pure competition, the market of each seller is perfectly merged with those of his rivals; now it is to be recognized that each is in some measure isolated, so that the whole is not a single large market of many sellers, but a network of related markets, one for each seller. The theory brings into the foreground the monopoly elements arising from ubiquitous partial independence. These elements have received but fragmentary recognition in economic literature, and never have they been allowed as a part of the general explanation of prices, except under the heading of "imperfections" in a theory which specifically excludes them. It is now proposed to give due weight to whatever degree of isolation exists by focusing attention on the market of the individual seller. A study of "competition" from this point of view gives results which are out of harmony with accepted competitive theory.

# Chapter 18

# Keynes on the Socialization of Investment

Inasmuch as an entire body of macroeconomic theory bears his name, John Maynard Keynes (1883-1946) is certainly one of the most recognized economists of the twentieth century. His international fame as an economist was established almost two decades before the appearance of his revolutionary *General Theory*, however, by his *Economic Consequences of the Peace* (1919), with its baleful but accurate predictions of the consequences of the harsh settlement imposed on Germany by the victors in World War I. Apart from his talents as a theorist, Keynes was also a keen student of financial markets and a shrewd speculator and investor. He not only amassed a personal fortune by financial speculation, he also greatly improved through successful investments the endowment of Cambridge University entrusted to him.

The excerpt presented here is from Keynes's *General Theory*, but as he himself tells us, its treatment is quite different from other parts of that theoretical treatise. Here Keynes discusses the nature, role, and influence of expectations, that slippery element of investment behavior that defies precise, technical treatment. Pay particular attention to Keynes's discussion of the difference between *speculation* and *enterprise,* of the upside and downside of highly-developed financial markets, and the importance he places on psychology, or what he refers to as "animal spirits." Note also, his concluding remarks, which predict an incresing role for the State in directing investment decisions.

Source:　Keynes, J. M. *The General Theory of Employment, Interest and Money.* New York: Harcourt, Brace and Company, 1936. Pages 147-164.

## Chapter 12

### THE STATE OF LONG-TERM EXPECTATION

I

We have seen in the previous chapter that the scale of investment depends on the relation between the rate of interest and the schedule of the marginal efficiency of capital corresponding to different scales of current investment, whilst the marginal efficiency of capital depends on the relation between the supply price of a capital-asset and its prospective yield. In this chapter we shall consider in more detail some of the factors which determine the prospective yield of an asset.

II

It would be foolish, in forming our expectations, to attach great weight to matters which are very uncertain. It is reasonable, therefore, to be guided to a considerable degree by the facts about which we feel somewhat confident, even though they may be less decisively relevant to the issue than other facts about which our knowledge is vague and scanty. For this reason the facts of the existing situation enter, in a sense disproportionately, into the formation of our long-term expectations; our usual practice being to take the existing situation and to project it into the future, modified only to the extent that we have more or less definite reasons for expecting a change.

The state of long-term expectation, upon which our decisions are based, does not solely depend, therefore, on the most probable forecast we can make. It also depends on the *confidence* with which we make this forecast—on how highly we rate the likelihood of our best forecast turning out quite wrong. If we expect large changes but are very uncertain as to what precise form these changes will take, then our confidence will be weak.

The *state of confidence,* as they term it, is a matter to which practical men always pay the closest and most anxious attention. But economists have not analysed it carefully and have been content, as a rule, to discuss it in general terms. In particular it has not been made clear that its relevance to economic problems comes in through its important influence on the schedule of the marginal efficiency of capital. There are not two separate factors affecting the rate of investment, namely, the schedule of the marginal efficiency of capital and the state of confidence. The state of confidence is relevant because it is one of the major factors determining the former, which is the same thing as the investment demand-schedule.

There is, however, not much to be said about the state of confidence *a priori.* Our conclusions must mainly depend upon the actual observation of markets and business psychology. This is the reason why the ensuing digression is on a different level of abstraction from most of this book.

For convenience of exposition we shall assume in the following discussion of the state of confidence that there are no changes in the rate of interest; and we shall write, throughout the following sections, as if changes in the values of investments were solely due to changes in the expectation of their prospective yields and not at all to changes in the rate of interest at which these prospective yields are capitalised. The effect of changes in the rate of interest is, however, easily superimposed on the effect of changes in the state of confidence.

192

# III

The outstanding fact is the extreme precariousness of the basis of knowledge on which our estimates of prospective yield have to be made. Our knowledge of the factors which will govern the yield of an investment some years hence is usually very slight and often negligible. If we speak frankly, we have to admit that our basis of knowledge for estimating the yield ten years hence of a railway, a copper mine, a textile factory, the goodwill of a patent medicine, an Atlantic liner, a building in the City of London amounts to little and sometimes to nothing; or even five years hence. In fact, those who seriously attempt to make any such estimate are often so much in the minority that their behaviour does not govern the market.

In former times, when enterprises were mainly owned by those who undertook them or by their friends and associates, investment depended on a sufficient supply of individuals of sanguine temperament and constructive impulses who embarked on business as a way of life, not really relying on a precise calculation of prospective profit. The affair was partly a lottery, though with the ultimate result largely governed by whether the abilities and character of the managers were above or below the average. Some would fail and some would succeed. But even after the event no one would know whether the average results in terms of the sums invested had exceeded, equalled or fallen short of the prevailing rate of interest; though, if we exclude the exploitation of natural resources and monopolies, it is probable that the actual average results of investments, even during periods of progress and prosperity, have disappointed the hopes which prompted them. Business men play a mixed game of skill and chance, the average results of which to the players are not known by those who take a hand. If human nature felt no temptation to take a chance, no satisfaction (profit apart) in constructing a factory, a railway, a mine or a farm, there might not be much investment merely as a result of cold calculation.

Decisions to invest in private business of the old-fashioned type were, however, decisions largely irrevocable, not only for the community as a whole, but also for the individual. With the separation between ownership and management which prevails to-day and with the development of organised investment markets, a new factor of great importance has entered in, which sometimes facilitates investment but sometimes adds greatly to the instability of the system. In the absence of security markets, there is no object in frequently attempting to revalue an investment to which we are committed. But the Stock Exchange revalues many investments every day and the revaluations give a frequent opportunity to the individual (though not to the community as a whole) to revise his commitments. It is as though a farmer, having tapped his barometer after breakfast, could decide to remove his capital from the farming business between 10 and 11 in the morning and reconsider whether he should return to it later in the week. But the daily revaluations of the Stock Exchange, though they are primarily made to facilitate transfers of old investments between one individual and another, inevitably exert a decisive influence on the rate of current investment. For there is no sense in building up a new enterprise at a cost greater than that at which a similar existing enterprise can be purchased; whilst there is an inducement to spend on a new project what may seem an extravagant sum, if it can be floated off on the Stock Exchange at an immediate profit. Thus certain classes of investment are governed by the average expectation of those who deal on the Stock Exchange as revealed in the price of shares, rather than by the genuine expectations of the professional entrepreneurs. How then are these highly significant daily, even hourly, revaluations of existing investments carried out in practice?

## IV

In practice we have tacitly agreed, as a rule, to fall back on what is, in truth, a *convention*. The essence of this convention—though it does not, of course, work out quite so simply—lies in assuming that the existing state of affairs will continue indefinitely, except in so far as we have specific reasons to expect a change. This does not mean that we really believe that the existing state of affairs will continue indefinitely. We know from extensive experience that this is most unlikely. The actual results of an investment over a long term of years very seldom agree with the initial expectation. Nor can we rationalise our behaviour by arguing that to a man in a state of ignorance errors in either direction are equally probable, so that there remains a mean actuarial expectation based on equi-probabilities. For it can easily be shown that the assumption of arithmetically equal probabilities based on a state of ignorance leads to absurdities. We are assuming, in effect, that the existing market valuation, however arrived at, is uniquely *correct* in relation to our existing knowledge of the facts which will influence the yield of the investment, and that it will only change in proportion to changes in this knowledge; though, philosophically speaking, it cannot be uniquely correct, since our existing knowledge does not provide a sufficient basis for a calculated mathematical expectation. In point of fact, all sorts of considerations enter into the market valuation which are in no way relevant to the prospective yield.

Nevertheless the above conventional method of calculation will be compatible with a considerable measure of continuity and stability in our affairs, *so long as we can rely on the maintenance of the convention.*

For if there exist organised investment markets and if we can rely on the maintenance of the convention, an investor can legitimately encourage himself with the idea that, the only risk he runs is that of a genuine change in the news *over the near future,* as to the likelihood of which he can attempt to form his own judgment, and which is unlikely to be very large. For, assuming that the convention holds good, it is only these changes which can affect the value of his investment, and he need not lose his sleep merely because he has not any notion what his investment will be worth ten years hence. Thus investment

194

becomes reasonably "safe" for the individual investor over short periods, and hence over a succession of short periods however many, if he can fairly rely on there being no breakdown in the convention and on his therefore having an opportunity to revise his judgment and change his investment, before there has been time for much to happen. Investments which are "fixed" for the community are thus made "liquid" for the individual.

It has been, I am sure, on the basis of some such procedure as this that our leading investment markets have been developed. But it is not surprising that a convention, in an absolute view of things so arbitrary, should have its weak points. It is its precariousness which creates no small part of our contemporary problem of securing sufficient investment.

V

Some of the factors which accentuate this precariousness may be briefly mentioned.

(1) As a result of the gradual increase in the proportion of the equity in the community's aggregate capital investment which is owned by persons who do not manage and have no special knowledge of the circumstances, either actual or prospective, of the business in question, the element of real knowledge in the valuation of investments by those who own them or contemplate purchasing them has seriously declined.

(2) Day-to-day fluctuations in the profits of existing investments, which are obviously of an ephemeral and non-significant character, tend to have an altogether excessive, and even an absurd, influence on the market. It is said, for example, that the shares of American companies which manufacture ice tend to sell at a higher price in summer when their profits are seasonally high than in winter when no one wants ice. The recurrence of a bank-holiday may raise the market valuation of the British railway system by several million pounds.

(3) A conventional valuation which is established as the outcome of the mass psychology of a large number of ignorant individuals is liable to change violently as the result of a sudden fluctuation of opinion due to factors which do not really make much difference to the prospective yield; since there will be no strong roots of conviction to hold it steady. In abnormal times in particular, when the hypothesis of an indefinite continuance of the existing state of affairs is less plausible than usual even though there are no express grounds to anticipate a definite change, the market will be subject to waves of optimistic and pessimistic sentiment, which are unreasoning and yet in a sense legitimate where no solid basis exists for a reasonable calculation.

(4) But there is one feature in particular which deserves our attention. It might have been supposed that competition between expert professionals, possessing judgment and knowledge beyond that of the average private investor, would correct the vagaries of the ignorant individual left to himself. It happens, however, that the energies and skill of the professional investor and speculator are mainly occupied otherwise. For most of these

persons are, in fact, largely concerned, not with making superior long-term forecasts of the probable yield of an investment over its whole life, but with foreseeing changes in the conventional basis of valuation a short time ahead of the general public. They are concerned, not with what an investment is really worth to a man who buys it "for keeps", but with what the market will value it at, under the influence of mass psychology, three months or a year hence. Moreover, this behaviour is not the outcome of a wrong-headed propensity. It is an inevitable result of an investment market organised along the lines described. For it is not sensible to pay 25 for an investment of which you believe the prospective yield to justify a value of 30, if you also believe that the market will value it at 20 three months hence.

Thus the professional investor is forced to concern himself with the anticipation of impending changes, in the news or in the atmosphere, of the kind by which experience shows that the mass psychology of the market is most influenced. This is the inevitable result of investment markets organised with a view to so-called "liquidity". Of the maxims of orthodox finance none, surely, is more anti-social than the fetish of liquidity, the doctrine that it is a positive virtue on the part of investment institutions to concentrate their resources upon the holding of "liquid" securities. It forgets that there is no such thing as liquidity of investment for the community as a whole. The social object of skilled investment should be to defeat the dark forces of time and ignorance which envelop our future. The actual, private object of the most skilled investment to-day is "to beat the gun", as the Americans so well express it, to outwit the crowd, and to pass the bad, or depreciating, half-crown to the other fellow.

This battle of wits to anticipate the basis of conventional valuation a few months hence, rather than the prospective yield of an investment over a long term of years, does not even require gulls amongst the public to feed the maws of the professional; it can be played by professionals amongst themselves. Nor is it necessary that anyone should keep his simple faith in the conventional basis of valuation having any genuine long-term validity. For it is, so to speak, a game of Snap, of Old Maid, of Musical Chairs—a pastime in which he is victor who says *Snap* neither too soon nor too late, who passes the Old Maid to his neighbour before the game is over, who secures a chair for himself when the music stops. These games can be played with zest and enjoyment, though all the players know that it is the Old Maid which is circulating, or that when the music stops some of the players will find themselves unseated.

Or, to change the metaphor slightly, professional investment may be likened to those newspaper competitions in which the competitors have to pick out the six prettiest faces from a hundred photographs, the prize being awarded to the competitor whose choice most nearly corresponds to the average preferences of the competitors as a whole; so that each competitor has to pick, not those faces which he himself finds prettiest, but those which he thinks likeliest to catch the fancy of the other competitors, all of whom are looking at the problem from the same point of view. It is not a case of choosing those

196

which, to the best of one's judgment, are really the prettiest, nor even those which average opinion genuinely thinks the prettiest. We have reached the third degree where we devote our intelligences to anticipating what average opinion expects the average opinion to be. And there are some, I believe, who practise the fourth, fifth and higher degrees.

If the reader interjects that there must surely be large profits to be gained from the other players in the long run by a skilled individual who, unperturbed by the prevailing pastime, continues to purchase investments on the best genuine long-term expectations he can frame, he must be answered, first of all, that there are, indeed, such serious-minded individuals and that it makes a vast difference to an investment market whether or not they predominate in their influence over the game-players. But we must also add that there are several factors which jeopardise the predominance of such individuals in modern investment markets. Investment based on genuine long-term expectation is so difficult to-day as to be scarcely practicable. He who attempts it must surely lead much more laborious days and run greater risks than he who tries to guess better than the crowd how the crowd will behave; and, given equal intelligence, he may make more disastrous mistakes. There is no clear evidence from experience that the investment policy which is socially advantageous coincides with that which is most profitable. It needs more intelligence to defeat the forces of time and our ignorance of the future than to beat the gun. Moreover, life is not long enough; human nature desires quick results, there is a peculiar zest in making money quickly, and remoter gains are discounted by the average man at a very high rate. The game of professional investment is intolerably boring and over-exacting to anyone who is entirely exempt from the gambling instinct; whilst he who has it must pay to this propensity the appropriate toll. Furthermore, an investor who proposes to ignore near-term market fluctuations needs greater resources for safety and must not operate on so large a scale, if at all, with borrowed money—a further reason for the higher return from the pastime to a given stock of intelligence and resources. Finally it is the long-term investor, he who most promotes the public interest, who will in practice come in for most criticism, wherever investment funds are managed by committees or boards or banks. For it is in the essence of his behaviour that he should be eccentric, unconventional and rash in the eyes of average opinion. If he is successful, that will only confirm the general belief in his rashness; and if in the short run he is unsuccessful, which is very likely, he will not receive much mercy. Worldly wisdom teaches that it is better for reputation to fail conventionally than to succeed unconventionally.

(5) So far we have had chiefly in mind the state of confidence of the speculator or speculative investor himself and may have seemed to be tacitly assuming that, if he himself is satisfied with the prospects, he has unlimited command over money at the market rate of interest. This is, of course, not the case. Thus we must also take account of the other facet of the state of confidence, namely, the confidence of the lending institutions towards those who seek to borrow from them, sometimes described as the state of credit. A collapse in the price of equities, which has had disastrous reactions on the marginal efficiency of

capital, may have been due to the weakening either of speculative confidence or of the state of credit. But whereas the weakening of either is enough to cause a collapse, recovery requires the revival of *both*. For whilst the weakening of credit is sufficient to bring about a collapse, its strengthening, though a necessary condition of recovery, is not a sufficient condition.

VI

These considerations should not lie beyond the purview of the economist. But they must be relegated to their right perspective. If I may be allowed to appropriate the term *speculation* for the activity of forecasting the psychology of the market, and the term *enterprise* for the activity of forecasting the prospective yield of assets over their whole life, it is by no means always the case that speculation predominates over enterprise. As the organisation of investment markets improves, the risk of the predominance of speculation does, however, increase. In one of the greatest investment markets in the world, namely, New York, the influence of speculation (in the above sense) is enormous. Even outside the field of finance, Americans are apt to be unduly interested in discovering what average opinion believes average opinion to be; and this national weakness finds its nemesis in the stock market. It is rare, one is told, for an American to invest, as many Englishmen still do, "for income"; and he will not readily purchase an investment except in the hope of capital appreciation. This is only another way of saying that, when he purchases an investment, the American is attaching his hopes, not so much to its prospective yield, as to a favourable change in the conventional basis of valuation, *i.e.* that he is, in the above sense, a speculator. Speculators may do no harm as bubbles on a steady stream of enterprise. But the position is serious when enterprise becomes the bubble on a whirlpool of speculation. When the capital development of a country becomes a by-product of the activities of a casino, the job is likely to be ill-done. The measure of success attained by Wall Street, regarded as an institution of which the proper social purpose is to direct new investment into the most profitable channels in terms of future yield, cannot be claimed as one of the outstanding triumphs of *laissez-faire* capitalism—which is not surprising, if I am right in thinking that the best brains of Wall Street have been in fact directed towards a different object.

These tendencies are a scarcely avoidable outcome of our having successfully organised "liquid" investment markets. It is usually agreed that casinos should, in the public interest, be inaccessible and expensive. And perhaps the same is true of Stock Exchanges. That the sins of the London Stock Exchange are less than those of Wall Street may be due, not so much to differences in national character, as to the fact that to the average Englishman Throgmorton Street is, compared with Wall Street to the average American, inaccessible and very expensive. The jobber's "turn", the high brokerage charges and the heavy transfer tax payable to the Exchequer, which attend dealings on the London Stock Exchange,

198

sufficiently diminish the liquidity of the market (although the practice of fortnightly accounts operates the other way) to rule out a large proportion of the transactions characteristic of Wall Street. The introduction of a substantial Government transfer tax on all transactions might prove the most serviceable reform available, with a view to mitigating the predominance of speculation over enterprise in the United States.

The spectacle of modern investment markets has sometimes moved me towards the conclusion that to make the purchase of an investment permanent and indissoluble, like marriage, except by reason of death or other grave cause, might be a useful remedy for our contemporary evils. For this would force the investor to direct his mind to the long-term prospects and to those only. But a little consideration of this expedient brings us up against a dilemma, and shows us how the liquidity of investment markets often facilitates, though it sometimes impedes, the course of new investment. For the fact that each individual investor flatters himself that his commitment is "liquid" (though this cannot be true for all investors collectively) calms his nerves and makes him much more willing to run a risk. If individual purchases of investments were rendered illiquid, this might seriously impede new investment, so long as *alternative ways* in which to hold his savings are available to the individual. This is the dilemma. So long as it is open to the individual to employ his wealth in hoarding or lending *money,* the alternative of purchasing actual capital assets cannot be rendered sufficiently attractive (especially to the man who does not manage the capital assets and knows very little about them), except by organising markets wherein these assets can be easily realised for money.

The only radical cure for the crises of confidence which afflict the economic life of the modern world would be to allow the individual no choice between consuming his income and ordering the production of the specific capital-asset which, even though it be on precarious evidence, impresses him as the most promising investment available to him. It might be that, at times when he was more than usually assailed by doubts concerning the future, he would turn in his perplexity towards more consumption and less new investment. But that would avoid the disastrous, cumulative and far-reaching repercussions of its being open to him, when thus assailed by doubts, to spend his income neither on the one nor on the other.

Those who have emphasised the social dangers of the hoarding of money have, of course, had something similar to the above in mind. But they have overlooked the possibility that the phenomenon can occur without any change, or at least any commensurate change, in the hoarding of money.

## VII

Even apart from the instability due to speculation, there is the instability due to the characteristic of human nature that a large proportion of our positive activities depend on spontaneous optimism rather than on a mathematical expectation, whether moral or hedonistic or economic. Most, probably, of our decisions to do something positive, the full consequences of which will be drawn out over many days to come, can only be taken as a result of animal spirits—of a spontaneous urge to action rather than inaction, and not as the outcome of a weighted average of quantitative benefits multiplied by quantitative probabilities. Enterprise only pretends to itself to be mainly actuated by the statements in its own prospectus, however candid and sincere. Only a little more than an expedition to the South Pole, is it based on an exact calculation of benefits to come. Thus if the animal spirits are dimmed and the spontaneous optimism falters, leaving us to depend on nothing but a mathematical expectation, enterprise will fade and die; though fears of loss may have a basis no more reasonable than hopes of profit had before.

It is safe to say that enterprise which depends on hopes stretching into the future benefits the community as a whole. But individual initiative will only be adequate when reasonable calculation is supplemented and supported by animal spirits, so that the thought of ultimate loss which often overtakes pioneers, as experience undoubtedly tells us and them, is put aside as a healthy man puts aside the expectation of death.

This means, unfortunately, not only that slumps and depressions are exaggerated in degree, but that economic prosperity is excessively dependent on a political and social atmosphere which is congenial to the average business man. If the fear of a Labour Government or a New Deal depresses enterprise, this need not be the result either of a reasonable calculation or of a plot with political intent; it is the mere consequence of upsetting the delicate balance of spontaneous optimism. In estimating the prospects of investment, we must have regard, therefore, to the nerves and hysteria and even the digestions and reactions to the weather of those upon whose spontaneous activity it largely depends.

We should not conclude from this that everything depends on waves of irrational psychology. On the contrary, the state of long-term expectation is often steady, and, even when it is not, the other factors exert their compensating effects. We are merely reminding ourselves that human decisions affecting the future, whether personal or political or economic, cannot depend on strict mathematical expectation, since the basis for making such calculations does not exist; and that it is our innate urge to activity which makes the wheels go round, our rational selves choosing between the alternatives as best we are able, calculating where we can, but often falling back for our motive on whim or sentiment or chance.

## VIII

There are, moreover, certain important factors which somewhat mitigate in practice the effects of our ignorance of the future. Owing to the operation of compound interest combined with the likelihood of obsolescence with the passage of time, there are many individual investments of which the prospective yield is legitimately dominated by the returns of the comparatively near future. In the case of the most important class of very long-term investments, namely buildings, the risk can be frequently transferred from the investor to the occupier, or at least shared between them, by means of long-term contracts, the risk being outweighed in the mind of the occupier by the advantages of continuity and security of tenure. In the case of another important class of long-term investments, namely public utilities, a substantial proportion of the prospective yield is practically guaranteed by monopoly privileges coupled with the right to charge such rates as will provide a certain stipulated margin. Finally there is a growing class of investments entered upon by, or at the risk of, public authorities, which are frankly influenced in making the investment by a general presumption of there being prospective social advantages from the investment, whatever its commercial yield may prove to be within a wide range, and without seeking to be satisfied that the mathematical expectation of the yield is at least equal to the current rate of interest, though the rate which the public authority has to pay may still play a decisive part in determining the scale of investment operations which it can afford.

Thus after giving full weight to the importance of the influence of short-period changes in the state of long-term expectation as distinct from changes in the rate of interest, we are still entitled to return to the latter as exercising, at any rate, in normal circumstances, a great, though not a decisive, influence on the rate of investment. Only experience, however, can show how far management of the rate of interest is capable of continuously stimulating the appropriate volume of investment.

For my own part I am now somewhat sceptical of the success of a merely monetary policy directed towards influencing the rate of interest. I expect to see the State, which is in a position to calculate the marginal efficiency of capital-goods on long views and on the basis of the general social advantage, taking an ever greater responsibility for directly organising investment; since it seems likely that the fluctuations in the market estimation of the marginal efficiency of different types of capital, calculated on the principles I have described above, will be too great to be offset by any practicable changes in the rate of interest.

# Chapter 19

## Friedman on the Quantity Theory of Money

Milton Friedman (b. 1912), 1976 Nobel Laureate in Economics, gives credence to the idea that good students are the work of good teachers. As a student at Rutgers, Chicago, and Columbia, Friedman studied under such prominent economists as Arthur Burns, Frank Knight, Lloyd Mints, Jacob Viner, Harold Hotelling, J. M. Clark, and Wesley Clair Mitchell. One of the most influential economists of the twentieth century, Friedman has that rare combination of talents that allows him to interpret complex ideas in a seemingly simple way (concentrating on essentials and lucidity of exposition) *and* to interpret simple ideas in a most sophisticated way. The sheer sway of his contributions has been monumental, touching theory and method, microeconomics and macro-economics, domestic and international trade, econometrics and policy. There is hardly a topic of contemporary economic theory or policy that has not been submitted in some way or other to Friedman's deft handling. Nevertheless, it is in the area of monetary economics that Friedman has made his greatest mark. And among his many contributions to this area, his restatement of the quantity theory of money is a shining example of Friedman's firm blend of theory and facts.

One of the oldest ideas in economics, although generally discredited by Keynesian macro theory, the quantity theory of money in the late 1950s was beset by a murky methodology, slim statistical support, and obscure linkages between data and theory. Almost single-handedly, Friedman restored monetary economics to a place of theoretical prominence. He did so first and foremost by restating the quantity theory in terms of the *demand* for money, and by concentrating empirical work on specifying its degree of stability. In his restatement, Friedman presented the demand for money as a portfolio decision with respect to alternative assets rather than a demand related to the flow of transactions and income. In the minds of some economists, this made Friedman a closet Keynesian. Make up your own mind on this issue after reading the following abridged selection.

Source: Friedman, Milton. "The Quantity Theory Of Money—A Restatement," in *Studies on the Quantity Theory of Money*. Chicago: University of Chicago Press, 1956. Pages 3-21.

The quantity theory of money is a term evocative of a general approach rather than a label for a well-defined theory. The exact content of the approach varies from a truism defining the term "velocity" to an allegedly rigid and unchanging ratio between the quantity of money defined in one way or another and the price level also defined in one way or another. Whatever its precise meaning, it is clear that the general approach fell into disrepute after the crash of 1929 and the subsequent Great Depression and only recently has been slowly re-emerging into professional respectability.

Chicago was one of the few academic centers at which the quantity theory continued to be a central and vigorous part of the oral tradition throughout the 1930's and 1940's, where students continued to study monetary theory and to write theses on monetary problems. The quantity theory that retained this role differed sharply from the atrophied and rigid caricature that is so frequently described by the proponents of the new income-expenditure approach  and with some justice, to judge by much of the literature on policy that was spawned by quantity theorists. At Chicago, Henry Simons and Lloyd Mints directly, Frank Knight and Jacob Viner at one remove, taught and developed a more subtle and relevant version, one in which the quantity theory was connected and integrated with general price theory and became a flexible and sensitive tool for interpreting movements in aggregate economic activity and for developing relevant policy prescriptions.

To the best of my knowledge, no systematic statement of this theory as developed at Chicago exists, though much can be read between the lines of Simons' and Mints's writings. And this is as it should be, for the Chicago tradition was not a rigid system, an unchangeable orthodoxy, but a way of looking at things. It was a theoretical approach that insisted that money does matter—that any interpretation of short-term movements in economic activity is likely to be seriously at fault if it neglects monetary changes and repercussions and if it leaves unexplained why people are willing to hold the particular nominal quantity of money in existence.

The purpose of this introduction is not to enshrine or, should I say, inter a definitive version of the Chicago tradition. To suppose that one could do so would be inconsistent with that tradition itself. The purpose is rather to set down a particular "model" of a quantity theory in an attempt to convey the flavor of the oral tradition. In consonance with this purpose, I shall not attempt to be exhaustive or to give a full justification for every assertion .

1. The quantity theory is in the first instance a theory of the *demand* for money. It is not a theory of output, or of money income, or of the price level. Any statement about these variables requires combining the quantity theory with some specifications about the conditions of supply of money and perhaps about other variables as well.

2. To the ultimate wealth-owning units in the economy, money is one kind of asset, one way of holding wealth. To the productive enterprise, money is a capital good, a source of productive services that are combined with other productive services to yield the products that the enterprise sells. Thus the theory of the demand for money is a special topic in the

theory of capital; as such, it has the rather unusual feature of combining a piece from each side of the capital market, the supply of capital (points 3 through 8 that follow), and the demand for capital (points 9 through 12).

3. The analysis of the demand for money on the part of the ultimate wealth-owning units in the society can be made formally identical with that of the demand for a consumption service. As in the usual theory of consumer choice, the demand for money (or any other particular asset) depends on three major sets of factors: *(a)* the total wealth to be held in various forms—the analogue of the budget restraint; (b) the price of and return on this form of wealth and alternative forms; and (c) the tastes and preferences of the wealth-owning units. The substantive differences from the analysis of the demand for a consumption service are the necessity of taking account of intertemporal rates of substitution in (b) and (c) and of casting the budget restraint in terms of wealth.

4. From the broadest and most general point of view, total wealth includes all sources of "income" or consumable services. One such source is the productive capacity of human beings, and accordingly this is one form in which wealth can be held. From this point of view, "the" rate of interest expresses the relation between the stock which is wealth and the flow which is income, so if Y be the total flow of income, and r, "the" interest rate, total wealth is

$$W = \frac{Y}{r}. \tag{1}$$

Income in this broadest sense should not be identified with income as it is ordinarily measured. The latter is generally a "gross" stream with respect to human beings, since no deduction is made for the expense of maintaining human productive capacity intact; in addition, it is affected by transitory elements that make it depart more or less widely from the theoretical concept of the stable level of consumption of services that could be maintained indefinitely.

5. Wealth can be held in numerous forms, and the ultimate wealth-owning unit is to be regarded as dividing his wealth among them (point [a] of 3), so as to maximize "utility" (point [c] of 3), subject to whatever restrictions affect the possibility of converting one form of wealth into another (point [b] of 3). As usual, this implies that he will seek an apportionment of his wealth such that the rate at which he *can* substitute one form of wealth for another is equal to the rate at which he is just willing to do so. But this general proposition has some special features in the present instance because of the necessity of considering flows as well as stocks. We can suppose all wealth (except wealth in the form of the productive capacity of human beings) to be expressed in terms of monetary units at the prices of the point of time in question. The rate at which one form can be substituted for another is then simply $1.00 worth for $1.00 worth, regardless of the forms involved. But this is clearly not a complete description, because the holding of one form of wealth instead of another involves a difference in the composition of the income stream, and it is

essentially these differences that are fundamental to the "utility" of a particular structure of wealth. In consequence, to describe fully the alternative combinations of forms of wealth that are available to an individual, we must take account not only of their market prices which except for human wealth can be done simply by expressing them in units worth $1.00 but also of the form and size of the income streams they yield.

It will suffice to bring out the major issues that these considerations raise to consider five different forms in which wealth can be held: (i) money (M), interpreted as claims or commodity units that are generally accepted in payment of debts at a fixed nominal value; (ii) bonds (B), interpreted as claims to time streams of payments that are fixed in nominal units; (iii) equities (E), interpreted as claims to stated pro-rata shares of the returns of enterprises; (iv) physical non-human goods (G); and (v) human capital (H).

......................................................

6. The tastes and preferences of wealth-owning units for the service streams arising from different forms of wealth must in general simply be taken for granted as determining the form of the demand function. In order to give the theory empirical content, it will generally have to be supposed that tastes are constant over significant stretches of space and time. However, explicit allowance can be made for some changes in tastes in so far as such changes are linked with objective circumstances. For example, it seems reasonable that, other things the same, individuals want to hold a larger fraction of their wealth in the form of money when they are moving around geographically or are subject to unusual uncertainty than otherwise. This is probably one of the major factors explaining a frequent tendency for money holdings to rise relative to income during war-time. But the extent of geographic movement, and perhaps of other kinds of uncertainty, can be represented by objective indexes, such as indexes of migration, miles of railroad travel, and the like. Let u stand for any such variables that can be expected to affect tastes and preferences (for "utility" determining variables).

7. Combining 4, 5, and 6 along the lines suggested by 3 yields the following demand function for money:

$$M = f(P, r_b - \frac{1}{r_b}\frac{dr_b}{dt}, r_e + \frac{1}{P}\frac{dP}{dt} - \frac{1}{r_e}\frac{dr_e}{dt}, \frac{1}{P}\frac{dP}{dt}; w; \frac{Y}{r}; u). \tag{7}$$

......................................................

From Equation (7) the usual quantity theory form, where v is velocity, may be derived as equation (13);

$$Y = v(r_b, r_e, \frac{1}{P}\frac{dP}{dt}, w, \frac{Y}{P}, u) \cdot M. \tag{13}$$

9. These equations are, to this point, solely for money held directly by ultimate wealth-owning units. As noted, money is also held by business enterprises as a productive

resource. The counterpart to this business asset in the balance sheet of an ultimate wealth-owning unit is a claim other than money. For example, an individual may buy bonds from a corporation, and the corporation use the proceeds to finance the money holdings which it needs for its operations. Of course, the usual difficulties of separating the accounts of the business and its owner arise with unincorporated enterprises.

10. The amount of money that it pays business enterprises to hold depends, as for any other source of productive services, on the cost of the productive services, the cost of substitute productive services, and the value product yielded by the productive service. Per dollar of money held, the cost depends on how the corresponding capital is raised whether by raising additional capital in the form of bonds or equities, by substituting cash for real capital goods, etc. These ways of financing money holdings are much the same as the alliterative forms in which the ultimate wealth-owning unit can hold its non-human wealth, so that the variables $r_b$, $r_e$, $P$, and $(1/P)(dP/dt)$ can be taken to represent the cost to the business enterprise of holding money. For some purposes, however, it may be desirable to distinguish between the rate of return received by the lender and the rate paid by the borrower; in which case it would be necessary to introduce an additional set of variables.

Substitutes for money as a productive service are numerous and varied, including all ways of economizing on money holdings by using other resources to synchronize more closely payments and receipts, reduce payment periods, extend use of book credit, establish clearing arrangements, and so on in infinite variety. There seem no particularly close substitutes whose prices deserve to be singled out for inclusion in the business demand for money.

The value product yielded by the productive services of money per unit of output depends on production conditions: the production function. It is likely to be especially dependent on features of production conditions affecting the smoothness and regularity of operations as well as on those determining the size and scope of enterprises, degree of vertical integration, etc. Again there seem no variables that deserve to be singled out on the present level of abstraction for special attention; these factors can be taken into account by interpreting $u$ as including variables affecting not only the tastes of wealth-owners but also the relevant technological conditions of production. Given the amount of money demanded per unit of output, the total amount demanded is proportional to total output, which can be represented by $Y$.

11. One variable that has traditionally been singled out in considering the demand for money on the part of business enterprises is the volume of transactions, or of transactions per dollar of final products; and, of course, emphasis on transactions has been carried over to the ultimate wealth-owning unit as well as to the business enterprise. The idea that renders this approach attractive is that there is a mechanical link between a dollar of payments per unit time and the average stock of money required to effect—it a fixed technical coefficient of production, as it were. It is clear that this mechanical approach is

very different in spirit from the one we have been following. On our approach, the average amount of money held per dollar of transactions is itself to be regarded as a resultant of an economic equilibrating process, not as a physical datum. If, for whatever reason, it becomes more expensive to hold money, then it is worth devoting resources to effecting money transactions in less expensive ways or to reducing the volume of transactions per dollar of final output. In consequence, our ultimate demand function for money in its most general form does not contain as a variable the volume of transactions or of transactions per dollar of final output; it contains rather those more basic technical and cost conditions that affect the costs of conserving money, be it by changing the average amount of money held per dollar of transactions per unit time or by changing the number of dollars of transactions per dollar of final output. This does not, of course, exclude the possibility that, for a particular problem, it may be useful to regard the transactions variables as given and not to dig beneath them and so to include the volume of transactions per dollar of final output as an explicit variable in a special variant of the demand function.

Similar remarks are relevant to various features of payment conditions, frequently described as "institutional conditions," affecting the velocity of circulation of money and taken as somehow mechanically determined—such items as whether workers are paid by the day, or week, or month; the use of book credit; and so on. On our approach these, too, are to be regarded as resultants of an economic equilibrating process, not as physical data. Lengthening the pay period, for example, may save book-keeping and other costs to the employer, who is therefore willing to pay somewhat more than in proportion for a longer than a shorter pay period; on the other hand, it imposes on employees the cost of holding larger cash balances or providing substitutes for cash, and they therefore want to be paid more than in proportion for a longer pay period. Where these will balance depends on how costs vary with length of pay period. The cost to the employee depends in considerable part on the factors entering into his demand curve for money for a fixed pay period. If he would in any event be holding relatively large average balances, the additional costs imposed by a lengthened pay period tend to be less than if he would be holding relatively small average balances, and so it will take less of an inducement to get him to accept a longer pay period. For given cost savings to the employer, therefore, the pay period can be expected to be longer in the first case than in the second. Surely, the increase in the average cash balance over the past century in this country that has occurred for other reasons has been a factor producing a lengthening of pay periods and not the other way around. Or, again, experience in hyperinflations shows how rapidly payment practices change under the impact of drastic changes in the cost of holding money.

...............................................................

14. It is perhaps worth noting explicitly that the model does not use the distinction between "active balances" and "idle balances" or the closely allied distinction between "transaction balances" and "speculative balances" that is so widely used in the literature.

The distinction between money holdings of ultimate wealth-owners and of business enterprises is related to this distinction but only distantly so. Each of these categories of money-holders can be said to demand money partly from "transaction" motives, partly from "speculative" or "asset" motives, but dollars of money are not distinguished according as they are said to be held for one or the other purpose. Rather, each dollar is, as it were, regarded as rendering a variety of services, and the holder of money as altering his money holdings until the value to him of the addition to the total flow of services produced by adding a dollar to his money stock is equal to the reduction in the flow of services produced by subtracting a dollar from each of the other forms in which he holds assets.

15. Nothing has been said above about "banks" or producers of money. This is because their main role is in connection with the supply of money rather than the demand for it. Their introduction does, however, blur some of the points in the above analysis: the existence of banks enables productive enterprises to acquire money balances without raising capital from ultimate wealth-owners. Instead of selling claims (bonds or equities) to them, it can sell its claims to banks, getting "money" in exchange: in the phrase that was once so common in textbooks on money, the bank coins specific liabilities into generally acceptable liabilities. But this possibility does not alter the preceding analysis in any essential way.

16. Suppose the supply of money in nominal units is regarded as fixed or more generally autonomously determined. Equation (13) then defines the conditions under which this nominal stock of money will be the amount demanded. Even under these conditions, equation (13) alone is not sufficient to determine money income. In order to have a complete model for the determination of money income, it would be necessary to specify the determinants of the structure of interest rates, of real income, and of the path of adjustment in the price level. Even if we suppose interest rates determined independently—by productivity, thrift, and the like—and real income as also given by other forces, equation (13) only determines a unique equilibrium level of money income if we mean by this the level at which prices are stable. More generally, it determines a time path of money income for given initial values of money income.

In order to convert equation (13) into a "complete" model of income determination, therefore, it is necessary to suppose either that the demand for money is highly inelastic with respect to the variables in $v$ or that all these variables are to be taken as rigid and fixed.

17. Even under the most favorable conditions, for example, that the demand for money is quite inelastic with respect to the variables in $v$, equation (13) gives at most a theory of money income: it then says that changes in money income mirror changes in the nominal quantity of money. But it tells nothing about how much of any change in $Y$ is reflected in real output and how much in prices. To infer this requires bringing in outside information,

as, for example, that real output is at its feasible maximum, in which case any increase in money would produce the same or a larger percentage increase in prices; and so on.

18. In light of the preceding exposition, the question arises what it means to say that someone is or is not a "quantity theorist." Almost every economist will accept the general lines of the preceding analysis on a purely formal and abstract level, although each would doubtless choose to express it differently in detail. Yet there clearly are deep and fundamental differences about the importance of this analysis for the understanding of short and long-term movements in general economic activity. This difference of opinion arises with respect to three different issues: (i) the stability and importance of the demand function for money; (ii) the independence of the factors affecting demand and supply; and (iii) the form of the demand function or related functions.

(i) The quantity theorist accepts the empirical hypothesis that the demand for money is highly stable—more stable than functions such as the consumption function that are offered as alternative key relations. This hypothesis needs to be hedged on both sides. On the one side, the quantity theorist need not, and generally does not, mean that the real quantity of money demanded per unit of output, or the velocity of circulation of money, is to be regarded as numerically constant over time; he does not, for example, regard it as a contradiction to the stability of the demand for money that the velocity of circulation of money rises drastically during hyperinflations. For the stability he expects is in the functional relation between the quantity of money demanded and the variables that determine it, and the sharp rise in the velocity of circulation of money during hyperinflations is entirely consistent with a stable functional relation. On the other side, the quantity theorist must sharply limit, and be prepared to specify explicitly, the variables that it is empirically important to include in the function. For to expand the number of variables regarded as significant is to empty the hypothesis of its empirical content; there is indeed little if any difference between asserting that the demand for money is highly unstable and asserting that it is a perfectly stable function of an indefinitely large number of variables.

The quantity theorist not only regards the demand function for money as stable; he also regards it as playing a vital role in determining variables that he regards as of great importance for the analysis of the economy as a whole, such as the level of money income or of prices. It is this that leads him to put greater emphasis on the demand for money than on, let us say, the demand for pins, even though the latter might be as stable as the former. It is not easy to state this point precisely, and I cannot pretend to have done so. (See item [iii] below for an example of an argument against the quantity theorist along these lines.)

The reaction against the quantity theory in the 1930's came largely, I believe, under this head. The demand for money, it was asserted, is a will-o'-the-wisp, shifting erratically and unpredictably with every rumor and expectation; one cannot, it was asserted, reliably specify a limited number of variables on which it depends. However, although the reaction came under this head, it was largely rationalized under the two succeeding heads.

(ii) The quantity theorist also holds that there are important factors affecting the supply of money that do not affect the demand for money. Under some circumstances these are technical conditions affecting the supply of specie; under others, political or psychological conditions determining the policies of monetary authorities and the banking system. A stable demand function is useful precisely in order  to trace out the effects of changes in supply, which means that it is useful only if supply is affected by at least some factors other than those regarded as affecting demand.

The classical version of the objection under this head to the quantity theory is the so-called real-bills doctrine: that changes in the demand for money call forth corresponding changes in supply and that supply cannot change otherwise, or at least cannot do so under specified institutional arrangements. The forms which this argument takes are legion and are still widespread. Another version is the argument that the "quantity theory" cannot "explain" large price rises, because the price rise produced both the increase in demand for nominal money holdings and the increase in supply of money to meet it; that is, implicitly that the same forces affect both the demand for and the supply of money, and in the same way.

(iii) The attack on the quantity theory associated with the Keynesian underemployment analysis is based primarily on an assertion about the form of (7). The demand for money, it is said, is infinitely elastic at a "small" positive interest rate. At this interest rate, which can be expected to prevail under underemployment conditions, changes in the real supply of money, whether produced by changes in prices or in the nominal stock of money, have no effect on anything. This is the famous "liquidity trap." A rather more complex version involves the shape of other functions as well: the magnitudes in (7) other than "the" interest rate, it is argued, enter into other relations in the economic system and can be regarded as determined there; the interest rate does not enter into these other functions; it can therefore be regarded as determined by this equation. So the only role of the stock of money and the demand for money is to determine the interest rate.

..........................................................

25. One of the chief reproaches directed at economics as an allegedly empirical science is that it can offer so few numerical "constants," that it has isolated so few fundamental regularities. The field of money is the chief example one can offer in rebuttal: there is perhaps no other empirical relation in economics that has been observed to recur so uniformly under so wide a variety of circumstances as the relation between substantial changes over short periods in the stock of money and in prices; the one is invariably linked with the other and is in the same direction; this uniformity is, I suspect, of the same order as many of the uniformities that form the basis of the physical sciences. And the uniformity is in more than direction. There is an extraordinary empirical stability and regularity to such magnitudes as income velocity that cannot but impress anyone who works extensively with monetary data. This very stability and regularity contributed to the

downfall of the quantity theory, for it was overstated and expressed in unduly simple form; the numerical value of the velocity itself, whether income or transactions, was treated as a natural "constant." Now this it is not; and its failure to be so, first during and after World War I and then, to a lesser extent, after the crash of 1929, helped greatly to foster the reaction against the quantity theory.

# Chapter 20

## Hayek on Knowledge in Economics

Friedrich A. Hayek (1899-1992), 1974 Nobel Laureate in Economics, was educated in the Austrian tradition, having attended the lectures of Friedrich von Wieser at the University of Vienna, where he obtained doctorates in law and political science. At the invitation of Lionel Robbins, Hayek began a series of lectures at the London School of Economics in 1931, and subsequently accepted the Tooke Chair at that institution. From his academic base in London, Hayek became an active participant in the debates in England during the 1930s concerning money, capital, and business cycles. Hayek's theory of business cycles was in stark opposition to Keynes's, but in the end it was Keynes's cycle theory that prevailed.

In the late 1930s and early 1940s Hayek turned his research toward the role of knowledge and discovery in the marketplace and toward the methodological underpinnings of the Austrian tradition. The emerging debate over the possibility of economic calculation under socialism formed the backdrop for his contributions in these areas. Menger's description of the *unintended* consequences of evolutionary change led easily to Hayek's conception of "spontaneous order"; and it was a short step from this last notion to the perception of the price system as a communication network.

As you read the following selection, be alert to Hayek's critical distinction between different kinds of knowledge. He contrasts scientific, or theoretical, knowledge (which is the proper concern of the economist) with the knowledge of particular circumstances of time and place (which is the proper concern of market participants). According to Hayek, failure to grasp this distinction can lead to two types of errors. The assumption that economists can assimilate both kinds of knowledge leads to the conclusion that 'rational planning' is superior to the decentralized decision making of the marketplace. And the assumption that market participants can assimilate both kinds of knowledge leads to the conclusion that they can nullify the systematic effects of monetary manipulation through anticipation of such effects (i.e., by 'rational expectations').

Source:  Hayek, F. A.  "The Use of Knowledge in Society," in *Individualism and Economic Order*. Chicago: The University of Chicago Press, 1948. Pages 77-91. Reprinted from the *American Economic Review*, vol. 35 (September 1945), pp. 519-530

What is the problem we wish to solve when we try to construct a rational economic order? On certain familiar assumptions the answer is simple enough. If we possess all the relevant information, if we can start out from a given system of preferences, and if we command complete knowledge of available means, the problem which remains is purely one of logic. That is, the answer to the question of what is the best use of the available means is implicit in our assumptions. The conditions which the solution of this optimum problem must satisfy have been fully worked out and can be stated best in mathematical form: put at their briefest, they are that the marginal rates of substitution between any two commodities or factors must be the same in all their different uses.

This, however, is emphatically *not* the economic problem which society faces. And the economic calculus which we have developed to solve this logical problem, though an important step toward the solution of the economic problem of society, does not yet provide an answer to it. The reason for this is that the "data" from which the economic calculus starts are never for the whole society "given" to a single mind which could work out the implications and can never be so given.

The peculiar character of the problem of a rational economic order is determined precisely by the fact that the knowledge of the circumstances of which we must make use never exists in concentrated or integrated form but solely as the dispersed bits of incomplete and frequently contradictory knowledge which all the separate individuals possess. The economic problem of society is thus not merely a problem of how to allocate "given" resources if "given" is taken to mean given to a single mind which deliberately solves the problem set by these "data." It is rather a problem of how to secure the best use of resources known to any of the members of society, for ends whose relative importance only these individuals know. Or, to put it briefly, it is a problem of the utilization of knowledge which is not given to anyone in its totality.

This character of the fundamental problem has, I am afraid, been obscured rather than illuminated by many of the recent refinements of economic theory, particularly by many of the uses made of mathematics. Though the problem with which I want primarily to deal in this paper is the problem of a rational economic organization, I shall in its course be led again and again to point to its close connections with certain methodological questions. Many of the points I wish to make are indeed conclusions toward which diverse paths of reasoning have unexpectedly converged. But, as I now see these problems, this is no accident. It seems to me that many of the current disputes with regard to both economic theory and economic policy have their common origin in a misconception about the nature of the economic problem of society. This misconception in turn is due to an erroneous transfer to social phenomena of the habits of thought we have developed in dealing with the phenomena of nature.

In ordinary language we describe by the word "planning" the complex of interrelated decisions about the allocation of our available resources. All economic activity is in this sense planning; and in any society in which many people collaborate, this planning, whoever does it, will in some measure have to be based on knowledge which, in the first instance, is not given to the planner but to somebody else, which somehow will have to be conveyed to the planner. The various ways in which the knowledge on which people base their plans is communicated to them is the crucial problem for any theory explaining the economic process, and the problem of what is the best way of utilizing knowledge initially dispersed among all the people is at least one of the main problems of economic policy or of designing an efficient economic system.

The answer to this question is closely connected with that other question which arises here, that of *who is* to do the planning. It is about this question that all the dispute about "economic planning" centers. This is not a dispute about whether planning is to be done or not. It is a dispute as to whether planning is to be done centrally, by one authority for the whole economic system, or is to be divided among many individuals. Planning in the specific sense in which the term is used in contemporary controversy necessarily means central planning direction of the whole economic system according to one unified plan. Competition, on the other hand, means decentralized planning by many separate persons. The halfway house between the two, about which many people talk but which few like when they see it, is the delegation of planning to organized industries, or, in other words, monopolies.

Which of these systems is likely to be more efficient depends mainly on the question under which of them we can expect that fuller use will be made of the existing knowledge. This, in turn, depends on whether we are more likely to succeed in putting at the disposal of a single central authority all the knowledge which ought to be used but which is initially dispersed among many different individuals, or in conveying to the individuals such additional knowledge as they need in order to enable them to dovetail their plans with those of others.

3

It will at once be evident that on this point the position will be different with respect to different kinds of knowledge. The answer to our question will therefore largely turn on the relative importance of the different kinds of knowledge: those more likely to be at the disposal of particular individuals and those which we should with greater confidence expect to find in the possession of an authority made up of suitably chosen experts. If it is today so widely assumed that the latter will be in a better position, this is because one kind of knowledge, namely, scientific knowledge, occupies now so prominent a place in public imagination that we tend to forget that it is not the only kind that is relevant. It may be admitted that, as far as scientific knowledge is concerned, a body of suitably chosen experts may be in the best position to command all the best knowledge available though this is of course merely shifting the difficulty to the problem of selecting the experts. What I wish to point out is that, even assuming that this problem can be readily solved, it is only a small part of the wider problem.

Today it is almost heresy to suggest that scientific knowledge is not the sum of all knowledge. But a little reflection will show that there is beyond question a body of very important but unorganized knowledge which cannot possibly be called scientific in the sense of knowledge of general rules: the knowledge of the particular circumstances of time and place. It is with respect to this that practically every individual has some advantage over all others because he possesses unique information of which beneficial use might be made, but of which use can be made only if the decisions depending on it are left to him or are made with his active cooperation. We need to remember only how much we have to learn in any occupation after we have completed our theoretical training, how big a part of our working life we spend learning particular jobs, and how valuable an asset in all walks of life is knowledge of people, of local conditions, and of special circumstances. To know of and put to use a machine not fully employed, or somebody's skill which could be better utilized, or to be aware of a surplus stock which can be drawn upon during an interruption of supplies, is socially quite as useful as the knowledge of better alternative techniques. The shipper who earns his living from using otherwise empty or half-filled journeys of tramp-steamers, or the estate agent whose whole knowledge is almost exclusively one of temporary opportunities, or the *arbitrageur* who gains from local differences of commodity prices are all performing eminently useful functions based on special knowledge of circumstances of the fleeting moment not known to others.

It is a curious fact that this sort of knowledge should today be generally regarded with a kind of contempt and that anyone who by such knowledge gains an advantage over somebody better equipped with theoretical or technical knowledge is thought to have acted almost disreputably. To gain an advantage from better knowledge of facilities of communication or transport is sometimes regarded as almost dishonest, although it is quite as important that society make use of the best opportunities in this respect as in using the latest scientific discoveries. This prejudice has in a considerable measure affected the attitude toward commerce in general compared with that toward production. Even economists who regard themselves as definitely immune to the crude materialist fallacies of the past constantly commit the same mistake where activities directed toward the acquisition of such practical knowledge are concerned apparently because in their scheme of things all such knowledge is supposed to be "given." The common idea now seems to be that all such knowledge should as a matter of course be readily at the command of everybody, and the reproach of irrationality leveled against the existing economic order is frequently based on the fact that it is not so available. This view disregards the fact that the method by which such knowledge can be made as widely available as possible is precisely the problem to which we have to find an answer.

4

If it is fashionable today to minimize the importance of the knowledge of the particular circumstances of time and place, this is closely connected with the smaller importance which is now attached to change as such. Indeed, there are few points on which the assumptions made (usually only implicitly) by the "planners" differ from those of their opponents as much as with regard to the significance and frequency of, changes which will make substantial alterations of production plans necessary. Of course, if detailed economic plans could be laid down for fairly long periods in advance and then closely adhered to, so that no further economic decisions of importance would be required, the task of drawing up a comprehensive plan governing all economic activity would be much less formidable.

It is, perhaps, worth stressing that economic problems arise always and only in consequence of change. As long as things continue as before, or at least as they were expected to, there arise no new problems requiring a decision, no need to form a new plan. The belief that changes, or at least day-to-day adjustments, have become less important in modern times implies the contention that economic problems also have become less important. This belief in the decreasing importance of change is, for that reason, usually held by the same people who argue that the importance of economic considerations has been driven into the background by the growing importance of technological knowledge.

Is it true that, with the elaborate apparatus of modern production, economic decisions are required only at long intervals, as when a new factory is to be erected or a new process to be introduced ? Is it true that, once a plant has been built, the rest is all more or less mechanical, determined by the character of the plant, and leaving little to be changed in adapting to the ever changing circumstances of the moment ?

The fairly widespread belief in the affirmative is not, as far as I can ascertain, borne out by the practical experience of the businessman. In a competitive industry at any rate and such an industry alone can serve as a test the task of keeping cost from rising requires constant struggle, absorbing a great part of the energy of the manager. How easy it is for an inefficient manager to dissipate the differentials on which profitability rests and that it is possible, with the same technical facilities, to produce with a great variety of costs are among the commonplaces of business experience which do not seem to be equally familiar in the study of the economist. The very strength of the desire, constantly voiced by producers and engineers, to be allowed to proceed untrammeled by considerations of money costs, is eloquent testimony to the extent to which these factors enter into their daily work.

One reason why economists are increasingly apt to forget about the constant small changes which make up the whole economic picture is probably their growing preoccupation with statistical aggregates, which show a very much greater stability than the movements of the detail. The comparative stability of the aggregates cannot, however, be accounted for as the statisticians occasionally seem to be inclined to do by the "law of large numbers" or the mutual compensation of random changes. The number of elements with which we have to deal is not large enough for such accidental forces to produce stability. The continuous flow of goods and services is maintained by constant deliberate adjustments, by new dispositions made every day in the light of circumstances not known the day before, by B stepping in at once when A fails to deliver. Even the large and highly mechanized plant keeps going largely because of an environment upon which it can draw for all sorts of unexpected needs: tiles for its roof, stationery or its forms, and all the thousand and one kinds of equipment in which it cannot be self-contained and which the plans for the operation of the plant require to be readily available in the market.

This is, perhaps, also the point where I should briefly mention the fact that the sort of knowledge with which I have been concerned is knowledge of the kind which by its nature cannot enter into statistics and therefore cannot be conveyed to any central authority in statistical form. The statistics which such a central authority would have to use would have to be arrived at precisely by abstracting from minor differences between the things, by lumping together, as resources of one kind, items which differ as regards location, quality, and other particulars, in a way which may be very significant for the specific decision. It follows from this that central planning based on statistical information by its nature cannot take direct account of these circumstances of time and place and that the central planner will have to find some way or other in which the decisions depending on them can be left to the "man on the spot."

5

If we can agree that the economic problem of society is mainly one of rapid adaptation to changes in the particular circumstances of time and place, it would seem to follow that the ultimate decisions must be left to the people who are familiar with these circumstances, who know directly of the relevant changes and of the resources immediately available to meet them. We cannot expect that this problem will be solved by first communicating all this knowledge to a central board which, after integrating all knowledge, issues its orders. We must solve it by some form of decentralization. But this answers only part of our problem. We need decentralization because only thus can we insure that the knowledge of the particular circumstances of time and place will be promptly used. But the "man on the spot" cannot decide solely on the basis of his limited but intimate knowledge of the facts of his immediate surroundings. There still remains the problem of communicating to him such further information as he needs to fit his decisions into the whole pattern of changes of the larger economic system.

How much knowledge does he need to do so successfully ? Which of the events which happen beyond the horizon of his immediate knowledge are of relevance to his immediate decision, and how much of them need he know ?

There is hardly anything that happens anywhere in the world that *might* not have an effect on the decision he ought to make. But he need not know of these events as such, nor of *all* their effects. It does not matter for him *why* at the particular moment more screws of one size than of another are wanted, *why* paper bags are more readily available than canvas bags, or *why* skilled labor, or particular machine tools, have for the moment become more difficult to obtain. All that is significant for him *is how much more or less* difficult to procure they have become compared with other things with which he is also concerned, or how much more or less urgently wanted are the alternative things he produces or uses. It is always a question of the relative importance of the particular things with which he is concerned, and the causes which alter their relative importance are of no interest to him beyond the effect on those concrete things of his own environment.

It is in this connection that what I have called the "economic calculus" (or the Pure Logic of (Choice) helps us, at least by analogy, to see how this problem can be solved, and in fact is being solved, by the price system. Even the single controlling mind, in possession of all the data for some small, self-contained economic system, would not  every time some small adjustment in the allocation of resources had to be made go explicitly through all the relations between ends and means which might possibly be affected. It is indeed the great contribution of the Pure Logic of Choice that it has demonstrated conclusively that even such a single mind could solve this kind of problem only by constructing and constantly using rates of equivalence (or "values," or "marginal rates of substitution"), that is, by attaching to each kind of scarce resource a numerical index which cannot be derived from any property possessed by that particular thing, but which reflects, or in which is condensed, its significance in view of the whole means-end structure. In any small change he will have to consider only these quantitative indices (or "values") in which all the relevant information is concentrated; and, by adjusting the quantities one by one, he can appropriately rearrange his dispositions without having to solve the whole puzzle *ab initio* or without needing at any stage to survey it at once in all its ramifications.

Fundamentally, in a system in which the knowledge of the relevant facts is dispersed among many people, prices can act to co-ordinate the separate actions of different people in the same way as subjective values help the individual to co-ordinate the parts of his plan. It is worth contemplating for a moment a very simple and commonplace instance of the action of the price system to see what precisely it accomplishes. Assume that somewhere in the world a new opportunity for the use of some raw material, say, tin, has arisen, or that one of the sources of supply of tin has been eliminated. It does not matter for our purpose and it is significant that it does not matter which of these two causes has made tin more scarce. All that the users of tin need to know is that some of the tin they used to consume is now more profitably employed elsewhere and that, in consequence, they must economize tin. There is no need for the great majority of them even to know where the more urgent need has arisen, or in favor of what other needs they ought to husband the supply. If only some of them know directly of the new demand, and switch resources over to it, and if the people who are aware of the new gap thus created in turn fill it from still other sources, the effect will rapidly spread throughout the whole economic system and influence not only all the uses of tin but also those of its substitutes and the substitutes of these substitutes, the supply of all the things made of tin, and their substitutes, and so on; and all his without the great majority of those instrumental in bringing about these substitutions knowing anything at all about the original cause of these changes. The whole acts as one market, not because any of its members survey the whole field, but because their limited individual fields of vision sufficiently overlap so that through many intermediaries the relevant information is communicated to all. The mere fact that there is one price for any commodity or rather that local prices are connected in a manner determined by the cost of transport, etc. brings about the solution which (it is just conceptually possible) might have been arrived at by one single mind possessing all the information which is in fact dispersed among all the people involved in the process.

6

We must look at the price system as such a mechanism for communicating information if we want to understand its real function  a function which, of course, it fulfils less perfectly as prices grow more rigid. (Even when quoted prices have become quite rigid, however, the forces which would operate through changes in price still operate to a considerable extent through changes in the other terms of the contract.) The most significant fact about this system is the economy of knowledge with which it operates, or how little the individual participants need to know in order to be able to take the right action. In abbreviated form, by a kind of symbol, only the most essential information is passed on and passed on only to those concerned. It is

more than a metaphor to describe the price system as a kind of machinery for registering change, or a system of telecommunications which enables individual producers to watch merely the movement of a few pointers, as an engineer might watch the hands of a few dials, in order to adjust their activities to changes of which they may never know more than is reflected in the price movement.

Of course, these adjustments are probably never "perfect" in the sense in which the economist conceives of them in his equilibrium analysis. But I fear that our theoretical habits of approaching the problem with the assumption of more or less perfect knowledge on the part of almost everyone has made us somewhat blind to the true function of the price mechanism and led us to apply rather misleading standards in judging its efficiency. The marvel is that in a case like that of a scarcity of one raw material, without an order being issued, without more than perhaps a handful of people knowing the cause, tens of thousands of people whose identity could not k ascertained by months of investigation, are made to use the material or its products more sparingly; that is, they move in the right direction. This is enough of a marvel even if, in a constantly changing world, not all will hit it off so perfectly that their profit rates will always be maintained at the same even or "normal" level.

I have deliberately used the word "marvel" to shock the reader out of the complacency with which we often take the working of this mechanism for granted. I am convinced that if it were the result of deliberate human design, and if the people guided by the price changes understood that their decisions have significance far beyond their immediate aim, this mechanism would have been acclaimed as one of the greatest triumphs of the human mind. Its misfortune is the double one that it is not the product of human design and that the people guided by it usually do not know why they are made to do what they do. But those who clamor for "conscious direction" and who cannot believe that anything which has evolved without design (and even without our understanding it) should solve problems which we should not be able to solve consciously should remember this: The problem is precisely how to extend the span of our utilization of resources beyond the span of the control of any one mind; and, therefore, how to dispense with the need of conscious control and how to provide inducements which will make the individuals do the desirable things without anyone having to tell them what to do.

The problem which we meet here is by no means peculiar to economics but arises in connection with nearly all truly social phenomena, with language and with most of our cultural inheritance, and constitutes really the central theoretical problem of all social science. As Alfred Whitehead has said in another connection, "It is a profoundly erroneous truism, repeated by all copybooks and by eminent people when they are making speeches, that we should cultivate the habit of thinking what we are doing. The precise opposite is the case. Civilization advances by extending the number of important operations which we can perform without thinking about them." This is of profound significance in the social field. We make constant use of formulas, symbols, and rules whose meaning we do not understand and through the use of which we avail ourselves of the assistance of knowledge which individually we do not possess. We have developed these practices and institutions by building upon habits and institutions which have proved successful in their own sphere and which have in turn become the foundation of the civilization we have built up.

The price system is just one of those formations which man has learned to use (though he is still very far from having learned to make the best use of it) after he had stumbled upon it without understanding it. Through it not only a division of labor but also a coordinated utilization of resources based on an equally divided knowledge has become possible. The people who like to deride any suggestion that this may be so usually distort the argument by insinuating that it asserts that by some miracle just that sort of system has spontaneously grown up which is best suited to modern civilization. It is the other way round: man has been able to develop that division of labor on which our civilization is based because he happened to stumble upon a method which made it possible. Had he not done so, he might still have developed some other, altogether different, type of civilization, something like the "state" of the termite ants, or some other altogether unimaginable type. All that we can say is that nobody has yet succeeded in designing an alternative system in which certain features of the existing one can be preserved which are dear even to those who most violently assail it such as particularly the extent to which the individual can choose his pursuits and consequently freely use his own knowledge and skill.

7

It is in many ways fortunate that the dispute about the indispensability of the price system for any rational calculation in a complex society is now no longer conducted entirely between camps holding different political views. The thesis that without the price system we could not preserve a society based on such extensive division of labor as ours was greeted with a howl of derision when it was first advanced by Von Mises twenty-five years ago. Today the difficulties which some still find in accepting it are no longer mainly political, and this makes for an atmosphere much more conducive to reasonable discussion. When we find Leon Trotsky arguing that "economic accounting is unthinkable without market relations"; when Professor Oscar Lange promises Professor von Mises a statue in the marble halls of the future Central Planning Board; and when Professor Abba P. Lerner rediscovers Adam Smith and emphasizes that the essential utility of the price system consists in inducing the individual, while seeking his own interest, to do what is in the general interest, the differences can indeed no longer be ascribed to political prejudice. The remaining dissent seems clearly to be due to purely intellectual, and more particularly methodological, differences.

A recent statement by Joseph Schumpeter in his *Capitalism, Socialism, and Democracy* provides a clear illustration of one of the methodological differences which I have in mind. Its author is preeminent among those economists who approach economic phenomena in the light of a certain branch of positivism. To him these phenomena accordingly appear as objectively given quantities of commodities impinging directly upon each other, almost, it would seem, without any intervention, of human minds. Only against this background can I account for the following (to me startling) pronouncement. Professor Schumpeter argues that the possibility of a rational calculation in the absence of markets for the factors of production follows for the theorist "from the elementary proposition that consumers in evaluating ('demanding') consumers' goods *ipso facto* also evaluate the means of production which enter into the production of these goods.''

Taken literally, this statement is simply untrue. The consumers do nothing of the kind. What Professor Schumpeter's *"ipso facto"* presumably means is that the valuation of the factors of production is implied in, or follows necessarily from, the valuation of consumers' goods. But this, too, is not correct. Implication is a logical relationship which can be meaningfully asserted only of propositions simultaneously present to one and the same mind. It is evident, however, that the values of the factors of production do not

222

depend solely on the valuation of the consumers' goods but also on the conditions of supply of the various factors of production. Only to a mind to which all these facts were simultaneously known would the answer necessarily follow from the facts given to it. The practical problem, however, arises precisely because these facts are never so given to a single mind, and because, in consequence, it is necessary that in the solution of the problem knowledge should be used that is dispersed among many people.

The problem is thus in no way solved if we can show that all the facts, if they were known to a single mind (as we hypothetically assume them to be given to the observing economist), would uniquely determine the solution; instead we must show how a solution is produced by the interactions of people each of whom possesses only partial knowledge. To assume all the knowledge to be given to a single mind in the same manner in which we assume it to be given to us as the explaining economists is to assume the problem away and to disregard everything that is important and significant in the real world.

That an economist of Professor Schumpeter's standing should thus have fallen into a trap which the ambiguity of the term "datum" sets to the unwary can hardly be explained as a simple error. It suggests rather that there is something fundamentally wrong with an approach which habitually disregards an essential part of the phenomena with which we have to deal: the unavoidable imperfection of man's knowledge and the consequent need for a process by which knowledge is constantly communicated and acquired. Any approach, such as that of much of mathematical economics with its simultaneous equations, which in effect starts from the assumption that people's *knowledge* corresponds with the objective *facts* of the situation, systematically leaves out what is our main task to explain. I am far from denying that in our system equilibrium analysis has a useful function *to* perform. But when it comes *to* the point where it misleads some of our leading thinkers into believing that the situation which it describes has direct relevance to the solution of practical problems it is high time that we remember that it does not deal with the social process at all and that it is no more than a useful preliminary to the study of the main problem.

# Chapter 21

# Tullock on the Welfare Costs of Tariffs, Monopolies and Theft

The following selection affords an example of *continuity* in the history of economic thought. Certain ideas resonate through the corridors of time, stimulating one development after another, until the sum of the refinements produces a major leap forward. In a certain sense, the field of public choice fits this mold. Adam Smith provided the original premise that monopolies harm society by limiting output and raising prices. Subsequent economists generally accepted this premise, but the first attempt to actually measure the welfare costs of monopoly did not occur until the middle of the nineteenth century, when the French engineer Jules Dupuit explicitly broached this question. Dupuit invented the "welfare triangle," a device later refined by Marshall, and through Marshall's hands it passed into the economist's standard tool kit.

In the reading below, Gordon Tullock underscores the shortcomings of the standard measure of the welfare cost of monopoly by exposing some of the hidden costs that accompany economic transfers. In the process Tullock explains the rationale of "rent seeking", or the general theory of transfer activity. James Buchanan (1986 Nobel Laureate) and Tullock pioneered the field of public choice—which examines the economic motivation of individuals (e.g., politicians) who operate in the public sector rather than the private sector. Public choice improves our understanding of the theory of regulation as well, because economic regulations constitute a legal framework for effecting economic transfers. The seminal idea of the "rent-seeking" paradigm is found near the end of Tullock's article, when he notes that

> Surely we should expect that...potential monopolists would be willing to invest large resources in the activity of monopolizing....The potential customers [of a monopoly] would also be interested in preventing the transfer and should be willing to make large invest-ments to that end. Once the monopoly is formed, continual efforts to to either break the monopoly or muscle into it would be predictable. Here again considerable resources might be invested. The holders of the monopoly, on the other hand, would be willing to put quite sizable sums into the defense of their power to receive these transfers.

Source: Tullock, Gordon. "The Welfare Costs of Tariffs, Monopolies and Theft," *Western Economic Journal*, vol. 5 (June 1967), pp. 224-232.

In recent years a considerable number of studies have been published that purport to measure the welfare costs of monopolies and tariffs. The results have uniformly shown very small costs for practices that economists normally deplore. This led Mundell to comment in 1962 that "Unless there is a thorough theoretical re-examination of the validity of the tools upon which these studies are founded. . .someone will inevitably draw the conclusion that economics has ceased to be important." Judging from conversations with graduate students, a number of younger economists are in fact drawing the conclusion that tariffs and monopolies are not of much importance. This view is now beginning to appear in the literature. On the basis of these measurements Professor Harvey Leibenstein has argued "Microeconomic theory focuses on allocative efficiency to the exclusion of other types of efficiencies that, in fact, are much more significant in many instances."

It is my purpose to take the other route suggested by Mundell and demonstrate that the "tools on which these studies are founded" produce an underestimation of the welfare costs of tariffs and monopolies. The classical economists were not concerning themselves with trifles when they argued against tariffs, and the Department of Justice is not dealing with a miniscule problem in its attacks on monopoly.

## STATICS

The present method for measuring these costs was pioneered by Professor Harberger. Let us, therefore, begin with a very simple use of his diagram to analyze a tariff. Figure 1 shows a commodity that can be produced domestically at the constant cost of $P_1$ and imported at $P_0$. With the given demand and no tariff $Q_0$ units will be purchased at a price of $P_0$. If a prohibitive tariff is imposed $Q_1$ units will be bought at a price of $P_1$. The increase in price, it is argued, is merely a transfer from some members of the community to others, and the only welfare loss is consequently the shaded triangle. The studies purporting to measure the welfare costs of tariffs have simply computed the value of this triangle. From the geometry it is fairly obvious that the amount would normally be small.

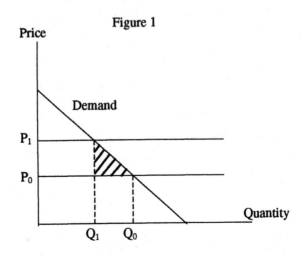

Figure 1

There are a considerable number of costs that are ignored by this procedure. As a starter, collection of a tariff involves expenditure on customs inspectors, etc., who do the actual collection and coast guards who prevent smuggling. Further, customs brokers are normally hired by the shipper to expedite the movement of their goods through customs. Normally we pay little attention to collections costs because they are small, but in this case they may well be larger than the welfare triangle which is also small. Thus by simply adding in collection costs we significantly increase the "social cost" of the tariff.

For a more significant criticism of this method of measuring the welfare cost let us apply the procedure to a standard excise tax instead of a tariff. Assume that Figure 1 shows a constant supply cost and a declining demand for some commodity in some country. $Q_0$ units are bought at a price, $P_0$. Now suppose that a tax is imposed, raising the price to $P_1$, and reducing sales to $Q_1$. The welfare cost of this tax is measured by the shaded triangle. But suppose further, that the revenues raised by this tax are completely wasted, building tunnels, for example, which go nowhere. Now the social cost of the total package of tax and wasteful expenditure is the welfare triangle plus the total tax revenue, or the trapezoid bounded by the lines showing cost, the cost-plus-tax, and the demand function. The people buying the product pay more than the cost, but no one benefits from the expenditure. The funds are not transferred because no one benefits from the existence of the tax. The whole economy is poorer not just by the triangle, but by the whole amount of wasted resources.

The tariff involves a similar waste of resources and consequently its social cost cannot be measured simply by the welfare triangle. Figure 1 can also be used to show the foreign and domestic costs of some type of good and the national demand for it. Since domestic cost is higher than the (delivered) cost of the foreign good, none would be produced domestically in the absence of a tariff. $Q_0$ units would be imported and consumed at a price shown by $P_0$. The country now puts on a prohibitive tariff and the higher cost domestic production takes over the complete market. $Q_1$ units are sold at $P_1$. The welfare triangle has been used to measure the welfare cost of this operation. The argument for this procedure is, essentially, that the higher prices paid by the consumers represent a transfer payment, not a real loss to the economy. But who receives this transfer? The owners of the resources now engaged in inefficiently producing the commodity receive no more than they would have received had the tariff never been introduced and they had been employed in other industries. These resources, however, are being inefficiently utilized, and the rectangle between $P_1$ and $P_0$ and bounded by the vertical axis and $Q_1$ measures the social cost of this waste. Thus the total welfare cost of the tariff is the triangle plus the much larger rectangle to its left.

The situation is identical to that which would arise if the government required an established domestic industry to abandon an efficient method of production and adopt an inefficient. This could be graphed on the same diagram, and it would be generally agreed that the welfare loss would not be just the welfare triangle, but would also include the inefficient use of resources required by the governmental regulation shown in the rectangle to the left of the triangle. Since a tariff shifting production from the production of export goods to import-replacement goods where the country has a comparative disadvantage is in fact, a governmental requirement that the goods be obtained in an inefficient manner, the cases are identical. The cost of a protective tariff is the triangle plus the difference between domestic cost of production and the price at which the goods could be purchased abroad.

Let us, however, consider the situation in which there is some domestic production before the imposition of a tariff. Figure 2 shows a commodity part of the consumption of which is imported and part produced domestically. The supply elasticity of the commodity from foreign sources is assumed infinite, but domestic production is carried on in conditions of increasing costs. Without the tariff, the price is $P_0$, domestic producers turn out $D_0$ units, and $Q_0 - D_0$ units are imported to make up the total consumption of $Q_0$. Suppose now, that Mr. Gladstone is prime minister and imposes a tariff on imports and an excise tax of the same amount on domestic production. With the new price, $P_1$, consumers will want only $Q_1$ units, and the shaded triangle measures the excess burden. Domestic production will remain $D_0$, but imports will shrink from $Q_0 - D_0$ to $Q_1 - D_0$. The government will receive a tax revenue equivalent to the entire rectangle bounded by the two price lines, the vertical axis and $Q_1$.

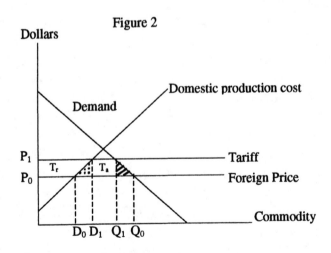

Figure 2

Let us now change our example by assuming that the domestic excise tax is repealed, so that we have only a protective tariff. Domestic consumption and price would remain the same, but domestic production would expand to $D_1$ and imports would shrink accordingly. There would be an inefficient use of resources in producing things which would be better imported represented by the dotted triangle. Governmental revenues would shrink to the rectangle marked $T_a$ and the owners of the resources in the domestic industry would receive an amount of resources equal to the area of the trapezoid $T_r$. Clearly the social cost of the tariff is not just the shaded triangle, but also the dotted triangle which shows a net waste of resources in inefficient production.

## DYNAMICS: THE COST OF TRANSFERS

The trapezoid $T_r$, however, would appear to be a pure transfer, and hence not to be included in the computation of the cost of the tariff. Strictly speaking this is so, but looking at the matter dynamically, there is another social cost involved, and its magnitude is a function of the size of this transfer trapezoid. Generally governments do not impose protective tariffs on their own. They have to be lobbied or pressured into doing so by the expenditure of resources in political activity. One would anticipate that the domestic producers would invest resources in lobbying for the tariff until the marginal return on the last dollar so spent was equal to its likely return producing the transfer. There might also be other interests trying to prevent the transfer and putting resources into influencing the government in the other direction. These expenditures, which may simply offset each other to some extent, are purely wasteful from the standpoint of society as a whole; they are spent not in increasing wealth, but in attempts to transfer or resist transfer of wealth. I can suggest no way of measuring these expenditures, but the potential returns are large, and it would be quite surprising if the investment was not also sizable.

Monopolies involve costs of a somewhat similar nature, and it follows that I will not be able to produce a method to measure their social costs. I will, however, be able to demonstrate that the welfare triangle method greatly underestimates these costs. The argument is customarily explained with the aid of a figure like Figure 1. The monopolist charges the monopoly price $P_1$ instead of the cost $P_0$ for the commodity, and consumption is reduced from $Q_0$ to $Q_1$. The welfare triangle is a clear loss to the community but the rectangle to its left is merely a transfer from the consumers to the owners of the monopoly. We may object to the monopolist getting rich at the expense of the rest of us, but this is not a reduction in the national product.

In order to demonstrate that this line of reasoning ignores important costs I should like to take a detour through the economics of theft. Theft, of course, is a pure transfer, and therefore might be assumed to have no welfare effects at all. Like a lump sum tax, it produces no welfare triangle at all, and hence would show a zero social cost if measured by the Harberger method. This would, of course, be incorrect. In spite of the fact that it involves only transfers, the existence of theft has very substantial welfare costs. Our laws against theft do not deal with a trivial and/or unimportant problem any more than our laws against monopoly.

Figure 3 shows the situation confronting the potential thief. On the horizontal axis is shown the quantity of effort and capital (burglars' tools, etc.) he might invest in a career of crime. On the vertical axis are shown potential returns. The "opportunity cost" line shows the returns he could get for the same investment of work and material in other occupations. It is assumed to be constant. Let us begin by assuming that taking another's property is not illegal. Under these circumstances the returns on various amounts of investment in the activity are shown by line R. The potential thieves would invest the quantity of resources shown at A in theft, the cost to him would be the rectangle AA'DC, and his net return on the investment would be the triangular area above A'D.

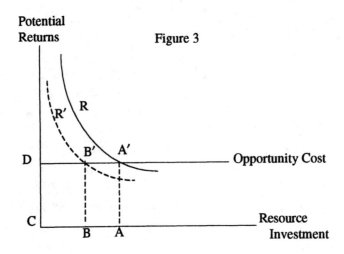

Figure 3

230

The situation of a person who wished to guard his own assets, who might, of course, be the thief hoping to hold onto his loot, may also be shown on Figure 3. On the horizontal axis are shown the resources invested in loss minimizing activities. The cost of each unit of resources put to this use is shown by the horizontal opportunity line, and the savings are on the vertical axis. The line $R$ now shows the returns in the form of savings for each unit of "theft prevention." The total amount of resources invested would again be A.

The two situations are interrelated by more than the fact that they can be shown on the same diagram. The height of the $R$ curve for the thief would depend upon the amount of resources invested by other members of the community in locks and other protections. Similarly, the individual in considering how many locks to buy would find that his $R$ curve depended upon the resources being invested in attempts at theft by the rest of the population. When a potential thief invests money, say, in an improved lock pick, the $R$ curve for people trying to protect their property moves downward. Similarly, hiring an armed guard to watch your valuables moves the $R$ curve for potential thieves down. Putting a new lock on my door reduces the chance that I will be robbed, but whether the gain will be worth the cost will depend upon the effort the thieves are willing to put into getting in. Over time the interaction between the investment in locks, the payoff on lock picks and the investment in nitroglycerin and safes would come to equilibrium.

This equilibrium, however, would be extremely costly to the society in spite of the fact that the activity of theft only involves transfers. The cost to society would be the investments of capital and labor in the activity of theft and in protection against theft. If we consider Figure 3 as representing the entire society instead of individuals, then the social costs would be the area covered by the rectangle AA'DC. Transfers themselves cost society nothing, but for the people engaging in them they are just like any other activity, and this means that large resources may be invested in attempting to make or prevent transfers. These largely offsetting commitments of resources are totally wasted from the standpoint of society as a whole.

This lesson has been learned by almost all societies that have adopted a collective method of reducing this sort of income transfer. This collective procedure, laws against theft and police and courts to enforce them, can also be shown on Figure 3. On the horizontal axis we now have resources invested by police and courts, with their opportunity cost shown as a horizontal line. The "protection" given by each unit of resources invested in these activities is shown by the $R$ line. The society would purchase A amount of protective services, and the total cost would be the usual rectangle. The effect of this would be to reduce the expected returns on theft and the savings to be made by private investment in locks, etc. The new returns are shown by $R'$ on Figure 3, and there is a corresponding reduction in the resources invested in each of these fields to B'. Whether the establishment of a police force is wise or not, depends upon an essentially technological question. If police activities are, for a range, more efficient than private provision of protection, then the $R$ line will have the shape shown, and the police and court rectangle will have an area smaller than the sum of the two "savings" rectangles, for theft and locks. This is, of course, what we normally find in the real world.

Note, however, that we do not carry investment in police protection to the extent that it totally replaces private protective expenditures. Clearly it is more efficient to have some protective expenditures by the owners of property. Automobiles are equipped with locks and keys, presumably because the expansion of the police force which could be paid for from the cost of leaving them off would be less effective in preventing theft than they are. The total social cost of theft is the sum of the efforts invested in the activity of theft, private protection against theft, and the public investment in police protection. The theft itself is a pure transfer, and has no welfare cost, but the existence of theft as a potential activity results in very substantial diversion of resources to fields where they essentially offset each other, and produce no positive product. The problem with income transfers is not that they directly inflict welfare losses, but that they lead people to employ resources in attempting to obtain or prevent such transfers. A successful bank robbery will inspire potential thieves to greater efforts, lead to the installation of improved protective equipment in other banks, and perhaps result in the hiring of additional policemen. These are its social costs, and they can be very sizable.

But this has been a detour through the criminal law, our major subject is monopoly. To return to Figure 1, the rectangle to the left of the welfare triangle is the income transfer that a successful monopolist can extort from the customers. Surely we should expect that with a prize of this size dangling before our eyes, potential monopolists would be willing to invest large resources in the activity of monopolizing. In fact the investment that could be profitably made in forming a monopoly would be larger than this rectangle, since it represents merely the income transfer. The capital value, properly discounted for risk, would be worth much more. Entrepreneurs should be willing to invest resources in attempts to form a monopoly until the marginal cost equals the properly discounted return. The potential customers would also be interested in preventing the transfer and should be willing to make large investments to that end. Once the monopoly is formed, continual efforts to either break the monopoly or muscle into it would be predictable. Here again considerable resources might be invested. The holders of the monopoly, on the other hand, would be willing to put quite sizable sums into the defense of their power to receive these transfers.

As a successful theft will stimulate other thieves to greater industry and require greater investment in protective measures, so each successful establishment of a monopoly or creation of a tariff will stimulate greater diversion of resources to attempts to organize further transfers of income. In Gladstone's England few resources were put into attempts to get favorable tariff treatment. In present day United States large and well financed lobbies exist for this purpose. The welfare cost in the first case was very low, in the

232

second it must be quite sizable. An efficient police force reduces the resources put into the activity of theft, and free trade or an active antitrust policy will reduce the resources invested in lobbying or attempting to organize monopolies.

The problem of identifying and measuring these resources is a difficult one, partly because the activity of monopolizing is illegal. The budget of the antitrust division and the large legal staffs maintained by companies in danger of prosecution would be clear examples of the social cost of monopoly, but presumably they are only a small part of the total. That very scarce resource, skilled management, may be invested to a considerable extent in attempting to build, break, or muscle into a monopoly. Lengthy negotiations may be in real terms very expensive, but we have no measure of their cost. Similarly, a physical plant may be designed not for maximum efficiency in direct production, but for its threat potential. Again, no measure is possible. As a further problem, probably much of the cost of monopoly is spread through companies that do not have a monopoly but have gambled resources on the hopes of one. The cost of a football pool is not measured by the cost of the winner's ticket, but by the cost of all tickets. Similarly the total costs of monopoly should be measured in terms of the efforts to get a monopoly by the unsuccessful as well as the successful. Surely most American businessmen know that the odds are against their establishing a paying monopoly, and they therefore discount the potential gain when investing resources in attempting to get one. The successful monopolist finds that his gamble has paid off, and the unsuccessful "bettor" in this particular lottery will lose, but the resources put into the "pool" would be hard to find by economic techniques. But regardless of the measurement problem, it is clear that the resources put into monopolization and defense against monopolization would be a function of the size of the prospective transfer. Since this would be normally large, we can expect that this particular socially wasteful type of "investment" would also be large. The welfare triangle method of measurement ignores this important cost, and hence greatly understates the welfare loss of monopoly.

# Chapter 22

## Stigler on the Economics of Information

Information, and its role in economizing behavior, was a key theme of the Austrian School, as demonstrated in earlier selections by Menger and Hayek. These earlier treatments have in turn stimulated interest beyond the narrow confines of the Austrian circle. In the following selection, University of Chicago economist George Stigler (1911-1990), 1982 Nobel Laureate in Economics, probes a particular aspect of information that had formerly been neglected, namely the cost of acquiring information. Standard economic analysis tended to ignore these so-called "search costs," which are themselves part of a broader class of costs to which economists have given the name of "transaction costs." Succinctly, transaction costs are the costs that accompany a transaction, other than the outright price of the particular product or service. A buyer, for example, must obtain information about the product's price, quality and availability, in addition to incurring the necessary expenditure of time, effort and money to complete the transaction. Likewise sellers must incur costs in order to provide knowledge about their product (e.g., advertising). Many purchases require additional service costs before they can be completed (e.g., legal fees, delivery charges, etc.). All of these "additional" costs are transaction costs. Despite their inevitablilty, this category of costs was slow in entering the main body of economic analysis.

The mathematical embellishments of Stigler's argument notwithstanding, his central point is clear enough: the acquisition of information is costly, and in general, individuals will engage in search for more information until the added cost of search is equated to its expected marginal return. Note how Stigler's inquiry starts with a commonplace of experience and leads logically to the enumeration of certain *determinants* of search. These determinants are related to the magnitude of the purchase price, the frequency of repetitive purchases, and the geographical size of the market.

Source:   Stigler, G. J. "The Economics of Information," *Journal of Political Economy*, vol. 69 (June 1961), pp. 213-224.

One should hardly have to tell academicians that information is a valuable resource: knowledge is power. And yet it occupies a slum dwelling in the town of economics. Mostly it is ignored: the best technology is assumed to be known; the relationship of commodities to consumer preferences is a datum. And one of the information producing industries, advertising, is treated with a hostility that economists normally reserve for tariffs or monopolists.

There are a great many problems in economics for which this neglect of ignorance is no doubt permissible or even desirable. But there are some for which this is not true, and I hope to show that some important aspects of economic organization take on a new meaning when they are considered from the viewpoint of the search for information. In the present paper I shall attempt to analyze systematically one important problem of information—the ascertainment of market price.

## I. THE NATURE OF SEARCH

Prices change with varying frequency in all markets, and, unless a market is completely centralized, no one will know all the prices which various sellers (or buyers) quote at any given time.  A buyer (or seller) who wishes to ascertain the most favorable price must canvass various sellers (or buyers)—a phenomenon I shall term "search."

The amount of dispersion of asking prices of sellers is a problem to be discussed later, but it is important to emphasize immediately the fact that dispersion is ubiquitous even for homogeneous goods. Two examples of asking prices, of consumer and producer goods respectively, are displayed in Table 1. The automobile prices (for an identical model) were those quoted with an average amount of "higgling": their average was $2,436, their range from $2,350 to $2,515, and their standard deviation $42. The prices for anthracite coal were bids for federal government purchases and had a mean of $16.90 per ton, a range from $15.46 to $18.92, and a standard deviation of $1.15. In both cases the range of prices was significant on almost any criterion.

TABLE 1

ASKING PRICES FOR TWO COMMODITIES

A. CHEVROLETS, CHICAGO, FEBRUARY 1959

| Price (Dollars) | | No. of Dealers |
|---|---|---|
| 2,350-2,400 | . . . . | 4 |
| 2,400-2,450 | . . . . | 11 |
| 2,450-2,500 | . . . . | 8 |
| 2,500-2,550 | . . . . | 4 |

B. ANTHRACITE COAL, DELIVERED
(WASHINGTON, D.C.), APRIL, 1953

| Price per Ton (Dollars) | | No. of Bids |
|---|---|---|
| 15.00-15.50 | | 2 |
| 15.50-16.00 | . . . . | 2 |

| | | |
|---|---|---|
| 16.00-16.50 | . . . . | 2 |
| 16.50-17.00 | . . . . | 3 |
| 17.00-18.00 | . . . . | 1 |
| 18.00-19.00 | | 4 |

Price dispersion is a manifestation—and, indeed, it is the measure—of ignorance in the market. Dispersion is a biased measure of ignorance because there is never absolute homogeneity in the commodity if we include the terms of sale within the concept of the commodity. Thus, some automobile dealers might perform more service, or carry a larger range of varieties in stock, and a portion of the observed dispersion is presumably attributable to such differences. But it would be metaphysical, and fruitless, to assert that all dispersion is due to heterogeneity.

At any time, then, there will be a frequency distribution of the prices quoted by sellers. Any buyer seeking the commodity would pay whatever price is asked by the seller whom he happened to canvass, if he were content to buy from the first seller. But, if the dispersion of price quotations of sellers is at all large (relative to the cost of search), it will pay, on average, to canvass several sellers. Consider the following primitive example: let sellers be equally divided between asking prices of $2 and $3. Then the distribution of minimum prices, as search is lengthened, is shown in Table 2. The buyer who canvasses two sellers instead of one has an expected saving of 25 cents per unit, etc.

The frequency distributions of asking (and offering) prices have not been studied sufficiently to support any hypothesis as to their nature. Asking prices are probably skewed to the right, as a rule, because the seller of reproducible goods will have some minimum but no maximum limit on the price he can accept.

TABLE 2

DISTRIBUTION OF HYPOTHETICAL MINIMUM PRICES BY NUMBERS OF BIDS CANVASSED

| No. of Prices Canvassed | Probability of Minimum Price of | | Expected Minimum Price |
|---|---|---|---|
| | $2.00 | $3.00 | |
| 1 | .5 | .5 | $2.50 |
| 2 | .75 | .25 | 2.25 |
| 3 | .875 | .125 | 2.125 |
| 4 | .9375 | .0625 | 2.0625 |
| ∞ | 1 | 0 | 2.00 |

If the distribution of asking prices is normal, the distributions of minimum prices encountered in searches of one, two, and three sellers will be those displayed in Figure 1.

237

## A. NORMAL DISTRIBUTION

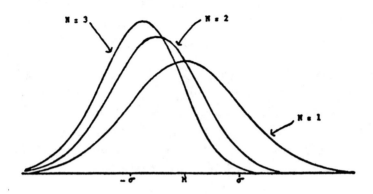

## B. UNIFORM DISTRIBUTION

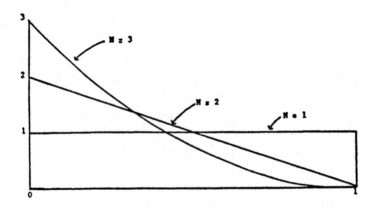

Figure 1. —Distribution of Minimum Prices with Varying Amounts of Search

If the distribution is rectangular, the corresponding distributions would be those shown in Panel B. The latter assumption does not receive strong support from the evidence, but it will be used for a time because of its algebraic simplicity.

In fact, if sellers' asking prices ($p$) are uniformly distributed between zero and one, it can be shown that: (1) The distribution of minimum prices with n searches is

$$n(1-p)^{n-1}, \tag{1}$$

2) the average minimum price is

$$\frac{1}{n+1},$$

and (3) the variance of the average minimum price is

$$\frac{n}{(n+1)^2(n+2)}$$

Whatever the precise distribution of prices, it is certain that increased search will yield diminishing returns as measured by the expected reduction in the minimum asking price. This is obviously true of the rectangular distribution, with an expected minimum price of $1/(n + 1)$ with n searches, and also of the normal distributions. In fact, if a distribution of asking prices did not display this property, it would be an unstable distribution for reasons that will soon be apparent.

For any buyer the expected savings from an additional unit of search will be approximately the quantity $(q)$ he wishes to purchase times the expected reduction in price as a result of the search, or

$$q\left|\frac{\partial P_{min}}{\partial_n}\right| \qquad (2)$$

The expected saving from given search will be greater, the greater the dispersion of prices. The saving will also obviously be greater, the greater the expenditure on the commodity. Let us defer for a time the problem of the time period to which the expenditure refers, and hence the amount of expenditure, by considering the purchase of an indivisible, infrequently purchased good say, a used automobile.

The cost of search, for a consumer, may be taken as approximately proportional to the number of (identified) sellers approached, for the chief cost is time. This cost need not be equal for all consumers, of course: aside from differences in tastes, time will be more valuable to a person with a larger income. If the cost of search is equated to its expected marginal return, the optimum amount of search will be found.

Of course, the sellers can also engage in search and, in the case of unique items, will occasionally do so in the literal fashion that buyers do. In this—empirically unimportant—case, the optimum amount of search will be such that the marginal cost of search equals the expected increase in receipts, strictly parallel to the analysis for buyers.

With unique goods the efficiency of personal search for either buyers or sellers is extremely low, because the identity of potential sellers is not known—the cost of search must be divided by the fraction of potential buyers (or sellers) in the population which is being searched. If I plan to sell a used car and engage in personal search, less than one family in a random selection of one hundred families is a potential buyer of even a popular

239

model within the next month. As a result, the cost of search is increased more than one hundredfold per price quotation.

The costs of search are so great under these conditions that there is powerful inducement to localize transactions as a device for identifying potential buyers and sellers. The medieval markets commonly increased their efficiency in this respect by prohibiting the purchase or sale of the designated commodities within a given radius of the market or on non-market days. The market tolls that were frequently levied on sellers (even in the absence of effective restrictions on non-market transactions) were clear evidence of the value of access to the localized markets.

Advertising is, of course, the obvious modern method of identifying buyers and sellers: the *classified* advertisements in particular form a meeting place for potential buyers and sellers. The identification of buyers and sellers reduces drastically the cost of search. But advertising has its own limitations: advertising itself is an expense, and one essentially independent of the value of the item advertised. The advertising of goods which have few potential buyers relative to the circulation of the advertising medium is especially expensive. We shall temporarily put advertising aside and consider an alternative.

The alternative solution is the development of specialized traders whose chief service, indeed, is implicitly to provide a meeting place for potential buyers and sellers. A used car dealer, turning over a thousand cars a year, and presumably encountering three or five thousand each of buying and selling bids, provides a substantial centralization of trading activity. Let us consider these dealer markets, which we shall assume to be competitive in the sense of there being many independent dealers.

Each dealer faces a distribution of (for example) buyers' bids and can vary his selling prices with a corresponding effect upon purchases. Even in the markets for divisible (and hence non-unique) goods there will be some scope for higgling (discrimination) in each individual transaction: the buyer has a maximum price given by the lowest price he encounters among the dealers he has searched (or plans to search), but no minimum price. But let us put this range of indeterminacy aside, perhaps by assuming that the dealer finds discrimination too expensive, and inquire how the demand curve facing a dealer is determined.

Each dealer sets a selling price, $p$, and makes sales to all buyers for whom this is the minimum price. With a uniform distribution of asking prices by dealers, the number of buyers of a total of $N_b$ possible buyers who will purchase from him is

$$N_t = KN_{b''}(1 - p)^{n-1} \tag{3}$$

where $K$ is a constant. The number of buyers from a dealer increases as his price is reduced, and at an increasing rate. Moreover, with the uniform distribution of asking prices, the number of buyers increases with increased search if the price is below the reciprocal of the amount of search. We should generally expect the high-price sellers to be small-volume sellers.

The stability of any distribution of asking prices of dealers will depend upon the costs of dealers. If there are constant returns to scale, the condition of equal rates of return dictates that the difference between a dealer's buying and selling prices be a constant. This condition cannot in general be met: any dealer can buy low, and sell high, provided he is content with a small volume of transactions, and he will then be earning more than costs (including a competitive rate of return). No other dealer can eliminate this noncompetitive rate of profit, although by making the same price bids he can share the volume of business, or by asking lower prices he can increase the rewards to search and hence increase the amount of search.

With economies of scale, the competition of dealers will eliminate the profitability of quoting very high selling and very low buying prices and will render impossible some of the extreme price bids. On this score, the greater the decrease in average cost with volume, the smaller will be the dispersion of prices. Many distributions of prices will be inconsistent with any possible cost conditions of dealers, and it is not evident that strict equalities of rates of return for dealers are generally possible.

If economies of scale in dealing lead to a smaller dispersion of asking prices than do constant costs of dealing, similarly greater amounts of search will lead to a smaller dispersion of observed selling prices by reducing the number of purchasers who will pay high prices. Let us consider more closely the determinants of search.

DETERMINANTS OF SEARCH

The equation defining optimum search is unambiguous only if a unique purchase is being made—a house, a particular used book, etc. If purchases are repetitive, the volume of purchases based upon the search must be considered.

If the correlation of asking prices of dealers in successive time periods is perfect (and positive!), the initial search is the only one that need be undertaken. In this case the expected savings of search will be the present value of the discounted savings on all future purchases, the future savings extending over the life of the buyer or seller (whichever is shorter). On the other hand, if asking prices are uncorrelated in successive time periods, the savings from search will pertain only to that period, and search in each period is independent of previous experience. If the correlation of successive prices is positive, customer search will be larger in the initial period than in subsequent periods.

The correlation of successive asking prices of sellers is usually positive in the handful of cases I have examined. The rank correlation of anthracite price bids (Table 1) in 1953 with those in 1954 was .68 for eight bidders; that for Chevrolet dealers in Chicago February and August of 1959 was .33 for twenty-nine dealers—but, on the other hand, it was zero for Ford dealers for the same dates. Most observed correlations will, of course, be positive

241

because of stable differences in the products or services, but our analysis is restricted to conditions of homogeneity.

As a rule, positive correlations should exist with homogeneous products. The amount of search will vary among individuals because of differences in their expenditures on a commodity or differences in cost of search. A seller who wishes to obtain the continued patronage of those buyers who value the gains of search more highly or have lower costs of search must see to it that he is quoting relatively low prices. In fact, goodwill may be defined as continued patronage by customers without continued search (that is, no more than occasional verification).

A positive correlation of successive asking prices justifies the widely held view that inexperienced buyers (tourists) pay higher prices in a market than do experienced buyers. The former have no accumulated knowledge of asking prices, and even with an optimum amount of search they will pay higher prices on average. Since the variance of the expected minimum price decreases with additional search, the prices paid by inexperienced buyers will also have a larger variance.

If a buyer enters a wholly new market, he will have no idea of the dispersion of prices and hence no idea of the rational amount of search he should make. In such cases the dispersion will presumably be estimated by some sort of sequential process, and this approach would open up a set of problems I must leave for others to explore. But, in general, one approaches a market with some general knowledge of the amount of dispersion, for dispersion itself is a function of the average amount of search, and this in turn is a function of the nature of the commodity:

1. The larger the fraction of the buyer's expenditures on the commodity, the greater the savings from search and hence the greater the amount of search.
2. The larger the fraction of repetitive (experienced) buyers in the market, the greater the effective amount of search (with positive correlation of successive prices).
3. The larger the fraction of repetitive sellers, the higher the correlation between successive prices, and hence, by condition (2), the larger the amount of accumulated search.
4. The cost of search will be larger, the larger the geographical size of the market.

An increase in the number of buyers has an uncertain effect upon the dispersion of asking prices. The sheer increase in numbers will lead to an increase in the number of dealers and, *ceteris paribus,* to a larger range of asking prices. But, quite aside from advertising, the phenomenon of pooling information will increase. Information is pooled when two buyers compare prices: if each buyer canvasses $s$ sellers, by combining they effectively canvass $2s$ sellers, duplications aside. Consumers compare prices of some commodities (for example, liquor) much more often than of others (for example, chewing gum)—in fact, pooling can be looked upon as a cheaper (and less reliable) form of search.

## SOURCES OF DISPERSION

One source of dispersion is simply the cost to dealers of ascertaining rivals' asking prices, but even if this cost were zero the dispersion of prices would not vanish. The more important limitation is provided by buyers' search, and, if the conditions and participants in the market were fixed in perpetuity, prices would immediately approach uniformity. Only those differences could persist which did not remunerate additional search. The condition for optimum search would be (with perfect correlation of successive prices):

$$q\left|\frac{\partial p}{\partial n}\right| = i \times marginal\ cost\ of\ search,$$

where $i$ is the interest rate. If an additional search costs \$1, and the interest rate is 5 per cent, the expected reduction in price with one more search would at equilibrium be equal to \$0.05/$q$—a quantity which would often be smaller than the smallest unit of currency. But, indivisibilities aside, it would normally be unprofitable for buyers or sellers to eliminate all dispersion.

The maintenance of appreciable dispersion of prices arises chiefly out of the fact that knowledge becomes obsolete. The conditions of supply and demand, and therefore the distribution of asking prices, change over time. There is no method by which buyers or sellers can ascertain the new average price in the market appropriate to the new conditions except by search. Sellers cannot maintain perfect correlation of successive prices, even if they wish to do so, because of the costs of search. Buyers accordingly cannot make the amount of investment in search that perfect correlation of prices would justify. The greater the instability of supply and/or demand conditions, therefore, the greater the dispersion of prices will be.

In addition, there is a component of ignorance due to the changing identity of buyers and sellers. There is a flow of new buyers and sellers in every market, and they are at least initially uninformed on prices and by their presence make the information of experienced buyers and sellers somewhat obsolete.

The amount of dispersion will also vary with one other characteristic which is of special interest: the size (in terms of both dollars and number of traders) of the market. As the market grows in these dimensions, there will appear a set of firms which specialize in collecting and selling information. They may take the form of trade journals or specialized brokers. Since the cost of collection of information is (approximately) independent of its use (although the cost of dissemination is not), there is a strong tendency toward monopoly in the provision of information: in general, there will be a "standard" source for trade information.

## II. ADVERTISING

Advertising is, among other things, a method of providing potential buyers with knowledge of the identity of sellers. It is clearly an immensely powerful instrument for the elimination of ignorance—comparable in force to the use of the book instead of the oral discourse to communicate knowledge. A small $5 advertisement in a metropolitan newspaper reaches (in the sense of being read) perhaps 25,000 readers, or fifty readers per penny, and, even if only a tiny fraction are potential buyers (or sellers), the economy they achieve in search, as compared with uninstructed solicitation, may be overwhelming.

Let us begin with advertisements designed only to identify sellers; the identification of buyers will not be treated explicitly and the advertising of price will be discussed later. The identification of sellers is necessary because the identity of sellers changes over time, but much more because of the turnover of buyers. In every consumer market there will be a stream of new buyers (resulting from immigration or the attainment of financial maturity) requiring knowledge of sellers, and, in addition, it will be necessary to refresh the knowledge of infrequent buyers.

...............................................................

The information possessed by buyers, however, is not simply a matter of chance; those buyers who spend more on the commodity, or who search more for a given expenditure, will also search more for advertisements. The buyers with more information will, on average, make more extensive searches, so the value of information will be greater than this last formula indicates.

We may pause to discuss the fact that advertising in, say, a newspaper is normally "paid" for by the seller. On our analysis, the advertising is valuable to the buyer, and he would be willing to pay more for a paper with advertisements than for one without. The difficulty with having the sellers insert advertisements "free" and having the buyer pay for them directly is that it would be difficult to ration space on this basis: the seller would have an incentive to supply an amount of information (or information of a type) the buyer did not wish, and, since numerous advertisements are supplied jointly, the buyer could not register clearly his preferences regarding advertising. (Catalogues, however, are often sold to buyers.) Charging the seller for the advertisements creates an incentive for him to supply to the buyer only the information which is desired.

It is commonly complained that advertising is jointly supplied with the commodity in the sense that the buyer must pay for both even though he wishes only the latter. The alternative of selling the advertising separately from the commodity, however, would require that the advertising of various sellers (of various commodities) would be supplied jointly: the economies of disseminating information in a general-purpose periodical are so great that some form of jointness is inescapable. But the common complaint is much exaggerated: the buyer who wishes can search out the seller who advertises little (but, of course, enough to be discoverable), and the latter can sell at prices lower by the savings on advertising.

These remarks seem most appropriate to newspaper advertisements of the "classified" variety; what of the spectacular television show or the weekly comedian. We are not equipped to discuss advertising in general because the problem of quality has been (and will continue to be) evaded by the assumption of homogeneous goods. Even within our narrower framework, however, the use of entertainment to attract buyers to information is a comprehensible phenomenon. The assimilation of information is not an easy or pleasant task for most people, and they may well be willing to pay more for the information when supplied in an enjoyable form. In principle, this complementary demand for information and entertainment is exactly analogous to the complementary demand of consumers for commodities and delivery service or air-conditioned stores. One might find a paradox in the simultaneous complaints of some people that advertising is too elaborate and school *houses* too shoddy.

..........................................................

*Price* advertising has a decisive influence on the dispersion of prices. Search now becomes extremely economical, and the question arises why, in the absence of differences in quality of products, the dispersion does not vanish. And the answer is simply that, if prices are advertised by a large portion of the sellers the price differences diminish sharply. That they do not wholly vanish (in a given market) is due simply to the fact that no combination of advertising media reaches all potential buyers within the available time.

Assuming, as we do, that all sellers are equally convenient in location, must we say that some buyers are perverse in not reading the advertisements? Obviously not, for the cost of keeping currently informed about all articles which an individual purchases would be prohibitive. A typical household probably buys several hundred different items a month, and, if, on average, their prices change (in some outlets) only once a month, the number of advertisements (by at least several sellers) which must be read is forbiddingly large.

The seller's problem is even greater: he may sell two thousand items (a modest number for a grocery or hardware store), and to advertise each on the occasion of a price change—and frequently enough thereafter to remind buyers of his price—would be impossibly expensive. To keep the buyers in a market informed on the current prices of all items of consumption would involve perhaps a thousandfold increase of newspaper advertising.

From the manufacturer's viewpoint, uncertainty concerning his price is clearly disadvantageous. The cost of search is a cost of purchase, and consumption will therefore be smaller, the greater the dispersion of prices and the greater the optimum amount of search. This is presumably one reason (but, I conjecture, a very minor one) why uniform prices are set by sellers of nationally advertised brands: if they have eliminated price variation, they have reduced the cost of the commodity (including search) to the buyer, even if the dealers' margins average somewhat more than they otherwise would.

The effect of advertising prices, then, is equivalent to that of the introduction of a very large amount of search by a large portion of the potential buyers. It follows from our discussion in Section I that the dispersion of asking prices will be much reduced. Since advertising of prices will be devoted to products for which the marginal value of search is high, it will tend to reduce dispersion most in commodities with large aggregate expenditures.

## III. CONCLUSIONS

The identification of sellers and the discovery of their prices are only one sample of the vast role of the search for information in economic life. Similar problems exist in the detection of profitable fields for investment and in the worker's choice of industry, location, and job. The search for knowledge on the quality of goods, which has been studiously avoided in this paper, is perhaps no more important but, certainly, analytically more difficult. Quality has not yet been successfully specified by economics, and this elusiveness extends to all problems in which it enters.

Some forms of economic organization may be explicable chiefly as devices for eliminating uncertainties in quality. The department store, as Milton Friedman has suggested to me, may be viewed as an institution which searches for the superior qualities of goods and guarantees that they are good quality. "Reputation" is a word which denotes the persistence of quality, and reputation commands a price (or exacts a penalty) because it economizes on search. When economists deplore the reliance of the consumer on reputation—although they choose the articles they read (and their colleagues) in good part on this basis—they implicitly assume that the consumer has a large laboratory, ready to deliver current information quickly and gratuitously.

Ignorance is like subzero weather: by a sufficient expenditure its effects upon people can be kept within tolerable or even comfortable bounds, but it would be wholly uneconomic entirely to eliminate all its effects. And, just as an analysis of man's shelter and apparel would be somewhat incomplete if cold weather is ignored, so also our understanding of economic life will be incomplete if we do not systematically take account of the cold winds of ignorance.

# Chapter 23

## Shackle on What Makes an Economist

Excerpted below is a speech, almost in its entirety, given by George Lennox Sherman Shackle (1903-1992) on the occasion of his appointment as the Brunner Professor of Economics at the University of Liverpool (1951), a post he held until his retirement in 1969. Shackle came to economics relatively late in life. Prior to, and to some extent during, his student days, Shackle worked as a bank clerk and then as a schoolmaster. In 1935 he was able to study under Hayek at the London School of Economics. Influenced by the new work of Keynes, as well as his mentor, Hayek, Shackle concentrated his professional interests on developing a theory of uncertainty, expectations, and investment decisions. His writings encouraged the resurgence of Austrian economics in America during the post-war period, as well as the refinements of Keynesian economics by the post-Keynesians.

Shackle was a writer of great elegance and style, and a person of wit and charm. In this selection he displays all of these traits, while presenting his keen insights into the nature of knowledge in general (and economics in particular), as well as the relation of mathematics to the social sciences, and the proper training of aspiring economists. This reading is as much a fitting way to conclude this volume as it might have been to initiate it--the focus of Shackle's remarks will undoubtedly continue to be of interest to university students and budding economists everywhere and at all times.

Source: Shackle, G.L.S. "What Makes an Economist?" in *Time, Expectations and Uncertainty in Economics: Selected Essays of G. L. S. Shackle*, edited by J. L. Ford. Hants, U.K. Edward Elgar, 1990. Pages 220-242

# What Makes an Economist?

To be a complete economist, a man need only be a mathematician, a philosopher, a psychologist, an anthropologist, a historian, a geographer, and a student of politics; a master of prose exposition; and a man of the world with experience of practical business and finance, an understanding of the problems of administration, and a good knowledge of four or five foreign languages. All this in addition, of course, to familiarity with the economic literature itself. This list should, I think, dispose at once of the idea that there are, or ever have been, any complete economists, and we can proceed to the practical question of what arrangements are likely to provide us with men who will feel not wholly confounded when an important economic decision confronts them.

Thoroughness in attacking this problem requires us, I think, to start by considering the nature of theoretical knowledge in general, then the character and the scope of economic theory in particular. Having seen what kind of intellectual tasks the economist is required to perform with what material, we can hope to show what claims economics can make as a cultivation of the mind and as a background for the administrator and the statesman. And at last we can ask what ingredients the University itself should pour into the mold thus provided by nature and the schoolmaster.

The business of creating theoretical knowledge consists of describing structures which repeat themselves.  Here I use the word *structure* to name the very essence of all knowledge beyond the mere memory of direct impressions from our surroundings. It is our common experience that such impressions are classifiable. To each class we give a name, and then we arrange these names in patterns, linguistic, geometrical, pictorial, and so on, to indicate that impressions belonging to certain classes occur, in some sense, 'together', in logical, spatial, or temporal-sequential association.  The suggestion that some particular associations are repetitive or, we may say, invariant, is called a law or a theory. The paleontologist finds a bone of a certain shape, and his theory tells him that search in the locality will reward him with other bones, of whose sizes and shapes he has a mental image. Here we have structure in a very concrete and obvious form, that of a skeleton. The chemist weighs the water displaced by a piece of some solid, then weighs this piece. The ratio of the two numbers he gets puts him in mind of a whole group of impressions of various classes, color, softness, ease of melting, and so on, suggested by a theory summed up in the word 'lead'. The medical man notes his own headache and the dryness of his skin, and decides that it will be five days before he can work again: influenza is his name for a structure of impressions involving duration. I need not give more examples. We manage our lives on the assumption that under the infinitely various and changeful combinations of particular sights, sounds, scents, savors, and sensations there is a dependable repetitiveness. This kind of invariance of structure is the subject-matter and necessary pre-supposition of all theory.

You will have noticed that, if what I say is true, the materials which compose these structures are words, symbols, or images, and not things which nature gives us direct and ready-made. Some of these words are the names of classes of our impressions of nature, such as length, weight, color; or of crystallized patterns of such impressions, such as gold, flame, man. Some of them are the names not of patterns of receivable impressions but of ghosts or fictions which play a somewhat analogous part in our thinking; gravity and aether for the physicist, gene for the biologist, and so on. Lastly some words are names of different ways in which our impressions of nature, or our constructs from those impressions, can be *related*, the ideas of spatial or temporal relative location, of equality or of greater than or less than, of logical equivalence or definition, and perhaps, more hazardously and elusively, of cause and effect. The phenomena, the classes or the patterns of impressions, having been distinguished, and the possible relations between them conceived, how do we know what relations to postulate between given phenomena? How are the essential shapes of our theoretical structures determined? From the infinite variety of possible shapes the choosing of a few to be tried and used is an act of imaginative and even artistic commitment of a kind which is as near as mortal man can get to ultimate creation.

Some of us may recall the words with which Victorian children were admonished to tell the truth:

> Oh what a tangled web we weave
> When first we practice to deceive.

Any statement, whether we believe it to be true or false, carries implications far beyond what it explicitly says. What it says in so many words may not obviously conflict with some other statement which we accept. But when one or other of these statements is unravelled and interpreted and allowed as it were to grow from the acorn to the oak, so that some of what is latent in it is displayed, then we may find that the two statements in fact contradict each other. When we draw consequences from a set of premises we add nothing to what is already in the premises but merely make what is there more visible and thus easier to compare with other statements. If the agreement is unsatisfactory, we may decide to modify our premises and see, by drawing out the fresh consequences that our new assumptions yield, whether the coherence of our whole system of statements is thereby improved. Thus we seek progressively to satisfy one criterion of a good theory. Now this work of spreading out the content of a statement, of drawing out inferences from a set of premises, is the whole business of logic or mathematics. It is, as we all know, in its higher flights a business demanding very special aptitudes and rare kinds of insight, as well as intensive practice and much knowledge of certain stylized or crystallized forms of thinking, the formal mathematical methods which relieve our memories of part of the weight of long concatenations of argument. This exploration and mutual confrontation of hypotheses is as much a part of theory-making as the invention of the explicit hypotheses themselves.

The building-up of a body of theoretical knowledge calls then for two kinds of intellectual capacity and effort. One of these is imaginative or as we may say creatively selective, and thus creative in a primary and radical sense; the other is analytical or logical, and thus creative only in a secondary, a corrective or completive sense. There is no doubt in my mind that the majority of highly gifted men are specially endowed in one or other of these ways and not in both; when a man has both powers in superlative degree we have an Einstein or a Keynes. The only point I would make here is that we must not suppose analytical power alone is sufficient to make a great theorist. Many men have studied economics whose capacity for handling mathematical tools was by no means inferior to that of Keynes; but they did not produce the Keynesian revolution.

From this glance at the nature of theoretical knowledge in general let me pass to the character of economics in particular.

Explanation is the relating of the unfamiliar to the familiar. The essence and prime purpose of theory or explanation is to show that a large collection of seemingly diverse and unrelated appearances is in truth merely a large number of different views of the same thing, and that thing itself from some viewpoints familiar. Thus, explanation seeks in a sense to reduce the mysterious to the prosaic, and diversity to unity. Now science as a whole will never be able to start its explanations from nothing and carry them through the whole of human experience. A part of that experience must be treated as belonging so essentially to the very nature of human consciousness that men feel no need for any truth interior to these direct intuitions. Science as a unity must of course seek the minimum such basis and on it build up all else step by connected step into a coherent picture of the whole cosmos and of human life. But it would plainly defeat the whole purpose of the division of science into distinct disciplines, if each of these attempted to go right down to the minimum intuitional basis. The chemist assumes that you know what he means by weight and volume, and for an explanation of these refers you to the physicist. The biologist assumes that you know what he means by carbon, hydrogen, and oxygen, and for an explanation of these refers you to the chemist. The economist assumes that you know what he means by hunger and by fertility, and for an explanation of these refers you to the biologist. So there arises the question of the best place for the frontier between one discipline and each of the others, and this is peculiarly troublesome in the case of economics.

Some of you may remember a verse by Edward Clerihew Bentley which explains the difference between geography and biography:

Geography (it says) is about maps
But biography is about chaps.

I doubt whether a geographer would accept the suggestion here that geography is not a human science; it is very largely concerned with human activities. But far more so is economics. Economics is entirely concerned with men's doings and arrangements, their wants and their means of satisfying them, their hopes and fears, beliefs, ambitions, conflicts of interest, their valuations and decisions, their governments and their material well-being. Economics emphatically is about chaps.

Many men have attempted to say in a sentence or a paragraph what economics is about; it is better, in my view, to begin by saying that economics is about human nature, human conduct, and human institutions, and then to say which parts of this huge field the economist is willing to leave to others. Nevertheless he must set up his flag at some particular spot in order to show the kind of ground he wishes to regard as his own; and I think there is still good reason for saying that this spot must be the market-place. Men's conduct and decisions can be influenced in many ways; by threats of violence or duress, by the firing of their spirit and imagination by rhetoric or by example, by the preacher's eloquence and the teacher's toil, or by the blandishments of lovers; but the simplest and most reliable, the commonest and the easiest is to offer them something *in exchange* for what they are required to give or do; and the market-place, in the wide and rather abstract sense in which, of course, I am now using this word, is where exchanges of all kinds take place.

It is by coming together in the market-place that men are able to be *economical*, in the ordinary sense of that word. For it is there that they can find out what other men are most keenly anxious to obtain. If by a *given* sacrifice of ease and leisure I can produce any one of half-a-dozen different things, I shall do best for myself by producing the one that other men most eagerly desire; for that thing, of all the half-dozen, will elicit from them the most effort and sacrifice on my behalf; and thus by studying their interest I shall serve my own, and get the most possible satisfaction in return for a specified amount of effort; and that is precisely what we mean by 'economy'.

If this market mechanism plays a less predominant part to-day than it did forty years ago in answering the questions: How much work of this kind and of that shall be done? How much shall be produced of this stuff and of that? and: In what proportions shall each of these products be shared out amongst those who contributed in one way or another to their making? yet even to-day in western countries it does most of the work of answering those questions, which express between them the core of what is agreed to be the subject-matter of economics. If, then, the economist takes up his stand in the market-place, he is correctly indicating where his interests start from. But they will lead him far afield. What he is watching there is human conduct, and questions will arise in his mind about human motives and human nature. Economists have sometimes come to believe that they can get little help, in understanding the economic aspect of men's actions, from the psychologist. Such a feeling cries out for the most searching examination, since it is on the face of it absurd. This attitude has indeed, in my view, been rendered completely untenable by the development of economic theory itself in the past 20 years. I do not suggest that the fault is all on the side of the economist. Whether the psychologists can meet our needs I am not yet sure, but that we have needs that they ought to meet I am quite certain. Economics is concerned, solely concerned, with some of the manifestations of human nature, and psychology is the science of human nature. Somewhere at the heart of this estrangement there is a mistake which we must try to find. At any rate it is plain that on one side economics has a frontier with psychology, or rather, that there lies between them a no-man's-land crying out to be explored and appropriated, that we might call economic psychics. Here, in my view, interest should center on the workings of the individual mind rather than on the total behavior of huge human aggregates. We need, for example, to understand the processes of forming expectations and making decisions. The famous question of the form of the Keynesian consumption-function rests upon foundations of individual psychology which no one so far has seen fit to explore as a psychologist. By what kind of psychic test does a man detect just that stage in. the day's work at which the fruits of a further half-hour's effort will not quite compensate him for that effort? What scheme of incentives would make him postpone that judgment? A long list of other such questions will occur to every economist. Here indeed is a ripe field for imaginative research, if only the economists will haul up their iron curtain out of sight and seek appropriate help.

I said a moment ago that the market mechanism is no longer the only means by which the practical questions are answered: How much of this and of that shall be produced, by what means, and for whom? But since the manner in which these matters are decided is still the prime concern of the economist, he must study whatever it is that has partly ousted the market from this function. In western countries the individual, nominally and ultimately at least, can still make his contribution to the answering of those questions, but nowadays there is much that he can no longer influence by a continuous direct pressure in the market, where the smallest details of his preferences could be signaled to his suppliers and make themselves felt; there is much that he can only affect at long intervals, in an exceedingly crude and uncertain way, by means of the electoral vote that he can cast for one big bundle of ill-defined, ill-assorted, and changeable policies or another. The whole question of government: its nature, purpose, justification, and detailed working, the source of the authority exercised by statesmen, the basis of society's claim to the individual's acquiescence in its decrees, the justice and admissible scope of the administrator's interference in his life; all this, in a country where the central government takes away from the citizens some two-fifths of their income and spends it on their behalf, must loom large on the economist's horizon, and it is plain that just beyond another part of the boundary of his subject there lies political theory. But a very large part of the whole study of government activities is actually inside his province, and perhaps we are already well on the way to that situation where the Government, rather than the consumer or the enterpriser, will be the economic agent to which the economist will direct most of his attention. The revolutionary change which has come about since 1939 in the relation between the importance, in the economic field, of those impersonal market forces of competition which were the main concern of economists until the thirties, and the importance of those radically different mechanisms by which the inarticulate purposes of a people are channeled and rendered explicit stage by stage via the polling-booth, the parliament, the cabinet-room, and the Whitehall department, has not yet had time to revolutionize our text-books. Still less has there been any recognition in them of that other but closely related revolution whereby the international exchange of goods has become a game for governments, a field for all the arts of diplomacy, negotiation and bargaining, calling for a combination of the talents of the chess-master and the poker-player. It may surprise those of my audience who are not economists to be told that one of the most important and radically novel contributions to economic theory that appeared in the past 10 years was called The Theory of Games and Economic Behaviour. No longer can economic theory be called the pure logic of choice. It is many things besides, and this book has brought into it the pure logic of strategy in the widest sense of that term.

The study of government is the study of institutions, and there are other human institutions, in all three senses of organizations, of practices, and of social inventions or devices, which profoundly influence the character and largely govern the outward forms of the economic process. The most fundamentally important of these is perhaps the device of money, in all its manifold aspects. The history of the evolution of money, I could almost venture to suggest, is a strand in the history of the growth of civilization second in importance only to that of language. Money began as a commodity, and has ended as a system of recording transactions and bringing every act of purchase and sale, of borrowing and lending, of working and producing and consuming, that takes place anywhere in the whole world at any time, into some degree of relation with every other such act. In its tremendous power and radical simplicity this tool of human advancement, money in its basic meaning and role of an accounting system, ranks surely next to the alphabet itself. If, then, such things as money and monetary habits, and all the intricate machinery which has been built on them, are part of the very fiber of man's civilized existence and are things of gradual and painful growth from primitive beginnings, ought not the economist to call in the anthropologist, the student of cultures and social machinery in a general sense, to aid him to understand these things?

Economics is concerned with man; with man as a creature capable of thoughts and feelings, of likes and dislikes, of hopes and fears, of invention and imagination. But, perhaps you will say, all this, no doubt, is what makes him human and distinguishes him from the brute creation; yet he is an animal, and in the last resort his life is conditioned and his survival determined by biological factors; his needs are bodily needs. What has economics to say of hunger, of the body's need for warmth and shelter, of the capabilities of muscles, of the physiological basis of fatigue? Are not these things relevant? The economist will agree that they are, but he will enter a caveat. The sum of human happiness

253

is not arrived at by adding up calories and kilowatts, not reckoning working hours per week. There are people, I am told (I find it hard to believe) who can see nothing in the dancing flames upon the hearth, whose hearts, if they have any, are warmed as well by a hot-water pipe as by all Prometheus' magic. To them, no doubt, an open fire is so many terms per hour wastefully supplied. To the economist the question how most *heat* can be obtained from a given quantity of fuel is irrelevant. He is only concerned to know how most *happiness* can be obtained from it. This happiness may be derived from bodily warmth, or from spiritual comfort and inspiration. Man is the measure of all things. Every object and occurrence that has economic significance derives it wholly from the relation of this object or event to man's desires and beliefs and valuations. Thus although, beyond yet another frontier of economics, there lie engineering, chemistry, agricultural science, and all the gamut of technology, these things are not in themselves the economist's concern. The frontier here is clear and definite. This does not mean, of course, that the economist can dispense with *facts* from the technologist; on the contrary, before he can make economic statements of fact about particular industries in particular places, or give practical advice, he will need such facts in great quantity and detail.

There are yet two more directions in which the economist can look out from his own territory over that of other specialists, and here the frontier is again in doubt. For here he sees geography and history, one partly and the other wholly concerned with man himself. Whenever the economist is asked to give practical advice in the affairs of a nation or an industry, his thoughts will turn at once to his friend the geographer, without whose help he himself, *qua* economist, can say little to the point. All the physical and many of the human factors which should guide the location of industry are matters for the geographer. As for the frontier with history, there is a whole province in dispute. I have the impression that in the past the historians neglected it to their loss, and that it is the economists who on the whole have shown themselves apt to become historians, rather than the historians who have readily put on the spectacles of the economist.

Now, . . . [having] tried to survey very briefly the ground that economics calls its own and the ground of other disciplines whose aid the economist needs or whose findings he must treat as data,...what is the best use for the specialist years at school? This is, I think, only a question of expediency and not of principle. But to answer it we must consider a question that perhaps should have come earlier in this lecture. In short, why study economics?

First, because as an ocean on which to practice the art of intellectual navigation, economics has fathomless virtues. It presents every kind of difficulty which any scientific study can throw up; the area to be charted is so immense and covers so many mysterious deeps that there can be no end to the work, however many may engage in it. Once he is launched upon this sea, a man's life work, if he be of the true scholarly temper, spreads away before him to his life's horizon. Some have found their way across this ocean by a patient following of the coastline from one set of landmarks to another, never having to grapple with more than a small part of the whole problem at any one time. These were the Marshallians, working in the tradition of the great English empricists who distrusted vast structures reared upon a single supposedly all-conquering idea, and preferred a construction in the English spirit of trial and error, of many supports and a variety of building methods. Others, if I may return to my metaphor of navigation, believed, like Walras, that they had found a star to guide them across the ocean in one swoop. In the equi-marginal principle, embodied in a system of simultaneous equations, they believed they had found a key to unlock the whole economic universe and explain everything. Their system was very beautiful, as well it might be, since it made in effect the tremendous assumption that every economic decision is a choice between perfectly apprehended alternatives. In their world, man knows what he is doing. But though it may seem absurd to explain human conduct in abstraction from human ignorance and fallibility, the so-called General Equilibrium theory invented by Walras and developed by Pareto is one of the greatest creations of economists. It made unmistakably clear once for all that the whole economic world is *interdependent*. The ocean to which I have been comparing our economic world is an apt metaphor in yet another sense. We may think of every individual, every firm, and every government as a boat upon the surface of this ocean. Every movement made by any boat will set up waves which, after a shorter or longer time-lag, will affect much or little every other boat on the ocean. This conception of complete and all-embracing human inter-dependence is not one, I think, which occurs naturally to an unsophisticated mind. Yet what understanding of man's lot in this world, and of his own personal situation in a deeper sense, can any human being claim who has not grasped it?

Thus I claim for the study of economics two chief merits: First, that it is difficult, not, however, in the way that some parts of mathematics are difficult, because their proofs involve a tremendous concatenation of logical steps, but in the sense that the subject-matter of economics is elusive, subtle, and complex to an extreme degree, because it is, in the last resort, the unsearchable heart of man. Mathematics, maybe, teaches men to scale intellectual crags, where each ledge or handhold can only serve if it is part of a chain or ladder of such ledges; but economics teaches men to walk upon quicksand's or to find ways to overleap them. Now this call for resourceful and daring inventiveness in the manufacture of concepts to reason about is very well indeed for those who are already well-practiced in reasoning about ready-made familiar things which, although just as truly fictive as the notions of the economist, appear to be drawn more directly from observation. But to pile this added difficulty of finding the straw or top of the more ordinary labor of intellectual brick-making is, I think, too much to ask of those who are still at school. And for the second merit of economics; this is, that it teaches men who are about to embrace some policy or course of action, to bear in the back of their minds the warning that this step will affect, much or little and sooner or later, everything in the economic universe; this again, I think, is an idea more acceptable and assimilable by somewhat mature minds. Thus it is my own feeling that the schoolmaster, having seen with all his care and energy to the sharpening of the tools of thought and expression, should be content to see them exercised upon the natural sciences, and, except for geography, should leave the human sciences to the student's University years with their better opportunities for free and leisured meditation and their, perhaps, more developed skepticism.

And so to the University course in economics. The first task of the University teacher of any liberal art is surely to persuade his students that the most important things he will put before them are questions and not answers. He is going to put up for them a scaffolding, and leave them to build within it. He has to persuade them that they have not come to the University to learn as it were by heart things which are already hard-and-fast and cut-and-dried, but to watch and perhaps to help in a process, the driving of a causeway which will be made gradually firmer by the traffic of many minds. The ordinary student can perhaps contribute little to this except by striving to say clearly what are the, to him, unsatisfactory things, the gaps and puzzles, and the incantations that hide some secret he does not share. But this he can only do by thinking, and once he has begun to do that with a feeling of freedom and a sense of independent experiment and exploration, he is already a worthy member of the class.

You may have wondered why I traded so much upon your patience with a long discussion of what economics is about and what subjects lie next it in the great fabric of human knowledge. Economics is like a country of the plain, lacking sharp natural frontiers within which it could pursue a self-contained existence, and the greater versatility that this calls for in its citizens, who, because of the constant intellectual traffic with their neighbors, have to be able as it were to speak several languages, poses a serious problem for the designer of the syllabus. There is one problem in particular, which has been a cloud of steadily growing blackness upon our horizon for many years. This is the question of how far, and how, economists should become mathematically literate. No one nowadays would deny that economics is an essentially mathematical subject, even in the old-fashioned sense of mathematics as a discipline concerned always in some way with quantities, for the business of economics also is to reason about quantities. But this is far from saying that all economists should equip themselves to use the formal notations of algebra, the differential and integral calculus, matrices, the theory of sets, and so on. There is much to be said for acquiring some mathematical insight and technical competence, for as 'he moves easiest who has learned to dance,' the pedestrian tasks of the economist will be performed with all the more grace and efficiency if he has practiced something demanding a formal elegance of procedure, while the ready-made tools of thought which mathematics provides will save him as much trouble as a vacuum cleaner saves the modern house-wife. But let him beware of putting his vacuum cleaner on the mantelpiece as an ornament. The kinds of mathematics that economists use are humble and utilitarian, seldom of a sort to arouse the thrilled interest of the mathematician. However, the mathematically trained economist is exposed to a more subtle and far more serious danger than that of mere barbarity in the presentation of his argument. This arises from the domination of applied mathematics in the past by classical dynamics. The world which we explore in that well-known chapter on the dynamics of a particle is a wholly deterministic, predestinatory world, where, and this is the nub of the matter, there is no real or significant distinction between past and future. The astronomer feels as certain that a total eclipse of the sun will be visible in Cornwall in 1999 as he does that a total eclipse was visible in Birmingham in 1927. But the writer of the textbook of classical particle dynamics feels more certain even than the astronomer; he feels *absolutely* certain just where his particle will be at any given instant, for he has excluded *by assumption* every possible accident which could interfere with its career. Can the economist reasonably analyze the conduct of men and women, on the supposition that those men and women believe themselves to know for sure all the relevant consequences of their actions? It is a cardinal fact of human life that we do not know the future, we cannot calculate the consequences of our actions but only guess them. A world without uncertainty would be an utterly inhuman world, of a character which we cannot imagine, and which some have very plausibly suggested is actually logically impossible to conceive and self-contradictory. The assumption of perfect foresight makes nonsense of economics, and yet it is so natural and obvious an assumption for the economist trained in classical dynamics (as some great economists have been) that some have sometimes actually made it *unconsciously*. Now, of course, the physicist of today has greatly modified the views that his grandfather held in the nineteenth century, about the nature of determinism in the physical world. Let me quote to you a passage from a recent article in the *Times Literary Supplement*. *

> 'Do not the "social scientists"—the psychologists, political scientists, sociologists, and *par excellence* the now almost completely symbolical, formal, and econometrical economists—groan and travail for a nineteenth century certainty of "laws", two generations late, just when the most advanced physical scientists are rounding the bend towards chance, uncertainty, and all fortuitousness?'

I am delighted, as some of you will understand, to hear someone telling the economists, in effect, that they should regard uncertainty as the very nerve and essence of their subject, or great parts of it. I myself have been telling them so for a dozen years and more. My only doubt about the statement I have quoted is whether our friends the natural scientists are in truth as far round the bend as the anonymous writer says. The Heisenberg

---

* September 5th, front-page article.

uncertainty principle, even as interpreted by Sir James Jeans, does not, I think, involve for physics anything which can be easily recognized to resemble the consequences that human ignorance of the future has for economics.

Indeed, habits of thought derived from statistical procedures, or from the statistical interpretations of determinism to which the 'uncertainty principle' has driven the modern physicist, can be as dangerous for the economist as the outlook unconsciously induced by classical mechanics. Statistical methods are a means to increase *knowledge*, not a means for analyzing or describing men's feelings and conduct in face of true, irreducible uncertainty, which can be ascribed in the last resort, if to nothing else, then to the ultimate impossibility of their ever knowing whether or not, in any particular case, they have all the relevant information. The econometricians have invited rebuke by publicly declaring that only the present crudity of their techniques (which they will improve) prevents them from telling us in advance what future months and years will bring. There are great scientific tasks for econometrics to perform, but to confound science with prophecy is an unworthy blunder.

Let me, then, try to state briefly my own faith in the matter. Mathematics must be the servant of economics and not its master. The kinds of mathematics required (statistics apart) are relatively workaday ones, and when the occasional cry is heard that some particular branch of economics calls for some new branch of mathematics to be invented, we must not think that even if this appeal is gloriously answered by the mathematicians, anything will be fundamentally changed. The important and practical questions are, first, whether the modest equipment of mathematical conceptions and methods which is all that most economists have time or good reason for aspiring to, should be taught to them by mathematics teachers quite separately from their course in economics, or whether this instruction should be infiltrated into the economics course itself so that mathematical notions and their economic applications and illustrations are inseparably interwoven; and, secondly, if we opt for a separate course in mathematics for economists, whether this should precede the main attack on economic theory, as a necessary preparation for it, or whether the need for mathematical equipment should be allowed to arise in the students' minds as they grapple with their economics course, and should be satisfied by a series of mathematics lectures very carefully dovetailed into those on economics so that each need is met as it arises.

To require students who abandoned algebra two or three or five years ago and have never heard of the calculus, to embark suddenly on an intensive year's cold-blooded instruction in these things, before they are allowed a glimpse of the need for them in economics, is, it seems to me, as though one should ask a man to swallow a tablespoonful of coffee-berries and then pour a cupful of hot water down on top of them in the hope that the two ingredients will somehow get appropriately mixed up in his inside. Half the difficulty in teaching the art of manipulating symbols to those who are not natural symbol-riggers is that it seems to them a purposeless game whose rules cannot be understood. If, in spite of your best efforts, you are always off-side for no reason that is ever made clear in a game where the goal-posts are invisible, you are bound to lose interest in the affair. It is in order to make the goal-posts visible that I think we should interweave the two courses, letting the need for some mathematical notions arise in the economic context and satisfying it on the spot. We need a text-book, and it should be a book of economics which insinuates mathematics, not a book of mathematics illustrated from economics.